MULTITYPE LIBRARY COOPERATION

CONTRIBUTORS

Henry E. Bates, Jr., City Librarian, Milwaukee Public Library; Director, Milwaukee County Federated Library System

Susan Cady, Exec. Secretary, Indiana Library Association, Indiana Library Trustees Association

Mary Jordan Coe, Coordinator, Stone Hills Area Library

Ethel S. Crockett, California State Librarian

William B. Ernst, Jr., University of Illinois at Chicago Circle; President, Board of Directors, Illinois Regional Library Council

Sylvia G. Faibisoff, Associate Professor, Department of Library Science, Arizona State University

Anne Marie Falsone, Asst. Commissioner of Education, Colorado State Library

Morris A. Gelfand, President, Board of Trustees, New York Metropolitan Reference and Research Library Agency; Professor Emeritus, Department of Library Science, Queens College of the City University of New York

Melvin R. George, Director of Libraries, Northeastern Illinois University

Beth A. Hamilton, Exec. Director, Illinois Regional Library Council

Susan Keller, Exec. Director, Library Council of Metropolitan Milwaukee

Dorothy Kittel, Coordinator, LSCA Title III, U.S. Office of Education, Office of Libraries and Learning Resources

David O. Lane, Librarian, Hunter College, New York City

Evaline B. Neff, Exec. Director, Rochester Regional Research Library Council

W. Boyd Rayward, Asst. Professor, Graduate Library School, University of Chicago

Allen Sevigny, Officer, U.S. Office of Education, Region V Library Program

Donald B. Simpson, Exec. Director, Bibliographic Center for Research

Dorothy Sinclair, Exec. Secretary, Cleveland Area Metropolitan Libary System

Edward G. Strable, Vice President and Manager, Information Services, J. Walter Thompson Company, Chicago, Illinois

Roderick G. Swartz, Washington State Librarian, Washington State Library

Kenneth E. Toombs, Director of Libraries, The University of South Carolina

MULTITYPE LIBRARY COOPERATION

Edited by

BETH A. HAMILTON

Illinois Regional Library Council

and

WILLIAM B. ERNST, Jr.

University of Illinois
at Chicago Circle

R. R. BOWKER COMPANY
New York/London, 1977

Published by R. R. Bowker Company
1180 Avenue of the Americas, New York, N.Y. 10036

Library of Congress Cataloging in Publication Data

Main entry under title:

Multitype library cooperation.

  Bibliography: p.
  Includes index.
  1. Library cooperation—United States.
I. Hamilton, Beth A. II. Ernst, William B.,
1916-
Z731.M84   021.6'4'0973   77-24092
ISBN 0-8352-0980-6

CONTENTS

ONE INTRODUCTION AND
BACKGROUND

TWO RELATIONSHIPS OF
MULTITYPE COOPERATIVES
TO STATE, REGIONAL AND
FEDERAL AGENCIES

THREE CASE STUDIES AND SPECIAL PERSPECTIVES

FOUR SUMMARY

APPENDIXES

INDEX

ONE

INTRODUCTION
AND BACKGROUND

INTRODUCTION: WHY MULTITYPE?

Beth A. Hamilton

What is multitype library cooperation? What can it do, and do better, than other kinds of library cooperation? Multitype library cooperation is a means of mobilizing total library resources to meet the needs of the user without regard to the type of library involved and without classifying the user as a public, school, academic, or special library patron. The goal is to help all library users make more effective use of all library resources and services related to educational, work, and recreational needs. The primary responsibility of each type of library is respected, but no one library can economically satisfy all demands made upon it. This characterization of multitype library cooperation was made in 1969 by Orin F. Nolting, then a political scientist at the University of Chicago. He further suggested that multitype library cooperation calls for a master plan for sharing resources and the adoption of policies that establish freer access for all users.

Societal compartmentalization has resulted in artificial divisions by types of libraries, whereas the basic library functions are common to all types and are not, in fact, the province of any one type. Multitype cooperatives emphasize commonalities, not differences, and can bring into symbiosis all types of libraries with all types of problems and can stimulate imaginative solutions. They afford the opportunity for all types of librarians to present a unified front to the user community in order to demonstrate their intention to satisfy fully the needs of library patrons. Multitype library cooperatives have the potential of devising new and creative ways of sharing resources and services, of fostering joint efforts between the public and private sectors, and of stopping needless duplication of effort and resources. As is mentioned frequently in the chapters that follow, they can, as a whole, be greater than the sum of their parts. Most of all, they can promote increased understanding of mutual concerns among all types of member librarians and can rally broad support to achieve the fullest aspirations of librarianship.

FROM SINGLE TO MULTITYPE COOPERATIVES

The library community is accustomed to thinking of interlibrary cooperation as that which occurs between like types of libraries. These single-type cooperatives preceded multitype ones, of course, and have had nota-

3

bly successful programs. In the 1975 survey of academic library consortia by System Development Corporation, 38 kinds of cooperative activities were reported by 409 academic consortia. The 1976 *ASLA Report on Interlibrary Cooperation* identifies over 300 single-type cooperatives, many of which are public library systems. The special libraries' "old boy network" is well known for fostering exchange of all sorts of information and services. School libraries have cooperation within their own districts, as a natural precondition for existence. What brings us, then, to the widespread development of multitype library cooperatives, and why are they having such impact? Why are single-type cooperatives becoming reincarnated into multitype ones? What are the dimensions of the challenge of bringing all types of libraries into an effective working relationship? What is the potential of multitype cooperatives in the future? The papers in this volume address these and related questions.

Multitype library cooperatives have developed within the past decade at the local, regional, state, and national levels without a master plan, in an uncoordinated way, and in response to felt needs. During this period, there has been no single unit within the American Library Association (ALA) providing a forum for discussing the many facets of multitype library cooperation, for promulgating definitions, or for devising standards. An Interlibrary Cooperation Committee (ad hoc), appointed by ALA Council in July 1974, was charged with investigating the need for a Standing Committee on Intertype Library Cooperation, with exploring relationships with the U.S. Office of Education and the National Commission on Libraries and Information Science, and with providing maximum communication with each of the units of ALA and other organizations that have interests in this area. Although final results of this committee's work are not yet known, the committee's very existence did have the effect of partially fulfilling one of its charges. Representatives of active ALA divisional committees on interlibrary cooperation met together on several occasions to witness the deliberations of the ad hoc committee and, therefore, were beginning to share experiences at the time they sat down to plan the Opportunities in Multitype Library Cooperation program.

1976 ALA PROGRAM ON MULTITYPE COOPERATION

At the ALA midwinter meeting in Chicago in January 1976, plans were laid for a centennial conference program on multitype library cooperation. Robert L. Clark, chairman of the Public Library Association Interlibrary Cooperation Committee, invited members of all of the ALA divisional interlibrary cooperation committees and of the Committee on Networking of the Special Libraries Association to attend a planning session for the program.

The objectives of the ALA program were numerous: to provide exposure to multitype library cooperation for the uninitiated; to give attention to the several concerns then evident from the multitype experience; to share successes and problems in governance, funding, and operation of multitype cooperatives; to examine the possibility of developing guidelines and standards; and to create a ground swell of support for a single multitype cooperation/resources sharing unit within ALA. The program was also to serve as a platform for the distribution of the first ERIC bibliography on multitype library cooperation [see Appendix 1 in this volume] and of the first national survey of multitype library cooperative activities, the 1976 *ASLA Report on Interlibrary Cooperation*.

This book is an adaptation of the papers, entitled "Opportunities in Multitype Library Cooperation," presented on July 22, 1976, at the ALA Centennial Conference. Original conference papers have been revised in the light of audience discussions at the meeting, and additional papers have been solicited to present developments not fully covered in the program. The program was cosponsored by the American Association of School Librarians Networking-Interconnection of Learning Resources Committee, the Association of College and Research Libraries, the Association of State Library Agencies Interlibrary Cooperation Committee, the ALA Intertype Library Cooperation Committee (ad hoc), the Public Library Association Interlibrary Cooperation Committee, the Reference and Adult Services Division Interlibrary Loan Committee, and the Special Libraries Association Committee on Networking.

The editors express appreciation for the work of the program planning committee members: Robert L. Clark, Oklahoma Department of Libraries, chairman; Barry Booth, Illinois Valley Library System; Eva R. Brown, Chicago Library System; Mary D. Quint, Illinois State Library; and Robert B. Lane, Air University. Thanks are also due the distinguished contributors to the program and to this volume, as well as the divisions of ALA that cosponsored the Opportunities in Multitype Library Cooperation program.

QUESTIONS ADDRESSED

In single-type cooperatives, member institutions have been readily brought together into cohesive operations because they have similar *operational, funding, governance*, and *service patterns*. Single-type cooperatives have been able to achieve close interaction among their members and focus on numerous problems with which the majority of their members can identify. Elements that led to the success of the public library systems included their legal bases, tax support, and geographic proximity. They were, moreover, usually a part of a statewide plan for mobilizing library resources, with state library agencies providing backup services and resources.

Multitype library cooperatives differ in many ways, although they have the same overall goal as single-type cooperatives—to provide improved library service to all library users within a particular geographic region. Multitype cooperatives have been federally encouraged, state administered, and locally implemented. They are more loosely structured, with fewer options for close interaction among the majority of their members. They have the capability of focusing on fewer problems with which their dissimilar member institutions can identify. Because they are usually governed by professional leaders representative of all types of libraries who are accountable primarily to their colleagues and who are eager to show results, they have the opportunity to get projects accomplished quickly and with a minimum of red tape. Given their collective head, they can experiment and devise solutions where predominantly lay boards are likely to require more assurances before undertaking experiments.

If multitype library cooperatives can be so effective in mobilizing total library resources, why then the controversies that surround them? The most frequently expressed doubt is whether such widely diverse institutions can really share resources, services, and good ideas. Is this only an illusion, with the multitype cooperative "laying on" additional programs but not creating mechanisms that broadly affect the actual operations of member libraries?

A second controversy arises out of the fact that the majority of multitype cooperatives are being established and are surviving on "soft money," i.e., money coming from the federal government through the Library Services and Construction Act (LSCA), which is, in 1977, of uncertain duration. The hard money, coming from secure sources, is not easily attained. While enabling legislation and tax support have been achieved in a few states, these are in the minority. It will be of interest to discover how public support, and therefore decision making, affect the governance and performance of the statutory multitype cooperatives.

The effects of LSCA funding on the development of multitype cooperatives are far-reaching. This book may be considered one small tribute to these effects. As Sylvia Faibisoff suggests in her article, LSCA funding coincided with other factors in a timely manner to produce results that were perhaps undreamed of in 1956 when federal funding for library programs first became a reality. LSCA requires that funds be administered through state agencies; that state agencies produce long-range plans of service; and that they should coordinate state agency programs with library programs and projects operated by institutions of higher education, by local elementary and secondary schools, and by other public and private institutions offering library services. These requirements have sometimes inadvertently produced certain tensions for the multitype library cooperative development, as noted in this volume by Faibisoff, Cady, and Keller.

The planning process itself poses contradictions. The decision must be made whether to work for immediate and meaningful results in order to justify continued funding and membership participation or to plan carefully and democratically to ensure that programs will have a solid basis for future operation. As Sinclair notes, the Cleveland cooperative voted for the quick results, as have several others.

The matter of *local versus state orientation* needs consideration. In order for federal funds to be distributed to cooperative projects on an equitable basis, the role of the cooperatives in statewide development plans must be well defined. This means that the cooperatives must balance their plans between what their local members perceive as the most urgent local needs and what state agencies perceive to be most urgently needed for the whole state. While state librarians would like to have local cooperatives' plans be perfectly fitting subsets of state plans, this condition rarely exists to everyone's satisfaction. Where the role of the cooperative is well defined or relatively well defined in the state, plans can be telescoped more readily. Pinning down roles in very deliberate ways eliminates some of the flexibility of the cooperative's operation and flexibility is an absolute must in an operation that bases its *raison d'être* in bringing together in an effective working relationship the very diverse types of libraries along with the very diverse attitudes of their individualistic librarians. Yet where roles are not well defined there is likely to be time wasted in power plays, in unproductive debate, and in deciding who is to do what. The balance to be sought here is a well-defined role that has built-in flexibility for operation.

Bringing together representatives from all types of libraries to the *planning* exercise is not an easy task. Representatives reflect the points of view of their constituencies, which is needed. Each does not bring an equal awareness of the points of view of other types of libraries; thus, bringing all planners to an equivalent understanding of all other types is a time-consuming, energy-depleting process. Until this level of mutual insight is reached, however, effective planning cannot take place.

How multitype library agencies relate to state library agencies is dealt with by Crockett, Cady, and Coe. That some states have imposed boundaries upon the multitype library cooperatives is troublesome, as this practice precludes the possibility of natural service boundaries as agreed upon by local leaders. It is also evidence of the Big Brotherness that private institutions, particularly special libraries, expect to avoid in cooperative ventures. Both Strable and Cady comment upon the sensitivities of this situation. The whole question of the role of the local unit in emerging multitype library cooperatives is addressed by Rayward. He delineates the problems of interaction at the local level and suggests that local units provide the foundation for network operation over larger areas.

In very large cooperatives, there is the likelihood that member librarians are not always fully aware of how their libraries relate to others in the cooperative or how they relate to the cooperative itself. According to George and Rayward, *interrelationships* often are not emphasized, but must be articulated in order for each member institution to take full advantage of the cooperate arrangement. Relationships with other agencies, organizations, and cooperatives is of importance, too, as Faibisoff, Cady, Crockett, Kittell, and Sevigny suggest.

If a full merger of library resources is to take place to reach full library service for all citizens, it is imperative that all libraries participate in multitype library cooperation. A section of this book is devoted to *problems and opportunities* exemplified in specific case studies, as well as those generally characteristic of types of libraries. Falsone, Bates, Strable, Toombs, and George explore the benefits and barriers from the points of view of their respective types of libraries.

The sensitive problem of *potential overuse of the larger research libraries* within a cooperative is the central focus of several papers, notably those of Falsone, Swartz, Rayward, Toombs, and George. The latter three also consider the necessity of providing equitable reimbursement for the heavy demands consistently placed upon the most prestigious library available. George, Toombs, Strable, and Sinclair point out that there are methods of equalizing the burdens and advocate accessing down the collection size ladder.

Multitype cooperatives provide services in response to needs identified by their memberships. The details of the needs and responses in each instance are specific to a given situation. Cady, Coe, Bates, Neff, Gelfand, Lane, Sinclair, and Simpson have all dealt with the particular *services offered* by the cooperatives they represent. It is fairly obvious that these services were developed because no other organization provided them adequately in their areas.

In its final draft for a National Library Program published in 1975, the National Commission on Libraries and Information Science noted that typical library networks are those formed by the libraries of metropolitan areas. The greatest concentration of library resources is in metropolitan areas, as is the greatest concentration of library users, and hence, probably the greatest concentration of problems in bringing users and resources together. Keller has outlined services that certain *metropolitan cooperatives* offered in 1975, while Coe presents a perspective of cooperative operation in a *rural* community. Neff, working in a *mixed urban-rural situation*, does not believe that the configuration of the community makes that much difference in services offered.

One of the activities most amenable to multitype library cooperation is resource sharing. Resource sharing begins with cooperative and coordinated purchasing of materials and equipment. Lane describes the New York METRO cooperative acquisitions program and Sinclair and Keller mention plans for coordinated acquisitions programs. Such programs are difficult to carry out because they tend to infringe upon the prerogatives of member libraries. Until we have demonstrated the ability to offer well-conceived programs of joint purchase, coordinated purchase, and subsequent sharing of resources, we cannot claim to have reached the full potential of multitype library cooperation. Three related areas—the building of bibliographic data bases for locating local resources, the development of communication protocols for linking these data bases, and the strengthening of physical distribution systems that ensure economical and timely delivery—must be given more attention.

STANDARDS NEEDED

Not addressed in this volume are the troublesome and important matters of definitions and standards, for the obvious reason that concerted attempts have not yet been made to address or solve them. Many of the contributors have chosen to use the broad term "multitype library cooperatives," whereas they are accustomed to referring to council and network. The use of "network" throughout these papers would violate the often articulated definition of networks as organizations with computer-assisted activities. Multitype library cooperatives are broader in scope and do not necessarily preclude the use of computer technology. The time is overdue for the professional community to agree to call the same thing by the same name and to develop and endorse both bibliographic and service standards. It may be necessary to modify the democratic process to the point where a few go ahead and do the developing and hope that their work will be accepted. Unanimity will be long in coming and we cannot wait for it.

FUTURE GOALS

The overriding problem in library cooperation is in *getting people to work together* productively. In summarizing the conference papers, Ernst emphasizes the role of people in achieving success. It is the human resources, as well as the material ones, that are to be shared. It is the involvement of volunteers that produces solid results. It is the willingness to put aside personal concerns and to concentrate on those of the whole group and the determination to experiment until better ways are found that enable cooperatives to make progress.

Before the question of where multitype library cooperatives fit into the future national network can be addressed, those of national network goals and funding must be answered. It is reasonable to expect that a national network will consist of several components, one of which will be the multitype cooperatives providing assistance to the libraries that directly serve the library user. It is, after all, at circulation desks in the smallest libraries and at the telephone in the hands of the most uncertain reference librarians that the validity of a national network will be tested. Multitype library cooperatives can make a difference and must be nurtured. Optimists believe a start has been made. Critics view some multitype developments as trivial ones and that is inevitable, just as it is inevitable that progress is made through conflict. We must stop thinking in terms of the limitations and begin examining the possibilities. Our greatest failure could be not in overcoming faulty structures and uncertain funding but rather in not taking every opportunity to provide full service to the American public.

THE MULTITYPE LIBRARY COOPERATIVE RESPONSE TO USER NEEDS

Roderick G. Swartz

The major thrust of recent trends in library service patterns has been expansion of the traditional effort at library cooperation, that is, shared resources and in some cases shared jurisdictions, but with the addition of new cooperation on a multitype basis. It is essential to take a critical look at the validity of library cooperation, especially multitype library cooperation, from the viewpoint of the user, to determine whether or not cooperation really has been, and will continue to be, a major factor in meeting library and information demands and needs.

ASSUMPTIONS OF LIBRARY COOPERATION

Library cooperation has prospered in the United States, based upon the assumption that more is good and that a well-coordinated and well-financed more is even better. Regional public library development grew out of projections made by Carleton Joeckel[1] in 1935 that the answer to the poor distribution of library resources in the United States was a series of regional libraries that would provide nationwide library service, including service to rural and suburban areas. Joeckel argued that by forming regional units of communities and counties, too poor to provide library service, adequate levels of service would span the country. Aided by federal legislation, such as the Library Services Act of 1956, regional libraries did begin to provide a pattern of library service to the country.

Cooperation among college and university libraries was based upon the assumption that the problems of too much growth of any one library would be offset by well-coordinated and cooperatively financed efforts. Spurred by threatening projections, college and university librarians began to develop joint acquisitions programs, such as the Farmington Plan; cooperative storage centers, such as the Center for Research Libraries in Chicago; and a nationwide system of interlibrary loans.

In the last few years, librarians have begun to talk about multitype library cooperation and networking. The same thing is not always meant when these terms are used. In fact, the Joint AASL/ASLA/PLA/RASD/SLA Committee, in planning for the 1976 conference program on multitype cooperation, had to clarify these terms. Multitype library cooperation is defined as the cooperation of two or more legal library entities in sharing resources, personnel, facilities, and/or programs with a library or libraries of another type and having a different legal base. A multitype library network is a cooperative structure that crosses jurisdictional, institutional, and often political boundaries to join several types of libraries (academic, school, special, and public) in a common enterprise. The multitype library network is usually an interface between two more or less highly articulated single-type library cooperatives. In many areas of the country, these two definitions are not so precise, and multilibrary cooperation and networking blend into one definition.

The network approach many times involves electronic transfer and storage of information, and electronic networking continues to stress the best coordination of existing resources in all types of libraries. Bibliographic networks make possible a decrease in repetitious processing of library materials. Telecommunications networks improve resource sharing in all types of libraries. Network governance structures enable better coordination of library and information services. The National Commission on Libraries and Information Science (NCLIS), in developing its program for a national network, stresses the coordination factor as a means of rationalizing information resources.

Multitype library cooperation and networking have become characterized as a way to improve traditional library service. The pattern emphasizes the importance of improved access to a growing number of library materials. Cooperative library service is viewed as better than no library service. Similarly, access to several university libraries via interlibrary loan is considered better than the availability of just one university collection, and coordinated access to library materials in the United States through a national network is seen as even more advantageous.

TRADITIONAL USER STUDIES

From the point of view of library management, cooperation is perhaps reasonable, but how does it affect user needs and demands? User studies traditionally have been examinations of how, and by whom, libraries are used.[2] They have been analyses of circulation statistics, of particular library areas, such as the reference department, or of the socioeconomic background of library patrons. Over the years, little attention has been given to the potential user or to the citizen information demands or needs.

Before one proceeds, one should distinguish between an information demand or an articulated information need placed on the formal information community and an information need that the individual has not articulated. Information demands on formal information sources, such as libraries, have been a growing concern for a number of years, while the study of information needs is still in its infancy. There is little standardization at this point and the methodology is in a formative stage of development. The major tool of measurement is the written questionnaire, combined with an interview. These studies should be looked at in several ways: What do they say about the present library situation? What do they say about the future of multitype library cooperation?

THE INFORMATION POOR AND THE INFORMATION RICH

When one considers information demands and needs, one should distinguish between groups of information users. Edwin Parker[3] uses the terms "information poor" and "information rich." The former are those who have little acquaintance with traditional information sources, such as libraries, and whose information needs, in many cases, would not be met by these sources. The latter includes leaders from scholarly, government, and business communities who have an overabundance of information, who use libraries and other formal information sources, and who are familiar with techniques for securing information.

Studies of the Information Poor

Studies of the demands of the information poor have shown that the logical, formal information source, the public library, contributes little at present toward fulfilling their needs. A new outlook seems to be needed by the public library if it is to be responsive to the information needs and demands of the disadvantaged. A 1968 study by Mary Lee Bundy of the needs of the information poor showed the public libraries in a position of nonimportance.[4]

A study conducted by the University of Texas at Austin reported that one out of every five American adults is functionally illiterate and unable to cope in today's society. It showed that 20 percent, or more than 23 million persons, cannot read newspapers or the help-wanted ads, or figure the best grocery buy, or make a plane reservation. Some 10,000 adults (aged 18 to 65) were tested over a four-year period with the following results: 13 percent, or 15 million, could not address an envelope properly for mailing; 30 percent, or 50 million, could not select an airline flight to arrive at a distant city at the time prescribed for a meeting; 26 percent, or 30.7 million, could not determine the best unit price among three sizes of cereal boxes.[5]

In 1975 a study was published by the Gallup Organization on behalf of 16 state library agencies and the American Library Association.[6] It showed that 60 percent of Americans had not been in a public library within the last 12 months, and if they did visit the library, they were largely oriented to traditional book materials. John Humphry, assistant commissioner for libraries for the New York State Education Department, commented that "the study indicates that the library community needs to find ways in which to reach out more effectively to attract those Americans with less education whose information needs are even greater than those with high school and college degrees." He further commented that the report certainly points out "the need to acquaint users as well as non-users with a wide range of materials, facilities and services now available in most public libraries that go beyond book loans."[7]

Contrast with Finland. These U.S. figures contrast with the author's observations during a year spent abroad, one-half of that time in Finland, where there is an extremely high literacy rate, almost 100 percent, and heavy use of all library systems. In Tampere, for example, one normally had to wait in a line of 6 to 12 people while they checked out materials from the public library systems. The sharp contrast between what was observed in Finland and in the United States precipitated an examination of trends in library service patterns in an attempt to answer some of these problems in the United States.

Studies of the Information Rich

An investigation of the information needs of scholars, researchers, and professionals in the United States showed their use or potential use of libraries also to be discouraging. Startlingly, studies of the information rich accentuate many of the same points as did studies of the information poor. The most recurring theme is the frequent choice by scientists, researchers, and other professionals of an informal information network rather than a formal network of libraries. When such individuals are drawn into a formal information channel, such as a library, numerous studies have shown that the information rich are not sophisticated in their use of library and information science tools. Studies of citations from abstracting and indexing tools, for example, show a small number of references drawn from these sources. Librarians are not seen as active participants in the procurement of information. They are considered to be housekeepers, organizers, or managers, but not people who aid in the complexity of securing information and data.

NEEDED NEW APPROACH TO DELIVERY OF INFORMATION

From the Gallup study of library users, or from the University of Texas study of the functionally illiterate, or from a look at the information needs and demands of the library rich, certain problems are apparent in traditional library use and cooperation. Despite limited knowledge of information demands and needs, it is obvious that well-coordinated and well-financed library cooperation is not enough. More and better traditional library service is not the complete answer. What is necessary is some new approach to the local delivery of information.

The next logical question to ask is whether the current multitype library cooperation infused with a combination of computer and telecommunications technology will have a different effect from a user's point of view. In 1976, in the state of Washington, for example, legislation was passed that established the Washington Library Network, essentially a multitype library venture on a statewide basis that includes computer services, telecommunications services, interlibrary services, and reference and referral services. From the residents' point of view, will this improve library services and information delivery services in the state of Washington? There are some encouraging factors in users' studies indicating that it will. In formal information channels, such as libraries, the right amount of information is more important than access to a quantity of information. Studies among physicians and physicists show that their use is limited to a restricted number of primary journals in each field. Another study claims that the "quick fix" was more often the norm than an exhaustive use of the library or other available collections.

The question of accessibility, in fact, in terms of both time and geography, proves to be a factor of more importance than the quality of the source. One study asked individuals in a search sample to rank sources of information for several hypothetical problems. In each case, the sources of a personal library, a knowledgeable person close by, or the telephone were given priority over the services of a more distant library. One researcher speculated that the twin features of accessibility and the right amount of information were the reasons many researchers went to informal sources, where they received the right information in the right amount and within the time required.

Another effort to gain answers was the NCLIS Conference on User Needs, held in Denver in May 1973. The commission invited 16 specialists in user information needs to present papers on the requirements of a particular subgroup. Each participant found that the description of information needs is a difficult task, even when one is extremely knowledgeable of the subgroup and its interest. In all 16, however, two factors that remained consistent were the importance of time and the usability of format. Unless information arrived on a prescribed time schedule and was in a format that could be used, the information was useless.[8]

In both the information rich and information poor, there were three factors that were emphasized: accessibility (the importance of time in receiving information), the receipt of the right amount of information, and the usability of the information received. It is here that multitype library cooperation might have some real strengths in improving library services. The problems of time and accessibility of information should certainly be improved when a cooperative endeavor is backed by computer technology and improved telecommunications. Accessibility to information in a subject field, such as medicine, or in a geographically isolated situation, such as Alaska, has been improved by the use of this combination.

Telecommunications makes data accessible from the computer. There are other telecommunications facilities, such as cable television, microwave, and facsimile transmissions, which are having, and will continue to have, a tremendous impact on time and delivery. Variety of format is being improved through multitype library endeavors. Bibliographic information has moved from a card format, to a book format, to a microfiche format.

Care has to be exercised because the zeal for complete information service, combined with the electronic capabilities, may prove disconcerting to the user. The future ability to locate and provide such complete information service could overwhelm the client, who is looking for just the right amount of information.

INFORMATION NEEDS OF THE LIBRARY

While the thrust of this article is multitype library cooperation from the viewpoint of the ultimate user, that is, the client, it is important to comment on cooperative endeavors from the point of view of another user, that is, the library involved in multitype cooperation.

The problems of different types of libraries will be discussed elsewhere, but there are a few general comments that must be made if needs and demands can be used in a slightly different connotation. The institution as a participant in multitype library cooperation has certain needs and demands placed upon it as a member of a multitype library cooperative. Most of the following observations are based upon the experience of Washington State in developing the Washington Library Network, an example of a multitype library cooperative effort supported by computer-telecommunications technology. Each library within the cooperative has the right to be represented in the development of the goals, objectives, and day-to-day regulations and rules of the organization, in whatever format it may take. The effort toward group decision making and participatory management, seen within individual libraries, has to be extended to multitype library activities. While the technology that backs many of these cooperatives causes many a difficult day, it is still the management of people within that organization that is an even greater challenge.

Another factor that needs to be considered is the difference in size and service capabilities among the smaller and the larger libraries within the cooperative. In a statewide cooperative, the larger libraries, which will eventually contribute more in the way of resource sharing, should be compensated for their contributions. Washington State is looking forward toward a request in the state budget to meet that particular responsibility. The interrelationship of the private and the public sector is of great importance. Libraries in private colleges and business must be involved in the network. Collections in special libraries, although small, have much to offer the multitype cooperative.

The public sector has much to gain from interaction with private interests. In Washington State, technical work on the computer effort benefited greatly by the interaction between a state agency and a private computer service within the state. On the other side of the coin, there are certain demands upon a library entering into multitype library activities. It is necessary to reevaluate information and library services to determine which are important and to ascertain the types and extent of the clients' needs.

IMPROVED RESPONSE TO INFORMATION NEEDS OF THE USER

Before any library moves into cooperation, it has to have a better understanding of its potential users' information needs. Marketing research techniques have proved helpful in some developments. This does not imply the creation of false needs, but rather a true analysis of a segment of the potential clientele and an assessment of the information needs and the development or alteration of services to meet these needs.

The relationship between user and librarian needs to be strengthened within the walls of any library. The librarian needs to be more adept at isolating an information demand when it is articulated. Studies show that the librarian is deficient in responding to even elementary information demands. Merely to call on one of the vast resources of library cooperation-interlibrary loan is not enough. The importance of the professional's role in interpreting the demands and delivering the right amount of information is reflected in user studies. It is crucial for the librarian directly serving the public to identify correctly an information demand and then to produce the right amount of information to satisfy that demand appropriately.

Improved information demand analysis implies a greater concern with the interview process. The librarian needs to know not only the literature and the channels for securing it but also how to query the client to be sure that the correct demand has been ascertained. It indicates a greater responsibility for the librarian as an information transfer facilitator. Special librarians have long espoused this role in meeting the demands of their organizations, but librarians from other types of libraries have been slower to accept this responsibility. If even the information rich are partial to informal, personal channels of information and are unskilled in the use of library and information science tools, the growing importance of the trained librarian or information transfer specialist is obvious.

There is certainly a need for the library to explain its role to its potential user. Studies show that even if the user can overcome the difficulties of translating a generalized need into an information need and then into an information demand, it is very unlikely that the library is credited with satisfying that demand. To correct this poor public image, a total public relations program is required for the library, starting with the marketing of needs assessment and extending to the development of a revitalized program. It is only then that an individual library can expect to benefit from multitype library cooperation.

The user will be cheated if the local library does not reexamine its program. Just as libraries are encouraged to evaluate their service programs before they start a new building program, similar evaluations should be made before they move into multitype library cooperation. A library cannot afford to jump on a bandwagon that only expands traditional library service. If multitype library cooperation can help revitalize service concepts at the local level, it will be of great benefit to the individual client and the local library. Since traditional library service has been found inadequate for many users in the past, the approach now should be to attempt new service techniques. Multitype library cooperation presents untapped opportunities for experimentation that may result in new mechanisms to satisfy user needs.

NOTES

1. Carleton B. Joeckel, *The Government of the American Public Library* (Chicago: University of Chicago Press, 1939, c. 1935).

2. D. N. Wood, "User Studies: A Review of the Literature from 1966–1970," *ASLIB Proceedings* 23 (June 1971): 11–23.

3. Edwin B. Parker, "Information and Society," In *Library and Information Service Needs of the Nation: Proceedings of a Conference on the Needs of Occupational, Ethnic, and Other Groups in the United States* (Washington, D.C.: GPO, 1974).

4. Mary Lee Bundy, *Metropolitan Public Users: A Report of a Survey of Adult Library Use in the Maryland Baltimore–Washington Metropolitan Area* (College Park: University of Maryland School of Library and Information Services, 1968).

5. University of Texas, Division of Extension, *Adult Functional Competency: A Summary* (Austin, Tex., 1975).

6. Gallup Organization, Inc., *The Role of Libraries in America: A Study Conducted for Chief Officers of State Library Agencies* (Princeton, N.J., October 1975).

7. John A. Humphry, Chief Officers of State Library Agencies Committee for the Gallup Study, press release, Gallup Organization, Princeton, N.J., December 1975).

8. National Commission on Libraries and Information Science, *Library and Information Service Needs of the Nation: Proceedings of a Conference of Needs of Occupational, Ethnic, and Other Groups in the United States* (Washington: GPO, 1975).

PLANNING, GOVERNANCE, AND FUNDING: AN OVERVIEW

Sylvia G. Faibisoff

Future historians writing of post-World War II libraries will most certainly include a chapter on the emergence and growth of multitype library cooperatives and networks. In retrospect, it appears that this development was inevitable, since it appeared on both national and international levels. It was not unexpected that libraries, more traditionally reactors to than agents of change, would respond to pervasive societal trends toward cooperation and interdependence. These attitudes seemed to spill over into local library situations. A positive psychological attitude toward cooperation, coupled with such factors as advances in computer and communications technology, a heightened awareness and conscientious approach to interdependent library relationships, and emerging government financial support, subsequently resulted in the establishment of library systems and networks.

Although there is no complete directory of library systems and networks, it was possible, through literature searches, to identify as many as 300 single-type library cooperatives, approximately 220 intrastate multitype library cooperatives, 11 interstate library networks, and an emerging plan for developing a national library network.[1-4] It was also clear that in spite of the prevalence and continuing creation of multitype library cooperatives, such entities still appeared to be enigmas, shrouded in a cloud of misinformation and skepticism, and, in some instances, struggling for survival, yet persistently refusing to go away. Hard-nosed pessimists still questioned the viability and feasibility of these proliferating cooperative organizations and expressed doubts that they could overcome either mythical, psychological, jurisdictional, or economic barriers. They also doubted that all types of libraries could effectively or successfully merge. They claimed that the resulting structure could not be homologous, but would merely be incongruous.[5]

The objective of this paper is to provide an overview of the current state of the art on planning, governance, and funding of multitype library cooperatives. It does not support either those who commended or condemned these developments. Unfortunately, the breadth of the topic and the lack of data preclude a comprehensive study. Data on governance, planning, and funding are not only scattered but inadequate. As much information as possible was obtained from the literature, including annual reports and publications of individual councils, journal articles, and existing directories of library cooperatives. Telephone interviews, meetings with directors of multitype cooperatives, and professional experience added further insight.

DEFINITIONS

The definition of the term "multitype library cooperative" prepared by the Symposium Planning Committee was as follows:

A multitype library cooperative or network is a combination, merger or contractual association of two or more types of libraries (academic, public, special or school) crossing jurisdictional, institutional or political boundaries, working together to achieve maximum, effective use of funds to provide library and information services to all citizens above and beyond that which can be provided through one institution on a local level. Such cooperative networks may be designed to serve a community, a metropolitan area, a region within a region, or may serve a statewide or multistate area.[6]

Persons familiar with Raynard Swank's more extensive definition of interlibrary cooperation and networks[7] may feel that the following components he identified should also be included in the definition: information resources—collections of documents or data in whatever medium; readers or users—citizens mentioned in the above definition; schemes for the intellectual organization of documents or data; methods for the delivery of resources; formal organization; and bidirectional communications, preferably through high-speed, long-distance electrical signal transmission with switching capabilities and computer hookup.

DEVELOPMENT AND CONFIGURATION

Although the history of interlibrary cooperation can be traced back to antiquity, the development of the multitype library cooperative is primarily a post-World War II product influenced by the Library Services Act of 1956 and the Library Services and Construction Act of 1965.

John Cory drew an interesting comparison between the development of libraries and interlibrary cooperation with developments in computer capability. He made the following comparisons: the single-type library unit (the individual public or academic library) with the first generation of computers; the single-type interlibrary cooperatives (the public library systems or the academic library consortia) with the second generation of computers; the combination of several types of libraries (the multitype cooperatives) with the third generation of computers; and, finally, the ultimate type of combination, all types of libraries with nonlibrary agencies, to a fourth generation of computers.[8]

Although the above analogy is a handy way to conceptualize developments in interlibrary cooperation, one should not assume that the growth of multitype library cooperation is either lineal or sequential or that one type of interlibrary cooperative may supplant another. At the present time, each type of interlibrary cooperative organization exists concurrently with and yet independently of other types; each may elect to affiliate with or become a member of another type of interlibrary organization and still maintain its autonomy; and each type can achieve a level of sophistication comparable to that of a late generation computer. By comparing changes in library organization with the developments of computers, Cory is suggesting that through cooperation libraries may increase their levels of capacity (their resource input and output), increase their power and effectiveness, decrease unit costs, and provide for economies of operation.

Approximately 220 intrastate multitype library cooperatives and 11 interstate multitype library networks have been identified throughout the country. Although intrastate multitype library cooperatives were not found in Alabama, Arkansas, Delaware, Hawaii, Mississippi, Nevada, West Virginia, or Wyoming, it is quite possible that these were missed or that, since multitype library cooperatives seem to erupt like dandelions, one may now exist where it did not a month ago.

As will be noted in Table 1, interstate multitype library networks cover the country. With the exception of libraries in Ohio and West Virginia, academic, public, and special libraries in the remaining states are members of one or more multitype interstate library network. They join in order to take advantage of the bibliographic, educational, and resource services offered by these organizations.

The multitype library cooperative is defined as a combination of two or more types of libraries. In 1970, when multitype library cooperation was still in its infancy, Ralph Stenstrom expressed his skepticism about the possibility of merging all types of libraries:

> While a good deal of attention is currently being paid to the concept of statewide or regional networks which would link all types of libraries and make resources of large areas accessible, there is little indication from the literature cited here of widespread implementation of this type of program. A number of programs sponsored jointly by academic, public, and special libraries are in operation, but there are few which include all four types of libraries. Part of this explanation may rest with school libraries which do not fit easily into cooperative programs with academic and special libraries. School library needs are fairly distinct and the collections they build are rarely of value to the users of academic and special libraries. . . .[9]

In order to ascertain the extent to which two-, three-, and four-type library cooperatives existed in 1975, 167 multitype organizations were examined. Besides finding a trend toward four-type combinations, there was also widespread implementation of statewide and regional networks. The

Table 1   Interstate Multitype Library Networks

Name and Location of Headquarters	Date Founded	States/Libraries Served (As of March 1976)
AMIGOS Bibliographic Council Richardson, Tex.	1975	Arizona, Arkansas, New Mexico, Texas
Midwest Region Library Network (MIDLNET) Green Bay, Wis.	1975	Illinois, Iowa, Indiana, Michigan, Minnesota, Missouri, Wisconsin
New England Library and Information Network (NELINET) Wellesley, Mass.	1966	Connecticut, Maine, Vermont, Massachusetts, New Hampshire
PALINET Union Library Catalog Philadelphia, Pa.	1974	Delaware, New Jersey, Pennsylvania
Pacific Northwest Bibliographic Center Seattle, Wash.	1940	Idaho, Montana, Oregon, and Washington
SALINET Boulder, Colo.	1974	Natrona County Library, Denver Library School, University of Kansas Library, Wyoming State Library
Southeastern Library Network (SOLINET) Atlanta, Ga.	1974	Alabama, Florida, Georgia, Kentucky, Louisiana, Mississippi, North Carolina, South Carolina, Tennessee, Virginia
Southwest Library Interstate Cooperative Endeavor (SLICE) Dallas, Tex.	1971	Arizona, Arkansas, Louisiana, New Mexico, Oklahoma, Texas
Western Interstate Commission for Higher Education (WICHE) Boulder, Colo.	Mid-1960s	Alaska, Arizona, California, Colorado, Idaho, Kansas, Montana, Nebraska, Nevada, New Mexico, North Dakota, Oregon, South Dakota, Washington, Wyoming
Bibliographic Center for Research (BCR) Denver, Colo.	1935	Colorado, Iowa, Nebraska, New Mexico, North Dakota, Oklahoma, South Dakota, Utah, Wyoming
Research Libraries Group Branford, Conn.	1974	Columbia, Harvard, and Yale University libraries, New York Public Library

number of multitype cooperatives in each state ranged from 1 to 21. As may be seen from Table 2, the four-type combination (68 units, or 40.7 percent) ranked just ahead of the three-type combination of academic-public-special (65 units, or 38.9 percent). Three- and four-type combinations accounted for 90 percent of the organizations examined.

For the most part, libraries have combined for such general purposes

Table 2   Combinations of Types of Libraries in Multitype Cooperatives

Academic	Public	Special	School	Number of Combinations	Percent
x	x	x	x	68	40.7
x	x	x		65	38.9
x	x		x	17	10.2
x		x		8	4.8
x			x	1	.6
	x	x	x	3	1.8
	x	x		2	1.2
	x		x	3	1.8
				167	100.0

as the common good, the elimination of duplication of effort, economy, the sharing of resources, the more effective utilization of resources, and the improvement of services. G. Flint Purdy noted that libraries of the same type initially combined in cooperative experiments "of immediately manageable dimensions."[10] These experiments generally resulted in programs involving union lists and catalogs, efforts to coordinate collection development, or cooperative use arrangements. Keyes Metcalf noted that interlibrary cooperative efforts might result in joint storage programs or joint acquisitions projects or reciprocal use.[11] In summary, interlibrary cooperative arrangements have provided a method for sharing resources more generously, more systematically, and more expeditiously. They also have provided a means for strengthening those resources that are shared.

SINGLE-FUNCTION COOPERATIVES

Multitype library cooperatives can be classified by function as well as by types of library combinations. There are single-function as well as multifunction cooperatives. A single-function cooperative provides its members with only one service, i.e., a union list of serials, cooperative processing, interlibrary loan, or any program to meet a specified need. The multifunction multitype library cooperative provides a package containing two or more of these services.

Many single-function interlibrary cooperatives were organized to produce and maintain union lists of serials. FULS, formally organized and funded by the Florida State Library System in 1969, involved 143 libraries in the compilation of the Florida Union List of Serials. IMULS, the Intermountain Union List of Serials, is a product of 53 participating libraries in the Southwest, organized informally in 1968. The Miami Valley Cooperating Libraries was organized in 1966 by 35 libraries for the primary purpose of compiling a union list, as was OSSHE-OSL, the Oregon State System of Higher Education-Oregon State Library, in 1967. The

Quad City Union List of Periodicals in Illinois and Iowa was founded in 1968. With some exceptions, these lists were produced by informally organized multitype cooperatives without a formal administrative structure or budget, utilizing the staff of participating libraries. They were generally housed in space provided by one of the participants. A staff member usually was designated coordinator of the program and served gratuitously.

In contrast to the informal and loosely structured union list type of cooperative, multitype library cooperatives that provide the single-function interlibrary loan service are generally formally structured. They have a hired staff, make provision for responsible, continuous funding, and generally compensate resource libraries for the use of their materials. The costs of these services—staff, communications, delivery tools (TWX, telefacsimile, vans)—are generally underwritten by state and federal appropriations. There are many examples of such statewide, single-function, multitype library cooperatives: NYSILL, the New York State Interlibrary Loan Network; ILLINET, the Illinois Library and Information Network; CHAIN, the Arizona Channeled Interlibrary Loan Network; and TIE, the Texas Information Exchange.

MULTIFUNCTION COOPERATIVES

The existence of a statewide interlibrary loan network has not always precluded the organization and operation of such programs by local or regional multitype, multifunction cooperatives. In New York State, for instance, each of the 3 R's Councils (the Reference and Research Resources Councils) has an established regional interlibrary loan network. In Illinois, each of the 18 systems, along with 4 Reference and Research Centers, are part of the statewide interlibrary loan network. The Illinois Regional Library Council, the multitype, multifunction cooperative serving the Chicago metropolitan area, does not have a role in this network and therefore limits its activity in this area to a physical access program.

Regional intrastate multitype library cooperatives are generally multifunction and provide two or more of the following services: interlibrary loan; cooperative services in acquisition, cataloging, processing, delivery, reference, and storage; continuing education; union lists of serials and microforms; legislative assistance; reciprocal borrowing; audiovisual services; and computerized bibliographic services.

INTERSTATE LIBRARY NETWORKS

The functions and purposes of the interstate multitype library networks differ in many respects from those of the intrastate library cooperatives, as their sphere of operation is larger and transcends state lines. The member libraries may be drawn from as few as 4 states (PALINET/ ULC) to as many as 16 (WICHE), and membership may include over 100 libraries (SOLINET). Operating budgets are generally greater than those of the regional networks, with some over a million dollars (NELINET, SOLINET).

Although the interstate library networks may provide some of the same services as the intrastate ones, they generally utilize existing electronic data equipment and current communications technology in their operations. Some have been avant-garde in offering computerized cataloging services to their clientele (NELINET, for instance); several provide on-line bibliographic access to the machine-readable data bases (AMIGOS, NELINET, Bibliographic Center for Research); and one (SALINET) is investigating the feasibility of using satellite communication as a mechanism for continuing education programs. Consideration is being given to the possibility of delivery of materials by coterminous or long-distance telecommunication transmission.

Many directors see their interstate networks as part of a nationwide net. NELINET stated that its goals were not only to provide a regional center for the provision of computerized services to the New England states, to decrease the cost of cataloging operations, and to take advantage of computer technology but also to serve as a computer link between the New England libraries and other computer-based information services. It would also create a network of libraries to serve as a node in an evolving national bibliographic and information network. Similar goals were expressed for MIDLNET (Barbara Markuson) and for SOLINET (Charles Stevens). Step by step, and still without national direction, it appears that the plans and functions of these intrastate and interstate library cooperatives may yet serve as a framework for the creation of a national network.

PLANNING STUDIES AND SURVEYS

To those who may have thought that multitype library cooperatives have grown haphazardly and without direction, it must now be evident that the traditional passive approach to the planning of information services has been vigorously challenged. The administrators of multitype organizations recognize that planning is essential to survival and that statements of goals and objectives establish the credibility and viability of their operations. Although the "why" of planning may be obvious, Andrew Aines and Melvin Day clearly formulate the rationale for planning, namely, to make certain that the right resources are available within a specified region to meet the needs of its constituents; to make certain that funds will be available for the implementation of programs; and to ensure future evaluation of each program.[12]

The emphasis on planning studies and surveys is reflected in the extensive bibliographies prepared by Bunge (1965), Stenstrom (1970), Babcock (1971), Gilluly (1972), Palmini (1973), and Connor (1975) [see Appendix 1]. The Library Services Act (1956) and the Library Services and Construction Act (1965) encouraged the states to support planning studies and surveys. Charles Bunge, whose bibliography contains 96 library surveys and plans, made the following observation:

> The publication of a statewide library development plan based on a thorough survey of library resources and services has come to be accepted, indeed almost a mandatory responsibility of a state library. Evidence of the acceptance of this responsibility can be found in the accelerated pace with which press releases arrive announcing the appointment of another governor's committee, the hiring of a consultant or surveyor, the publication of another report or adoption of measures to achieve survey recommendations.[13]

Bunge's compilation lists plans, surveys, and reports for 1944–1964 for all the states but Arizona, Alabama, Alaska, Delaware, Georgia, Louisiana, North Dakota, South Carolina, Virginia, and Wyoming.

State agencies, however, have not been solely responsible for initiating and encouraging plans and surveys. The efforts and influence of local civic leaders, concerned educators, librarians, and other professionals should not be underestimated. In the early 1950s, for instance, a private organization called the Trustees Committee was founded. This committee represented the Yale, Harvard, Columbia, and New York Public Library interests and commissioned an exploratory study of the combined library resources of these institutions, prior to the possible establishment of a cooperative system among them. It was not until 1973 that such a cooperative came into being—the Research Library Group. This multitype library cooperative was organized only after yet another study had been prepared and further proposals for cooperation initiated.

In Pennsylvania, it was the influence of educators—the presidents of the University of Pennsylvania and the Carnegie Institute of Technology, the chancellor of the University of Pittsburgh, and the director of the Carnegie Library—that led to the establishment of the Pittsburgh Regional Library Center.

As recently as 1975, MIDLNET, a midwestern multitype interstate network, was established as the result of the efforts of a group of librarians from Iowa, Illinois, Minnesota, and Wisconsin. This group, with the support of the Committee on Interinstitutional Cooperation, insisted that planning studies should be undertaken and funded by the concerned private institutions, not with public or foundation funds.

The role of the professional associations in encouraging, promoting, and supporting planning studies should not be overlooked. SLICE (the Southwest Library Interstate Cooperative Endeavor), the product of the Southwest Library Association, is involved in continuing education and in a humanities project. The Louisiana Library Association promoted studies of SOLINET and the Arizona Library Association encouraged a regional planning study of that state. The Illinois Library Association commissioned a consultant study that led to the 1965 passage of the Network of Public Library Systems Act, from which the multitype network ILLINET eventually evolved.

Private agencies, such as the Kellogg and Rockefeller foundations and the Council on Library Resources, funded by the Ford Foundation, have also provided extensive funds for planning, research, and development of interstate and intrastate cooperatives.

ROLE OF TITLE III OF LSCA

It can generally be concluded from the literature that planning and surveys were the earmarks of multitype library development in the 1960s. Implementation and growth were the earmarks of the 1970s. A benchmark date was 1966. The inclusion of Title III in the Library Services and Construction Act not only encouraged state agencies to promote interlibrary cooperation but also fostered creative development by providing funds for demonstration programs. Long-range planning and evaluation were required. Each state had to submit comprehensive five-year program statements, including policies and procedures for their implementation.

ORGANIZATION AND GOVERNANCE

Traditionally, libraries have relied upon informal agreements to provide services to other libraries. The agreements were not binding since no official record was kept of services exchanged. As a rule, there was no well-defined organizational structure. As the requirements of multitype library cooperatives became more and more complex, it was apparent that informal agreements were insufficient and that networks required specialized skills. Thomas Parker noted that the management requirements of library networks are extremely complex and require a specialized and not widely recognized set of boundary spanning skills.[14] Planning, implementation, and evaluation of interlibrary programs could not be left to happenstance staff, direction, and agreements. In recent years, there has been a trend toward more formality. A comprehensive study of the progress that has been made in this direction has not yet been undertaken. All of the interstate multitype networks have some form of organizational structure (NELINET, MIDLNET, Bibliographic Center for Research, SOLINET, AMIGOS) as do most of the multifunction intrastate multitype cooperatives.

In most of these organizations, a written constitution defines executive and administrative responsibilities. The organizations are independent, autonomous, and generally, although not necessarily, incorporated.

Incorporation, however, is important. Ruth Patrick itemized the advantages.[15] Such a step provides the cooperative not only with the rights and privileges of a legal body but also makes it easier to enter into contracts, to fix legal responsibility, and to provide limited liability for individual members. Incorporation usually requires a board of directors that serves as a policymaking group. The composition of the boards varies. In the Reference and Research Resources Library Councils in New York State, some of the boards are composed of laypersons only, while others are a combination of laypersons and librarians. The members of the board are generally elected by the membership and serve for a period defined by the bylaws or constitution. The powers and responsibilities are carefully specified.

The administrative staff usually consists of a director and clerical assistance. Skills in systems analysis and design and networking, a knowledge of computer and communication technologies, and the ability to relate to people are not uncommon requirements for the position of director. The size of the staff is dependent upon the scope of the operation and the availability of funds. NELINET, for instance, has a very sophisticated operation as well as a staff composed of educators and technicians. The Illinois Regional Library Council and the Rochester 3R's Council have small staffs—a director, an assistant to the director, and secretarial and clerical help.

Because of limited staff, multitype library cooperatives depend on committees to help design, plan, and implement programs. This also ensures member participation. The staff of member libraries may be asked to serve on such committees as interlibrary loan, continuing education, serials, access, and media. Permitting staff to contribute time and services to these committees, without compensation, is an indication of the membership support of the cooperative's activities.

Finding suitable quarters for multitype cooperatives has been a problem. It is not uncommon for these organizations to be housed in office buildings or in space rented from or donated by their member libraries. The Illinois Regional Library Council has moved from space provided by the Suburban Library System to space donated by the Chicago Public Library. New York METRO is based in the New York Public Library, the North Country Library Resource Council has its headquarters in an academic institution, and the Central New York Library Reference Council rents office space in a commercial building. The Library Council of Metropolitan Milwaukee operates in space donated by the Milwaukee Public Library, while the Tri-County Council's space is donated by the University of Wisconsin at Parkside. The Indiana ALSAs are required to have their headquarters apart from member libraries; they usually rent commercial space located as near as possible to the center of their service areas.

Every effort has been made by the multitype cooperative to ensure democratic governance and participatory democracy. Alphonse Trezza noted that one of the major barriers to participation in library cooperatives by public, academic, and special libraries was fear of loss of local autonomy.[16] In order to overcome this apprehension, multitype library cooperatives regularly schedule meetings, provide progress reports for their members and governing boards, and make certain all are closely involved in decision and policymaking. The membership elects the governing board and participates in program development; governing boards vote on budget and policy matters. Most of these organizations operate within a framework provided by a constitution and bylaws. It is obvious that the multitype cooperatives will not knowingly jeopardize the autonomy of the individual library units that make up their memberships.

Although they are staffed, organized and housed, and governed by a constitution and bylaws, and are even incorporated, many cooperative organizations do not feel secure. Since multitype cooperatives cross local jurisdictional boundaries, they constantly petition for statutory recognition and funding, two basic needs that cannot be underemphasized and that have been vigorously pursued.

As shown in Table 3, about 80 percent of the states have some form of enabling legislation that at least encourages multitype development, even though it may not specifically authorize it. Only a few states (Maine, Michigan, Nevada, Ohio, and Utah) have passed legislation appropriating funds for multitype library cooperatives.[17]

Ed Sayre made the following observation regarding statutory authorization of multitype cooperatives:

> Statutes may not encourage library cooperation specifically, but they will authorize inter-jurisdictional mechanisms whereby regional library services may be instituted. This has been an issue of legislative concern for many years and most legislators are willing and anxious to tell their constituents how they promoted fiscal economies by promoting regional cooperation such as library systems.[18]

There are subtle differences in the wording of these statutes. The legislation in Maine, Illinois, Indiana, and Rhode Island specifically authorizes "all types of libraries to merge and provide more effective library service." Alaska, Arizona, Maryland, and Idaho authorize "some state agency to provide the necessary leadership and guidance that will result in coordinated library activities." In other states, a blanket law permitting "two or more public agencies to enter into agreements with any other agency for joint or cooperative action" is used as the basis for multitype cooperative development.

Table 3   Multitype Library Cooperation: State Enabling Legislation and Statutory Support

State	Statutory Funding	Enabling Legislation
Alabama	None	None
Alaska	None	Supportive: state library may coordinate library service of the state with other educational agencies to increase effectiveness and eliminate duplication.
Arizona	None	Supportive: allows Library Extension Service to give advice and assistance to "joint ventures" of different types of libraries. AR Rev Statutes: 41-708.A.4.
Arkansas	None	None.
California	None	None. There is a joint exercise of powers authority, enabling CLASS (California Library Authority for Systems and Services) to govern, direct, set policies, establish computerized networks, and make its services available to all libraries in California.
Colorado	None	Supportive: allows for regional library service systems: C.R.S. 1973, 24-90-108.
Connecticut	None	Connecticut Public Acts 75-316, 363 (1975).
Delaware	None	None.
Florida	None	None.
Georgia	None	None.
Hawaii	None	None.
Idaho	None	None.
Illinois	Yes	Illinois State Library Chapter 128; 106; 107; 118. Library Systems Act Chapter 81; 111; 117; 122. Local Libraries Chapter 81: 4-7, 22; 1004-10011. Corporation Law Chapter 32.
Indiana	None	Library Services Authority Act of 1967. Chapter 47, Acts of 1967 (Burns 41-1201-1214) IC 1971, 20-13-6-1–20-13-6-14). "It is the purpose of this act to en-

Table 3   Multitype Library Cooperation: State Enabling Legislation and Statutory Support, Continued

State	Statutory Funding	Enabling Legislation
		courage the development and improvement of all types of library service and to promote the efficient use of funds, personnel, materials, and properties enabling government authorities having library responsibilities to join together in a municipal corporation called a library services authority, which will provide such services and facilities as the governing authorities party to the establishment and support of the library services authority may determine."
Iowa	None	None.
Kansas	Yes	Kansas State Act 75-2547 et seq. Regional System of Cooperating Libraries: purpose of this act is for the state in cooperation with local libraries to provide adequate library services to all citizens of the state through the regional systems of cooperating libraries herein provided by use of joint planning and financing of library services to improve existing services, to utilize such federal aid funds as may be available, and to extend library service to persons not having the same at this time.
Kentucky	None	None.
Louisiana	None	None.
Maine	Yes	Specifically permitted: 1964 Maine revised statutes, Title 27, Chapter 626, Public, academic, school, and special libraries to serve collectively the entire population of the state by participating in a network of library districts for the purpose of organizing library resources for research, information. . . .

Table 3   Multitype Library Cooperation: State Enabling Legislation and Statutory Support, Continued

State	Statutory Funding	Enabling Legislation
Maryland	None	Supportive: the State Board of Education, and subject to its approval, the division of library development and services shall have the power to provide leadership and guidance for the planning of coordinated development . . . to develop public library and school library services, and library networks. . . .
Massachusetts	None	Supportive: Comprehensive Library Media Services Act (Chapter 78, section 19E).
Michigan	Yes	Specifically permitted: P.A. 286, 1965, providing for four classes of systems based on population size.
Minnesota	None	None.
Mississippi	None	Supportive: allowed by contract.
Missouri	None	Supportive: allowed by contract.
Montana	None	None.
Nebraska	None	Supportive: any two or more public agencies may enter into agreements with any other for joint or cooperative action.
Nevada	None	Specifically permitted: enabling multitype library cooperative development: NRS 378.080, paragraphs 7, 12, 14, 15, 16, 18 and NRS 378.085 (added 1973).
New Hampshire	Yes	Specifically permitted: enabling multitype library cooperative development: N.H. RSA 201-C:13, 1963 and 1973.
New Jersey	None	None.
New Mexico	None	None.
New York	None	No such legislation exists in New York; several bills in legislature.
North Carolina	None	Specifically permitted: enabling multitype library cooperative development: G.S. 125-2 (4) (1973).
North Dakota	None	None.

Table 3   Multitype Library Cooperation: State Enabling Legislation and Statutory Support, Continued

State	Statutory Funding	Enabling Legislation
Ohio	Yes	Ohio Rev. Code 3375.90-3375.93. Provides for organizing Metropolitan Library Systems involving four or more libraries of two or more types in a metropolitan area.
Oklahoma	None	None.
Oregon	None	Broad coverage permitting service contracts.
Pennsylvania	Yes	Library Code: authorizes the state library to receive funds allocated to the state for library purposes by the federal government or by private agencies and to administer such funds in library maintenance, improvement, or extension programs consistent with federal and state library objectives. The code also authorizes an appropriation of up to $100,000 for each regional resource center (designated centers: Carnegie Library of Pittsburgh, Free Library of Philadelphia, State Library of Pennsylvania).
Rhode Island	Yes	The State Department is authorized to establish five interrelated systems in order to coordinate, on a cooperative basis, library resources throughout the state, to provide improved library services . . . the Providence Public Library is designated as the principal library in the state and the University of Rhode Island, Brown University, and Rhode Island College are listed as special resource centers.
South Carolina	None	None.
South Dakota	None	The policy of the state provides that cooperation among and between libraries shall be encouraged and promoted by the State Library Agency. The agency is required to provide a network of li-

Table 3   Multitype Library Cooperation: State Enabling Legislation and Statutory Support, Continued

State	Statutory Funding	Enabling Legislation
		braries and a system whereby the resources of libraries in the state are made available to the citizens . . . to provide for state participation in regional, national or international networks . . . and allows the state agency to make rules and regulations under which libraries may have access to systems and networks.
Tennessee	None	Tennessee code provides encouragement of library development within the state . . . to enter into local, regional, or interstate compacts with competent agencies in the furtherance of library service.
Texas	None	Interlocal Cooperation Act, Article 4413.
Utah	None	Library laws of 1963 . . . boards of city libraries, county libraries, of education, and of other educational institutions, library agencies, and local political subdivisions are empowered to cooperate, merge, or consolidate in providing library services.
Vermont	None	None.
Virginia	Yes	Code of Virginia establishes the authority of the state library to enter into contracts for the purpose of providing cooperative service.
Washington	None	Chapter 31, laws of 1975–1976 . . . Senate bill establishes the Washington Library Network and places responsibility for Network with the Washington State Library.
West Virginia	None	None.
Wisconsin	None	Statute 43.05. Facilitate interlibrary loans and other forms of interlibrary cooperation among all libraries in this state, including

Table 3   Multitype Library Cooperation: State Enabling Legislation and Statutory Support, Continued

State	Statutory Funding	Enabling Legislation
		without limitation because of enumeration public, school, academic and special libraries, public library systems, regional resource centers and state level library and information centers.
Wyoming	None	None.

Source: ASLA Interlibrary Cooperation Subcommittee, comp. and ed., *ASLA Report on Interlibrary Cooperation* (Chicago, 1976).

For the past decade, state and federal library legislation has not only stimulated interlibrary cooperation but has concurrently strengthened library agencies at the state level. The Library Services Act of 1956 and the Library Services and Construction Act of 1966 and its amendments all placed the responsibility for the receipt and distribution of federal funds for the development of interlibrary cooperation at the state level. States that did not have appropriate machinery to handle these funds and responsibilities soon created them. Although the names of the agency units may vary (the Development Services Unit in Colorado, the Library Development Group in Connecticut, the Division of Library Development in New York), their functions are the same. According to the ASLA report, most states that do not yet have such units have plans for their future creation.[19]

Interstate as well as intrastate multitype library cooperatives also have expressed some concern regarding their legal status. The problem is primarily with the rights of libraries in one state to enter into interstate relationships. This matter is generally handled by interstate compacts and does not appear to be a significant problem. With the exceptions of Delaware, Idaho, Hawaii, New Jersey, and Texas, all states have statutes permitting libraries, as well as other agencies, to enter into interstate relationships. Even libraries in those states that do not have such permissive legislation have become members of interstate networks and their actions have not been constrained by legislative omission. Although multitype library cooperatives may have difficulty in obtaining statutory recognition and funding, there have been no legal barriers that have prohibited or limited their participation in statewide multitype library cooperative activities.

FUNDING SOURCES

There appears to be no question that funding is one of the principal problems facing multitype cooperatives. Unlike the public libraries that have been and undoubtedly will continue to be funded by local tax bases, the multitype cooperatives do not have dependable or continuing sources of funds. To date the primary source of funding has been the federal government. Should this source of funding be withdrawn, the effect would be catastrophic.

There are several factors that may account for the funding problem. First, the multitype cooperatives do not have a long tradition of service. Second, the concept of the multitype library cooperative is difficult to explain to the general public and to the legislator. For the past ten years, this type of organization has had to establish its feasibility and its need. It has had to prove itself to the library community and to explain its existence to everyone. Since it is not a walk-in type of library, its existence is invisible to the public. Multitype library cooperatives need publicity and a hard sell.

This country's present economic situation has created a very serious problem for the multitype library cooperative. State and federal legislators faced with continuing economic crises establish funding priorities, and education and libraries are not always high on their lists. Many agencies anticipate that levels of funding will remain stationary. While federal funds are still available through the Library Services and Construction Act, they must be lobbied for continuously. (Under the Nixon administration, withholding of funds became an executive pastime, and a source of frustration for state libraries anticipating funding.)

It is also possible that the present economic environment may have an effect on membership fees. Will academic, public, and special libraries, hard pressed to meet their own needs, feel a need to retrench and cut back services offered to other libraries? Will member libraries have to justify payment of fees? Will they have to charge additional service fees? It is becoming increasingly apparent that to survive, cooperatives will have to continue to offer creative and imaginative programs and to produce results.

There now appear to be about six sources of funding for the multitype cooperative. The following are the most common:

Membership fees. There is no common denominator or formula for charging fees. Some are set at a particular rate; others are on a scale, based on a percentage of the budget or expenditures for acquisitions. Within the same state, scales may vary. In New York, for instance, each of the 3R's Councils has a varying membership charge. In the South Central Research Library Council, it is $50; in the Rochester and METRO Councils, it is based on member library budgets.

Service charges. Although many services are considered part of the multitype library cooperative package, charges are imposed when the service must pay for itself. A number of cooperatives may be willing to pay for photocopies produced for interlibrary loan for their members, but will then impose a charge for delivery. In almost all instances, fees are levied for searching machine-readable data bases.

State and federal support. The extent of support from federal sources has been repeatedly emphasized. Multitype library cooperatives not only take advantage of funds from the Library Services and Construction Act but also apply for special grants offered through the Higher Education Act, the Elementary and Secondary School Act, and the Medical Library Assistance Act. The more desired funding comes from state sources on an ongoing basis. State funds may be appropriated by the legislature (Utah, Pennsylvania, Michigan, Illinois) or may be part of the executive budget (New York). In order for state funds to be distributed on a permanent and equitable basis, the role of the cooperative in the statewide library development plan must be well defined. In Illinois, for example, there is statutory funding for the public library systems that are converting to multitype cooperatives, but little likelihood for the Illinois Regional Library Council to obtain funding through the legislature until its role vis-à-vis the systems is defined.

Private and government foundations. Many cooperatives have investigated foundation support. In 1974, the National Endowment for the Humanities awarded the Southwestern Library Association a six-month grant in support of one of its projects. These funds were used to spearhead the SLICE Bibliographic Network Project. Ford and Kellogg foundations are among the organizations considered as possible sources of funding. The Kellogg Foundation awarded a $140,000 grant to the Michigan Library Consortium to enable its member libraries to take advantage of new technology. The Council on Library Resources, funded by the Ford Foundation, has provided grants to a number of organizations.

Professional associations. It has been noted earlier that professional associations have provided support and encouragement for the establishment of multitype cooperatives. They can provide assistance in lobbying for legislation and in providing a forum for the discussion of problems relating to all types of libraries within their memberships. The possibility of monetary support from professional organizations is another area that needs investigation.

Invisible sources of support. An area of support that will not be found in the annual budgets of the multitype cooperatives is the many hours of staff time contributed by participating member libraries. An unpublished study undertaken in the South Central Research Library Council in New

York State attempted to determine the number of free hours donated. It was found to be the equivalent of at least one full-time staff member at $10,000 per year.[20] Such contributions are an indication of member support of multitype library cooperation.

Attempts to collect information on sources of funding and on the cost of operating multitype library cooperatives have been at best frustrating, although such a study should be undertaken. The problems in collection of data are obvious. There is no uniformity in reporting statistics, no standardized vocabulary, and the functions of multitype cooperatives are such that the investigator is faced with unending variables. It is expected, however, that some enterprising economist will one day attempt such a study.

NOTES

1. *American Library Directory 1974/75* (New York: R. R. Bowker, 1975).

2. ASLA Interlibrary Cooperation Subcommitte, comp. and ed., *ASLA Report on Interlibrary Cooperation* (Chicago: Association of State Library Agencies, 1976).

3. Diana D. Delanoy and Carlos A. Cuadra, *Directory of Academic Library Consortia* (Santa Monica, Calif.: System Development Corporation, 1972).

4. Donald W. Black and Carlos A. Cuadra, *Directory of Academic Library Consortia*, 2d ed. (Santa Monica, Calif.: System Development Corporation, 1976).

5. Richard Dougherty, "Paradoxes of Library Cooperation," *Library Journal* 97 (May 15, 1972): 1867–1870.

6. Joint Divisional Planning Committee for a Symposium on Multitype Library Cooperation, "Program Manual" (typescript).

7. Raynard C. Swank, "Interlibrary Cooperation, Interlibrary Communications and Information Networks—Explanation and Definition," in *Proceedings of the Conference on Interlibrary Communications and Information Networks*, ed. Joseph Becker (Chicago: American Library Association, 1971), pp. 18–26.

8. John Cory, "Networks in a Major Metropolitan Center," *Library Quarterly* 39 (January 1969): 90–98.

9. Ralph J. Stenstrom, *Cooperation between Types of Libraries, 1940–1968: An Annotated Bibliography* (Chicago: American Library Association, 1970).

10. G. Flint Purdy, "Interrelationships among Public, Academic and School Libraries," *Library Quarterly* 39 (January 1969): 52–63.

11. Keyes D. Metcalf, "Cooperation among Maine Libraries" (Cambridge, Mass., 1961), p. 7.

12. Andrew A. Aines and Melvin S. Day, "National Planning of Information Systems," *Annual Review of Information Science and Technology* 10 (1975): 3–42.

13. Charles A. Bunge, "Statewide Public Library Surveys and Plans, 1944–1964," *ALA Bulletin* (May 1965): 364–374.

14. Thomas F. Parker, "Models and Methods: The Tools of Library Networking," *College and Research Libraries* (November 1975): 480–486.

15. Ruth Patrick, *Guidelines for Library Cooperation* (Santa Monica, Calif.: System Development Corporation, 1972).

16. Alphonse F. Trezza, "Fear and Funding," *Library Journal* 99 (December 15, 1974): 3174–3175.

17. ASLA Interlibrary Cooperation Subcommittee, op. cit.

18. Ed Sayre, "Five Vital Considerations," *Library Journal* 99 (December 14, 1974): 3178.

19. ASLA Interlibrary Cooperation Subcommittee, op. cit.

20. Betsy Ann Olive, "A Study of Contributed Time by Library Staff Members in an Academic Library Consortium" (Cornell University, Business and Public Administration Library, 1972) 2 pp. typescript.

TWO

RELATIONSHIPS OF MULTI-TYPE COOPERATIVES TO STATE, REGIONAL AND FEDERAL AGENCIES

THE FEDERAL ROLE

Dorothy Kittel

Many agencies in both the executive and legislative branches of the federal government are concerned with improving cooperation and coordination among different types of libraries. To cite some examples, the U.S. Congress has passed legislation supporting the coordination of library resources and services among libraries of different types. The National Commission on Libraries and Information Science has performed a number of research studies in many areas in order to develop a national plan. The Library of Congress is engaged in many sophisticated and complicated experiments in improving bibliographic access to resources. The Federal Library Committee, representing the national libraries and other federal departmental libraries, also promotes cooperation among its quite diverse institutions. The discussion here will focus on the role of the U.S. Office of Education in multitype library cooperative development, reflecting the situation and policies as they were during the 1975/76 fiscal year.

The Office of Libraries and Learning Resources, and its predecessors in the Office of Education, have played a key role in administering federal support programs for libraries since 1956. In hearings on the extension of the Library Services and Construction Act held before the Subcommittee on Select Education of the Committee on Education and Labor, House of Representatives, on December 15, 1975, administration officials stated:

> . . . the Federal Government has a joint role with states and localities to encourage, support, and provide incentive capital for comprehensive information services in interinstitutional cooperative patterns and to demonstrate these, as well as other related arrangements of new information delivery systems for libraries of all types.[1]

That the Library Services and Construction Act and the Higher Education Act, Title II-B, Library Research and Demonstration, have stimulated the development of library cooperatives and networks is a proposition taken largely on the basis of faith. Hopefully, in the near future, there will be more complete and in-depth factual and evaluative data to support this faith.

The National Center for Education Statistics is currently reviewing proposals for a "Survey of Library Cooperatives, Consortia, and Networks." The survey will identify such activities and acquire data from the

43

headquarters of cooperatives, consortia, and networks that serve academic, public, and special libraries. The data will be analyzed and the status and condition of these legal entities and organizations reported.

A second study under the direction of the USOE Office of Planning, Budgeting, and Evaluation will evaluate the impact of LSCA Title III and HEA Title II-B programs. Proposals are being reviewed for a "Study of Library Cooperative, Network, and Demonstration Programs and Projects." The study will be concerned with the direction and magnitude of changes and the impact resulting from these program efforts. The study will also attempt to answer these questions: How have changes been produced; whom have they affected; and how effective have they been? The two objectives for the study of LSCA Title III are to determine the degree (if any) to which support for this program has resulted in the establishment and/or expansion of cooperative networks; and to identify the factors that contribute to the success and failure of this program. The findings of these two studies should provide the data and information needed to establish criteria for planning and evaluation in the areas of cooperative development and networking for all types of libraries and information centers.

FEDERAL PARTICIPATION IN LIBRARY COOPERATIVE PROJECTS

Library legislation in the form of the Library Services Act (LSA) was first passed by Congress in 1956. The act provided federal funds to improve public library services to rural areas with less than 10,000 population. The Library Services and Construction Act (LSCA) was approved by Congress in 1964, amending the original rural program to include grants for public library services to urban as well as rural areas and to provide funds for public library construction.

LSCA did not mandate interlibrary cooperation but there was a thrust toward larger units of service and cooperative projects. In 1966, LSCA was amended by Congress to include a new Title III, Interlibrary Cooperation, "for the establishment and maintenance of local, regional, state or interstate cooperative networks of libraries, including state, school, college and university, public and special libraries and information centers, to provide maximum effective use of funds in providing services to all users." [For full text of LSCA see Appendix 2—Ed.]

Requirements of LSCA

LSCA is administered by legally authorized state library agencies under a state plan, which is submitted to the U.S. Commissioner of Education for approval. The purpose of the plan is to "provide a framework within which the State will encourage the establishment or expansion of programs to carry out the purposes of the Act and to provide the basis on which payments are made to the States."

The state plan consists of three parts:

1. A basic state plan that includes assurances and certifications that the state meets the legal and fiscal requirements of the law, a statement of criteria to be used in determining adequacy of services, and a listing of the statewide advisory councils.
2. A long-range program that identifies the state's present and projected library needs; describes a plan of action for meeting these needs; and outlines the policies, criteria, priorities, and procedures for the following: (a) periodic evaluation of the effectiveness of programs and projects supported under the act, (b) dissemination of the results of such evaluation, (c) the effective coordination of state agency programs with library programs and projects operated by institutions of higher education, by local elementary or secondary schools, and by other public and private institutions offering library services, and (d) criteria used in allocating funds under each title of the act.
3. An annual program for the use of funds under each title detailing specific activities that will fulfill library needs set forth in the long-range plan.

The state plan must be developed with the assistance of the statewide advisory council and in consultation with the U.S. Commissioner of Education, who has delegated this authority to the ten regional library services program officers (RLSPO). The statewide advisory councils on libraries are representative of public, school, academic, and special libraries; institutional libraries, such as hospital or reformatory libraries; and libraries serving the physically handicapped. Library users must comprise one third of the council membership. The functions of the council are to advise the state agency on the development of the state plan; advise on policy matters arising in the administration of the state plan; and assist in evaluating library programs, services, and activities under the state plan.

LOCAL PROPOSALS SHOULD RELATE TO THE STATE PLAN

Multitype library cooperative activities cannot be isolated from the total library development efforts within a state, as the state uses LSCA funds to improve library services for all its residents. Proposals for multitype library programs relate to the state plan for library development. Any potential applicant should, therefore, have a thorough knowledge of the state plan—its goals, objectives, criteria, and priorities. Information about a state plan is disseminated through state library publications, conferences, meetings, workshops, and announcements of the availability of LSCA funds for certain purposes. Any proposal should define the need for the project and the project's goals and objectives in relation to the state plan's goals and objectives. It should also describe the unique contribution this activity would make toward achieving state goals or improving or expanding ongoing efforts. It should describe the procedures by which the proposal was developed. Who was involved? How was the need for this activity identified? What evidence exists that the activity might be successful? What is the prospect that it will be continued if federal funds should be no longer available?

State library agencies have on their staffs consultants who provide assistance in developing proposals and are knowledgeable about both federal and state rules, regulations, and administrative requirements. It also has guidelines and forms for submitting proposals, and it has the final authority to determine which proposals will be funded. The proposals that are approved become the state's annual program and are then submitted to the appropriate USOE regional office to be reviewed for compliance with LSCA regulations and for conformity with the state's long-range program.

Once an activity is accepted as a part of the state plan, the process of accountability begins—at the local, state, and federal levels. The local level makes oral and written reports on program development and financial status to the state agency. Consultant services, local project monitoring, and annual reports to the federal government on the accomplishments and failures of the LSCA programs in achieving their goals and objectives are required at the state level.

At the federal level, USOE uses annual reports from the states to compile a national assessment of the effectiveness of LSCA for review by administrative and congressional officials. These must, therefore, include program data that are not merely descriptive but also evaluative of the degree to which objectives were achieved. This information is meaningful at the federal level to the Congress and administration and to the library profession. In spite of the complexity of the procedures to be followed, they enable programs to be initiated locally with federal support. The ultimate objective is to have a nationwide system of libraries and information services, a natural outgrowth of expressions of need at the state and local levels.

MULTITYPE LIBRARY COOPERATION IS NOT NEW

It is interesting to go back to 1936 and reflect upon an earlier expression of the library cooperative concept, which was articulated by the Special Committee on Federal Relations to the ALA Council. Members serving on that committee were Charles H. Compton, St. Louis Public

Library; James T. Gerould, Princeton University Library; Carleton B. Joeckel, University of Chicago Graduate Library School; Harriet C. Long, Oregon State Library; Milton E. Lord, Boston Public Library; Mary U. Rothrock, Tennessee Valley Authority; Clarence E. Sherman, Providence Public Library; Forrest B. Spaulding, Des Moines Public Library; and Louis Round Wilson, University of Chicago Graduate Library School, chairman.

Based on several years of study and investigation of federal grant-in-aid programs in education, agriculture, and highways, and of the contemporary library scene, the committee concluded that "A system of permanent annual Federal grants-in-aid to libraries is essential to the complete and adequate development of library service throughout the United States." While the committee directed its attention to the rationale and structure of federal aid to states for the development of public library services, it recognized the need for stimulation and assistance for library services in the public elementary and secondary schools and in public institutions of higher education. These institutions were seen as "essentially a part of any general plan for complete service to all the people, and in this sense, educational libraries belong to the 'public library system' of any State." Federal grants-in-aid would be essential to assist in a general program of library cooperation and in the coordination of library resources on a regional and national scale. The committee opposed, however, the use of federal subsidies to establish a single unified pattern of library service throughout the country. It saw the states, the local communities, and the nation all contributing to the development of a cooperative plan for the improvement of library service:

> The function of the federal library agency is to oversee the distribution of federal grants-in-aid and to assure the efficient use of federal appropriations through the exercise of reasonable supervisory powers. The state library agency is responsible for the formulation of state plans of library development and for the distribution of federal grants to the libraries in counties, cities and towns. Finally, the local units, as is now the case, have full authority in the administration of their libraries and also, as now, are responsible for the success or failure of library service.[2]

NOTES

1. U.S., Congress, House of Representatives, Committee on Education and Labor, *Hearing . . . on H.R. 11233 to Amend the Library Services and Construction Act to Extend the Authorizations of Appropriations in Such Act and for Other Purposes,* 94th Cong., 1st sess., December 15, 1975, p. 59.

2. American Library Association, Special Committee on Federal Relations, "Libraries and Federal Aid," *ALA Bulletin* 30 (May 1936): 425, 457, 459.

EMERGENCE OF THE MULTISTATE REGION

Allen Sevigny

The Library Services and Construction Act (LSCA) is a fully region-alized program; that is, full responsibility for the act is delegated by the U.S. Commissioner of Education to the regional commissioners of education. The ten regional USOE offices are in Boston, New York, Phila-delphia, Atlanta, Chicago, Dallas, Kansas City, Denver, San Francisco, and Seattle. Each regional office has a library program officer (RPO) who is a civil service employee and has the following responsibilities: the ad-ministration of the Library Services and Construction Act and the provi-sion of information and technical assistance in other federal programs that affect libraries, including Revenue Sharing, Community Development Act, Appalachian Regional Development Act, Older Americans Act, and others. The library program officer reports to the regional commissioner of education, has responsibilities to the Office of Libraries and Library Resources in Washington, and works closely with the state library agencies.

Although LSCA dollars represent a pittance compared to total ex-penditures for library service, their impact has been enormous. LSCA programs now permeate every corner of the library world. The majority of local and statewide cooperative activities originated as LSCA projects. Because LSCA required state library agencies to administer these pro-grams, it was necessary to strengthen these agencies so that they could assume a leadership role in statewide development. Twenty years ago, there was little awareness of the existence of a state library agency.

STATEWIDE PLANNING

The 1970 amendments to the Library Services and Construction Act called for the development in each state of a comprehensive statewide plan for library development.[1] Planning in most libraries, unfortunately, had consisted of waiting until one heard what one's budget level was to be, and then of trying to stretch it as far as it would go. In the early 1970s, most librarians had little experience in comprehensive long-range plan-ning and even less in program evaluation. Ray Fry of the U.S. Office of Education approached professionals in planning and evaluation and asked them to devise an institute for state library personnel. The Center on Planning and Evaluation of Ohio State University was selected to develop a year-long institute for the 50 state and territorial library agencies. The center's task had many facets:

1. The adaptation of existing disciplines of long-range planning and evaluation to the library context
2. The training of state library agency staff, USOE Washington staff, and the RPO's for planning and evaluation
3. The preparation of a guide for statewide planning and evaluation
4. The provision of assistance to the state library agencies in the preparation of the long-range programs mandated by the Library Services and Construction Act.

It is a tribute to Ray Fry's vision and tenacity that the institute worked. The state libraries have just completed their fifth year of long-range planning.

Planning is now at least as sophisticated as that which is carried on in other disciplines, as is exemplified by the Wisconsin and Illinois plans.[2, 3] Since the RPO's monitor the long-range planning of a state library agency, they tend to be very much aware of cooperative development and are strategically placed to work for multistate cooperation, since each covers a number of states.

EVOLUTION OF MULTITYPES FROM PUBLIC LIBRARY SYSTEMS

Public library systems have been in existence for four decades and have demonstrated the basic principle that the whole is greater than the sum of its parts. Within the last decade, with incentives provided by Title III of LSCA, and an increasing public demand for information, these systems have begun to encourage membership and participation by non-public libraries. Evolution of library systems into multitype councils has proceeded where conditions were conducive, but not according to a generally accepted blueprint or following widely accepted guidelines. There have been some haphazard results that could have been avoided if prescriptions for multitype library cooperative development had been available. Suggested minimum requirements for a sound multitype cooperative might be a firm basis in law relative to a government body; solid planning, with maximum input from the total constituency; firm funding formulas, based in law; and a mutually agreed upon role in the statewide library network.

As yet there is no commonly accepted terminology of library cooperation. Words like consortium, system, network, council, cooperative, intertype, and multitype are thrown about, but every writer gives them a different shade of meaning. In this article, "system" will refer to the classic public library system and "council" to the cooperative that involves two or more types of libraries. "Intertype" seems less precise than "multitype" as the adjective for that kind of council. Misuse of the word "regional" may create unnecessary confusion. There are two local offenders in nomenclature in Region V states (Illinois, Indiana, Michigan, Minnesota, Ohio, and Wisconsin). First, the local multitype cooperative is known as the Illinois Regional Library Council, which it is not at all. It is a local cooperative, serving metropolitan Chicago. Rather than listing its many excellencies, one might note that for several years as other councils have developed in the Midwest, one or the other of the aspects of IRLC's program has been imitated. Who has not heard of the INFOPASS it sponsored? The other offender is MIDLNET, the Midwest Region Library Network, which is, in fact, a multistate network and roughly parallels other regional networks. Both of these organizations are not-for-profit corporations, are not closely related to a government body, and are not permanently funded. Thus they do not meet the aforementioned minimum requirements for a sound multitype cooperative. It is expected, however, that in time they will.

In the early 1960s, public libraries were completing a period of experimentation in system development. There were cooperative, consolidated, and federated systems and a dozen variations and combinations of these. One state, New York, had succeeded in creating a network of public library systems covering the state. Other states were soon to follow. By the time the last New York public library system was formed, library leaders in the state perceived that while the systems were an effective and logical mechanism for cooperative activity, they did not go far enough.

Only public libraries could join the system *and* participate in its governance. As a rule, public library system charters did not permit them to serve other kinds of libraries and the earliest systems tended to ignore nonpublic library resources and services. Although informal activities were carried on, their success depended on the goodwill and service orientation of the participants in the arrangement. This was not a very sound basis for cooperative activity, which can thrive only where there is a carefully planned structure, sound legal authorization, and hard cash available for experimentation and for the reward of the haves for sharing with the have-nots.

In about the same period, the Commissioner's Committee on Reference-Research Library Resources proposed the creation of reference and research systems, paralleling the public library systems.[4] The language of the subsequent legislation authorizing the 3 R's Councils is interesting, because there is frequent mention of library service at the reference and research level. In retrospect, it seems a rather naive notion. Down here, as it were, there is ordinary library service, to be provided by public libraries and the public library systems that backstopped them. Somewhere up above, there is another level of service for a more demanding or sophisticated clientele. There was a major conceptual error in this dualism, but scarcely anyone realized it at the time. Now all library and information services are perceived to be at one unified level.[5]

In a major study of the decade, recommendations came precariously close to resolving the dilemma of two levels of service by suggesting two separate New York networks. The study refers to "the possibility of non-public libraries becoming system members. Public library systems would thus become library systems for all the public that uses libraries. Above the systems, specialized reference and research services should be organized into regions, each serving several library systems."[6] Note that the notion persists of two separate networks, developing independently of each other. There was some attempt at coordination through the requirement that council boundaries follow system boundaries and that public library systems have permanent representation on the 3 R's Council boards.

Multitype councils have been set up in a great many states but, unfortunately, some other states are moving toward two separate networks. In Region V, there are multitype organizations in Illinois, Indiana, Michigan, Ohio, and Wisconsin. In Minnesota, there is much multitype activity, but library groups are still searching for an appropriate design for multitype cooperatives.

No one quite realized how many multitype cooperatives, consortia, and networks there were until the Association of State Library Agencies' Subcommittee on Interlibrary Cooperation published its 1976 Report.[7] It seems to be time to bring order out of this proliferation of networks. The enormous amount of cooperative activity of the last dozen years is welcomed and taken as evidence of the continuing vitality of the library profession.

There are a number of issues to be resolved in multitype library cooperation. No state has yet achieved a statewide chain of multitype cooperatives that effectively coordinates all library and information services. There is time for debate and dialogue on these issues. An examination of the ASLA Report reveals that all over the land libraries have created multitype organizations in which all kinds of libraries have joined forces to meet the needs of a diverse public. Surely, in the time of single, isolated library units, no one would have believed that one day the lions and lambs would lie down together.

THE INDIANA PATTERN

The first advocate of a single, unified statewide network was Sam Prentiss, state librarian of New York in the early 1960s. His thinking was too far in advance of the times, and the idea seems to have been dropped. The really crucial date for the multitype cooperative is 1967, the year of the legislation in Indiana called the Library Services Authority Act.[8] The multitype cooperatives set up in Indiana are known as Area Library Service Authorities (ALSAs). An ALSA, like the definition of a word in *Alice in Wonderland*, is anything one wants it to be. In Indiana, any group of libraries, of any type, may join forces in a regional authority, the ideal pattern of organization for the multitype cooperative.

Thus Indiana bypassed the trap into which so many states have fallen, the creation of public library systems and subsequently the casting about for ways to coordinate the public library systems with academic or school or special libraries. At one stroke, all legal barriers to participation by a given library in the network because of its type had been precluded. Now Indiana has a network of unique multitype cooperatives that will soon cover the entire state.

This may be all well and good for service in a particular ALSA, but what about services that can be most effectively organized on a statewide basis? The answer is the statewide cooperative InCoLSA (Indiana Cooperative Library Services Authority), which concerns itself with such services as automated bibliographic services. The millenium has not been reached in Indiana. Of the requirements for multitype library cooperation, Indiana lacks one. There is a firm legal basis for the ALSAs and sound planning has gone into their development. What has not yet been achieved is state funding. Indiana has just appropriated its first state funding for library services, but it went not to the cooperatives but to local public libraries. The impact there will be much less than if it had been used for the cooperatives. Although the ALSAs subsist for the moment on Library Services and Construction Act funds, hopefully they will eventually achieve state funding.

ISSUES REQUIRING FURTHER INVESTIGATION

A few of the pressing questions in multitype cooperation that need further investigation are as follows:

Is the state the appropriate level for leadership in the development of multitype cooperatives? If one concedes that responsibility for education is a function of the state, it follows that responsibility for library and information services also rests at the state level. The fundamental unit is the statewide network, based in state library law and funded by formulas that are fixed in law. Funding formulas, then, will not vary with changes in political parties or priorities.

How truly comprehensive can statewide planning be? All state library agencies have developed long-range programs or five-year plans for their states. According to the mandates of LSCA, we must refer to these as long-range programs, while, in fact, they are five-year plans that are revised annually. They are not yet truly comprehensive, but in time will become so, as all types of institutions join statewide networks.

How unified are we in our position that multitype is the way we want to go? We must have a unified position, or at least the appearance of one, when the library community approaches funding bodies. The least hint of public dissent within the library world will cause legislators to draw back and support neither faction. Let the debate go on within the profession. This is the reason why "type-of-library" factionalism is so dangerous.

What are the real barriers to cooperative action? Legal organization and authorization, controlling parent body, and clientele were considered the barriers in the past. The barriers are disappearing. The Illinois Regional Library Council has proven that when there is goodwill and commitment to work together many of these barriers are overcome, disappear, or are seen to have been imaginary. The library question of 1965 was: "How can special libraries, which are creatures of the private sector, participate in the cooperatives, which are publicly supported?" With time the question has evaporated. In Chicago, special libraries were leaders in the development of the Illinois Regional Library Council.

What is the best legal configuration for multitype library cooperation? Any consortium or cooperative had better be firmly anchored in law and firmly related to a government unit, whether municipal, county, or state, or in multiples or a combination of these. No group of legislators is much interested in putting its money in a consortium existing in limbo. Legislators will fund a group or an activity only if that group reports to them and ultimately is responsible to the public. This is not to suggest that consortia should be located within the bureaucracy or that they should actually be departments of state or local government. There are many patterns of organization. The important thing is that the cooperative must be firmly related to a funding body and that it must be responsible to that body. Five years is about the minimum time frame for effective planning. Any group that is trying to survive on soft money is only kidding itself. The only secure money comes from funding formulas written into law or from membership assessments, and in the United States we have not had much luck with dues and assessments.

SUMMARY

Library and information services must be conceived of as a unity. A library, cooperative council, or system of libraries has primary responsibility to its own clientele. It also has a responsibility to all other libraries and all other clienteles, since the product with which it deals is the intellectual heritage of all mankind.

The multitype cooperative seems to be the best method yet devised for mobilizing all resources, all services, and all organizations into one single unified effort. Multistate cooperatives have only been mentioned in passing, because the programs of a given multistate cooperative depend on, and are limited by, the pattern of networking and cooperative activity in the member states. Implicit is the judgment that the state is the fundamental unit of organization, and that the state library agency is responsible for the development of all library and information services in the state. The multistate cooperative exists, then, at the will of the states. The next question of appropriate relationships among local, state, and multistate networks and the national program proposed by the National Commission on Libraries and Information Science has only begun to be examined. A good first step was made in a symposium sponsored by MIDLNET in 1976.[9] Here the roles of local, state, multistate, and federal levels were considered and many new questions were probed. Answers await developments in the field.

NOTES

1. *84 Stat.* 1934, 1970.
2. "Comprehensive Long-Range Program for Library Services in Wisconsin," *Wisconsin Library Bulletin* 72, no. 5 (September–October 1976):193–226.
3. "Meeting the Challenge: Illinois State Library's Long-Range Program for Library Development in Illinois 1975–1980," *Illinois Libraries* 57, no. 8 (October 1975):520–548.
4. New York Education Department, Commissioners Committee on Reference and Research Library Resources, *Cooperative Program for the Development of Reference and Research Library Resources in New York State: An Interim Report*, 1960.
5. *Toward a National Program for Library and Information Services: Goals for Action* (Washington, D.C.: National Commission on Libraries and Information Science, 1975).
6. New York Education Department, Division of Evaluation, *Emerging Library Systems: The 1963–66 Evaluation of the New York State Public Library System*, 1967.
7. ASLA Interlibrary Cooperation Subcommittee, comp. and ed., *ASLA Report on Interlibrary Cooperation* (Chicago: Association of State Library Agencies, 1976).
8. Burns Indiana Statutes Annotated, Sec. 41-1201-1214.
9. *First MIDLNET Symposium Report, 1976* (Green Bay, Wis.: Midwest Region Library Network, 1976).

THE ROLE OF THE STATE LIBRARY

Ethel S. Crockett

For many years library cooperation was informally based on personal friendships, goodwill, proximity, and local custom. In the last decade the practice of assisting one's neighbor has quickly evolved into more formal arrangements, the most sophisticated being the all-embracing multitype library cooperative. The primary impetus for this evolution was the Library Services and Construction Act Title III, which provided for expansion and establishment of programs to include all types of libraries. That same act provided funding to improve and strengthen the capacity of state library administrative agencies to meet the needs of the people of the states.

Many multitype cooperatives that exist today were created to serve a single type of library or to provide a single service for several types of libraries. These evolved into multitype units as librarians from different kinds of libraries asked to join them. Others began as multitype agencies, as a result of local, state, or multistate initiative. The trend throughout the country is toward organized multitype library cooperation, leading to regional (multistate) and ultimately national networking.

Some state librarians began their state service during the era of the Library Services Act (1956) or the Library Services and Construction Act (1966). The Library Services Act was a means of federal assistance to rural public libraries. It was so successful that it was expanded to LSCA, which in turn was amended to provide a broader program as it became quite clear that operating exclusively in a community of public libraries was unsatisfactory if users were to have the benefit of total library resources. State librarians are quite generally committed to the philosophy that it is necessary to include all types of libraries in cooperative units where all kinds of information may be readily shared.

STATE LIBRARY LEADERSHIP

We may start from the premise that it is logical for the state library agency to spearhead cooperative library development. How this is accomplished varies widely from state to state just as state agencies themselves vary. Their scope and authority range from the supervision of a single-purpose law library in the state capitol to the administration of the large multidepartment libraries of the most populous states, as well as to the large complex networks that provide services to all citizens of the state. Whether or not a state library is in a position to coordinate library activities outside its own walls depends largely on the statutory role of the library, the number and nature of libraries in the state, population size, geography, and proximity to out-of-state library resources. Where the state population is small, the state librarian may be responsible for all library services for the public. Utah, for example, has a single public library system directed by the state librarian. Such a structure would be impossible for a state librarian to handle in more populous states.

Information flows naturally to the state library, which provides an excellent vantage point from which to identify needs and to observe a multitude of current library activities and trends. It is a natural focal point for library development. Location in the capitol of a state is a prime factor. The climate at the hub of the state's political activities is favorable for meetings, statewide planning, and action. Activists of all professions travel to their state capitols to confer with legislators, to lobby for bills, and to tap resources lodged at the seat of government. A state librarian is in a position to seek out and to make friends for library programs, to ascertain the political realities, to keep legislators and government leaders informed on library matters, and to rally support. Not unimportant is the fact that advice and legal assistance is also close at hand.

Since the passage of the Library Services Act of 1956, state librarians have administered federal funding programs for libraries. As a result, they have had some influence on the development of public libraries. The fact that there has been money for cooperative purposes has enabled state librarians to promote the development of multitype systems; consequently, this has heightened the state library profile in the nonpublic library field. State funds for libraries are generally administered by the state librarians, who have thus been able to coordinate library programs with the support of both state and federal funds.

Intended or not, this casts the state librarian in a leadership role that cannot be lightly disregarded. A well-planned course of action must be followed to ensure that monies administered by the agency are used to the best advantage for all the citizens of the state. A certain amount of criticism from librarians who would spend the money differently is inevitable. Yet a state library agency is relatively neutral turf where planning and coordination can take place. Developments may progress on a trial-and-error basis as problems are worked out, all under the somewhat anonymous heading of a state librarian's project.

While coordination is an historic role of the state librarian, leadership is generally thrust upon him by librarians who press for programs they don't have the time, inclination, or resources to take on themselves. Unless this leadership role is abused, it encounters very little opposition. Dictation, however, is out of the question. No one will tolerate the dictates of state officialdom for long. So, going back to the premise that the state library agency is the proper agency for coordinating and funding multitype library cooperatives, one might well add some reservations:

Librarians need to have the roles of their state agencies well defined.

They want to have a voice in decisions made about statewide library development as it affects their libraries and patrons.

They look to their state agencies to develop legislation needed to support cooperative programs.

They hope to receive technical assistance to carry out cooperative programs; e.g., librarians in isolated geographic areas naturally form cooperative arrangements for maximum access to information. When linkage to other similar groups is planned, the state library staff is in a position to answer the logical questions of "to whom," "where," and "how."

They expect their state library agencies to have staff representative of all sectors of the library community in order that their problems are well understood when planning and development decisions are made; e.g., special librarians who frequently suffer job-related isolation are extremely ingenious and therefore quick to take advantage of all possible resources available to them. They are quite receptive to the state library's role in coordination of multitype cooperation when they perceive that the agency understands their needs and limitations.

THE CALIFORNIA STATE LIBRARY AND INTERLIBRARY COOPERATION

In California, the state library was established in 1850 for the purpose of serving the legislature. The state library traditionally has supported public library development. A union catalog of the holdings of many libraries in the state was started in 1909, and with enabling legislation voted in 1911 the state library worked to develop county library systems throughout the state.

Today, the California State Library has a general fund budget of $3.9 million, a staff of 197 with 55 professionals, and a collection of over 800,000 volumes and 3 million government publications. It administers $1 million in state aid, which is apportioned annually according to a complex formula (State Education Code Article 8, Sections 18770 and 18771), and approximately $4 million in federal aid from the Library Services and Construction Act. A new legislative proposal for state funding was approved by the California Library Association in December 1976 and will soon be introduced in the legislature.

There are no other government agencies charged with major responsibility for interlibrary cooperation. Within the state library, two units handle all such activities: the State Library Services Bureau (interlibrary loan and the union catalog) and the Library Development Services Bureau (advisory, informational, and technical assistance and specialized services).

State aid was enabled in 1963 with the passage of the Public Library Services Act, which has as its purpose the aid and encouragement of free public library systems. There are now 15 cooperative library systems and 5 single jurisdiction library systems covering over 90 percent of the state.

California is second to New York in having the largest number of libraries (*ASLA Report on Interlibrary Cooperation*). Estimates by type are public 177; academic 180; public schools 4,063 (1973-1974); private schools 331 (est. 1973-1974); special profit 400; and special nonprofit 75. This large library community has enormous and complex requirements for interaction.

With Title III of the Library Services and Construction Act as impetus, intertype library networks have sprung from the public library systems in almost every part of California in the last five years. TIE (Total Interlibrary Exchange), associated with the Black Gold Cooperative Library System, serves academic, public, school, and special libraries of five counties, centered at Santa Barbara. Similarly, CIN (Cooperative Information Network), operating out of Stanford University, has members in four counties served by three library systems. California maintains two regional reference centers with LSCA funds for interlibrary reference referral: the Bay Area Reference Center (BARC) in San Francisco and the Southern California Answering Network (SCAN) in Los Angeles. A study of public library systems was made by the consulting firm of Peat, Marwick, Mitchell and Company in 1975. Its report served as text for the Library Planning Institute of June 1975, wherein plans were initiated for the new legislative proposal to fund cooperative services that will now be introduced.

Finally, mention must be made of California's newest and most exciting development, CLASS, the California Library Authority for Systems and Services, which was formed in June 1976 as an independent public agency under California's Joint Exercise of Powers Act. The state librarian sits as one of a five-member board of directors for CLASS, representative of all types of libraries. Ronald F. Miller is the first executive director with an office in San Jose, Santa Clara County. The services of CLASS will be available to any library, public or private, upon payment of a low membership fee, and it will be possible for libraries to contract for just one or all of the services provided. It is expected that one of the first activities of CLASS will be to establish a computerized listing of publications in libraries throughout the state for cataloging, interlibrary loan, and reference use. Other services that CLASS may offer include a facility for storing little-used and last-copy books, the cooperative acquisition of library materials, and delivery systems for statewide interlibrary loan. CLASS will also provide an effective mechanism for interfacing with other state, regional, and/or national networks and utilities.

BIBLIOGRAPHY

1. ASLA Interlibrary Cooperation Subcommittee, comp. and ed. *ASLA Report on Interlibrary Cooperation*. Chicago: Association of State Library Agencies, 1976.

2. California State Library. *Library Planning Institute Proceedings, June 23–27, 1975*. Sacramento: California State Library, 1975.

3. Kittel, Dorothy A. "Trends in State Library Cooperation." *Library Trends* 24, no. 2 (October 1975): 245–255.

4. Martin, Lowell. *Public Library Service Equal to the Challenge of California*. Sacramento: California State Library, 1965.

5. Peat, Marwick, Mitchell and Company. *California Public Library Systems: A Comprehensive Review with Guidelines for the Next Decade*. June 1975.

6. Shank, Russell. "Emerging Programs of Cooperation." *Library Trends* 23, no. 2 (October 1974): 287–304.

7. Simpson, Donald B. *The State Library Agencies: A Survey Report 1975*. Chicago: Association of State Library Agencies, 1975.

8. "Stanford University BALLOTS System." *Journal of Library Automation* 8 (March 1975): 31–50.

THE LOCAL NODE

W. Boyd Rayward

PROBLEMS OF DEFINITION

Webster's *New Collegiate Dictionary* provides a number of meanings for "node," an ugly word that has achieved considerable currency in discussions of library networking. The first definition given is "an entangling complication"; another meaning is "a thickened or swollen enlargement." Both meanings are foreign to the ideology of library cooperation, though expressive of what may occur when libraries actually begin to cooperate. Surely one may dismiss "either of two points where the orbit of a planet or comet intersects the ecliptic." The meaning that would be most vigorously approved by librarians, however, is "a point at which subsidiary parts originate or center."

In the discussion that follows, "node" is taken to be an institutional point in a system of library relationships, ordered or structured according to a variety of forms of agreement, through which sustained communication can take place and by means of which bibliographic and other information, documentary materials, and expertise, of a kind and to a degree agreed upon, are transmitted. When this system is called a "network," there is usually an implication of considerable size either in terms of geographic area covered or in terms of numbers and kinds of libraries involved. Usually there is also an implication of carefully maintained institutional formality. Typically, a library's clientele has access to the network only through its own library (though there are controlled exceptions, as in the case of the Illinois Regional Library Council's INFOPASS program).

"Local" nodes in a network are those points at which particular libraries physically connect their own clienteles with the network, though some network services may be directed primarily to the library staffs of these nodes. In schematic representations of hierarchically organized networks, they are usually shown as being at the bottom of the pyramid. They are, however, points on which the whole weight of the network organization falls, and the major problem of local nodes in a network is to distribute, control, and support this weight. In a multitype library network, this problem is more serious than in other kinds of networks because of the different jurisdictions, institutions, and interests involved at the level of the local node.

PROBLEMS OF IDENTIFICATION

It should be recognized at the outset that the idea of a local node is not straightforward, that is to say, it can be difficult to identify actual local nodes and to determine the nature of their major interests. At one end of the scale, such a task is relatively simple. Local public, school, special, and college libraries are easily identified as clearly able to function as local nodes in a network. They have a primary constituency that they were created to serve, the support of whose bibliothecal interests is their first duty. This is also true of large university and research libraries, but these may also have responsibilities that require that they act in a secondary capacity in the network, as in the case of the medical library network, or in ILLINET (the Illinois Library and Information Network), or in New York's 3 R's (Reference and Research Library Resources) system, or the NYSILL (New York State Inter Library Loan) network.

A further loss of clarity in the identity of the local node occurs when one turns to state libraries and the several national libraries, the Library of Congress, the National Library of Medicine, and the National Agriculture Library. Each of these has a form of local clientele (even if one identifies this as "everyone" in the state or nation), though each may also represent the acme of a complicated network structure that is intended to facilitate access of organized units of its clientele to its services and collections. Stripped of explicit network responsibilities, the Illinois State Library or the National Library of Medicine, for example, would still be a library functioning for a particular constituency; they would be similar indeed to what they were before assuming such responsibilities. These libraries differentiate their network from their local responsibilities (insofar as they are actually separable) by the creation of structure—special personnel performing certain kinds of tasks through departments or offices created to incorporate the libraries' networking roles. Some of the forms taken by and the names given to these structures appear in the *ASLA Report on Interlibrary Cooperation* (Chicago, Association of State Library Agencies, 1976).

PROBLEMS OF ROLE

One needs to be aware of potential role conflict between network and local obligations in certain kinds of libraries that have prominent, continuous, well-defined (perhaps by law) network responsibilities. The actual existence of such conflict may well mirror fear in other libraries at the local level of potential conflict of obligation arising from network participation. If libraries so varied in size, location, scope, and clientele as public, special, school, state, and national libraries may function as potential local nodes in a network, one may well ask what does not have such a function. The answer is simply those organizations in a network whose primary constituencies are libraries. Such organizations may be managerial and act as coordinating agencies for parts or all of the network, or they may provide more tangible services as well. Examples of such bodies are the Illinois Regional Library Council and the headquarters organizations of OCLC (Ohio College Library Center) and of the public library systems in Illinois that are an integral part of ILLINET.

Several of the last provide illuminating examples of some of the problems of role conflict that can result from the lessening of the identity of the local node as a result of network participation. Several of these systems have set up their headquarters in one or more of the major public libraries located in their area. They have offered certain system services through these libraries. In some instances, these services have been integrated with those of the local libraries; in yet other instances, the director of the local library for a time has also acted as director of the system.

Involvement in system services has led to certain advantages to the local library—deposit of system-owned materials to enrich general or reference collections, the subsidy of additional professional and other staff, and assistance with overheads. While the system has been able to draw on larger collections and more varied staff than it could have provided alone, nevertheless, both the consolidation of system services with those of the local library and the merging of the role of director of the system with that of the local library have led to major difficulties of accountability, confused allegiance of staff, conflicting responsibilities, prejudiced self-interest, and professional embarrassment. A number of arrangements of the kind described in general terms here that were set up in the early history of Illinois systems have since been terminated as a result of the unexpected problems they engendered.

PROBLEMS OF PARTICIPATION

There are two major ways of looking at library cooperation: in a highly abstract rather moralistic way from the point of view of some nebulous but global good; or in a quite matter-of-fact pragmatic way in terms of particular or selfish interests. The local node is the point at which the network is activated and through which it delivers its goods and services. The network can justify, even legitimate, itself only in terms of what it can do for and through the local node. Continued participation in and support of the network at the local level ultimately depends on network performance in relation to specific needs and demands transmitted through the local node. There is an interesting reciprocity involved here because network survival is at stake. To survive, a network must obtain and sustain membership. The ultimate pressure to which it must conform is membership withdrawal. It must, therefore, adapt to the needs and demands of the local node to ensure membership support, and it must also attempt to shape the expression of those needs and demands to a form it can deal with most effectively.

The local nodes in a multitype library network present an unusually wide spectrum of interests that have to be assessed and accommodated if libraries of various types in various locations are to join the network. In each case, the libraries involved—school, public, college, university, or special—are creatures of other institutions that support them and provide them with quite specific constituencies: students and faculty, local residents, or organizational personnel. They are frequently attached to or draw financial support from different political and other jurisdictions. Public libraries are supported by taxes drawn in various ways from municipalities, villages, townships, library districts, counties, cities, or even states (as in the case of Hawaii, for example). School libraries function within the relatively narrow confines of schools, some of which are publicly supported in various ways, others of which are supported privately, for example, by religious bodies. Universities and colleges are also either public or private and are more or less closely associated jurisdictionally and geographically with particular communities—more closely in the case of community colleges, for example, less closely in the case of major state or private universities. Colleges also frequently function at different levels for different kinds of students. These characteristics are inevitably and necessarily reflected in their libraries. The special library may be a part of local, state, or federal government and is therefore supported by public funds. More commonly, it may belong to profit-oriented organizations that look to the justification of the expense it involves in terms of how it helps the organization maintain and improve products, services, and markets, sometimes but not always through its contribution to organizational research and development.

To bring libraries so variously situated into cooperative arrangements is a diplomatic task of the utmost delicacy. One of the major reasons that such a task is difficult is the enormous variability in sophistication of these libraries and their staffs. Sophistication may be partly a function of size and partly of support, which in turn may themselves be related. An important component of staff sophistication is professional orientation. While it is true that libraries are institutionally embedded, professional staff in particular are usually trained in professional schools in universities and colleges, meet frequently in various configurations of interest, and read a variously produced common literature. As a result librarians tend to develop an awareness of a commonality of objectives, services, methodologies, and so on that is recognized as extending beyond any particular organizational context.

This awareness is a matter of degree and has been expressed in the sociological literature in terms of the concepts of cosmopolitan and local opinion leaders. If a library staff has little or no professional orientation (perhaps because the library is so small and badly supported that it has few if any professional staff), then participation in networking or any form of cooperative activity that draws on shared beliefs in the commonality of professional endeavors will be inhibited. Such a staff may well be unable to gauge the reciprocal advantages that can stem from such activity. It will look inward and will emphasize and jealously guard the prerogatives of a simplistically conceived local institutional autonomy.

Certain factors will influence local participation in a multitype library network. The geographic extent or reach of the network—whether strictly local, regional (perhaps crossing one or more state boundaries), statewide, or involving several states—may encourage or discourage membership. Certain libraries may be reluctant or legally unable to participate in networks crossing state or other jurisdictional boundaries; others may see their major interests as best served by a network confined in scope to a region or extending to the area of one or more states. The size of the area involved will have implications for speed and quality of service. It will also determine the total size of the potential membership of the network and the proportion of various types of library. This in turn will help to determine what interests may predominate and will influence the expectations of different kinds of libraries as to what they may gain from the network.

The distribution of total membership geographically and by type of library will also have important consequences for the forms of representation chosen for the government of the network in order to achieve balanced representation or protection of majority or other selected interests. The presence of other networks and forms of cooperative arrangements and its own and other libraries' memberships in these will have some bearing on what individual libraries at the local level decide about a particular network. What is it that membership in a particular network has uniquely to offer? How does it complement or duplicate other memberships? Above all, libraries at the local level will assess the potential benefits a network offers, together with the costs and obligations of membership.

It is here that suspicious self-interest comes into play and this may permeate the entire local level of the network. A school library, for example, may fear that as a local node in a multitype library network, materials needed unexpectedly and immediately by its faculty and students may be whisked irrecoverably into the network for use by another library.

Larger university libraries may fear inequitable demands on their resources that will reduce their local effectiveness and increase their costs. Indeed, many fear having to take up an unacknowledged and unlooked for burden of implicit subsidy of the network, though the realities of networking have become sufficiently clear for this to be less of a problem than it may once have been.

In the crassest terms, however, each local node, whatever the kind of library, fears that more will be asked of it than it will receive. Participation in multitype library networks involves special problems of mutual suspicion that may not be present in other forms of networks. Can special libraries, in profit organizations especially, contribute sufficiently to warrant membership in a network that may have a majority of memberships from publicly supported libraries? What have small public and or school libraries to offer college and university libraries or special libraries? Such questions are likely to be less pressing in networks of the same type of library.

CONDITIONS FAVORING NETWORK SUCCESS

For a network to succeed, recognition of certain conditions having been met must be general enough to overcome these suspicions. These conditions are of two kinds: those that might be called environmental and those that are network related. It must be generally clear that a particular library's resources are inadequate for the provision of a desired level of service to its local clientele. Inadequacy may result from diminishing levels of support, increasing costs in relation to relatively stationary levels of support, or increasing demand, either absolutely or for materials or services that are unusual or difficult for a particular library to provide. It must be clear also that the network as set up will allow the demands originating at the local node to be met in a timely way and at an acceptable cost. This involves knowledge of the network's objectives and procedures and trust in its underlying organizational soundness, which in turn involves appropriate representation, suitable communication processes, and responsiveness to individual needs and changing conditions.

Where one library contributes proportionately more to the network than other libraries, some form of remuneration or recompense must be determined. Balance in levels of participation must be achieved either by routine operation of the network or by a kind of market process. The ideal network is one in which libraries participate equally in terms of costs and benefits; it is a system of moving parts without friction; it is one in which all libraries of whatever kind have full and immediate comprehension of and sympathy for the difficulties of others. Insofar as reality departs from the ideal, problems occur and must be resolved.

One major factor that influences the success of networks is affluence.

Networks are a phenomenon of relative affluence. They cannot be created unless each member at the local level has sufficient resources of time, staff, materials, and basic equipment and supplies to participate. It is astonishing, for example, how recently many school and public libraries have had telephones installed—and how many still have none. More sophisticated network technology, such as the computer, will require even higher levels of affluence of participant members.

Networks function best when based on strong local nodes. Weak libraries in a network create imbalance of demand and supply. Of course, strength is relative here, for an ideally strong library may well be considered one that is able instantly to supply anything its clientele needs. It is the recognition that an acceptable approximation to completeness and instantaneity is not possible that has led first to cooperative arrangements between similar kinds of library and latterly to arrangements involving all available resources within a defined area in whatever kind of library. Only if the local node is sufficiently strong and capable can it deliver the network's services to its clientele. The capacity of the local node, in terms of the kind of use it makes of the network or allows the network to make of it, determines the effectiveness of the network as a whole.

THREE

CASE STUDIES AND SPECIAL PERSPECTIVES

INDIANA CASE STUDY 1: INDIANAPOLIS, AN URBAN EXPERIENCE

Susan Cady

Multitype library cooperation in an urban setting is influenced both by demographic characteristics of the urban area and by the complexity of its bibliographic environment. With 70 percent of the U.S. population living within a Standard Metropolitan Statistical Area (SMSA), it is difficult to separate out those characteristics of library services that are unique to urban areas. For our purposes, urban refers to those areas that are located in or are adjacent to cities and that identify strongly with them, namely, the SMSAs.

Indianapolis is the location of the headquarters of the Central Indiana Area Library Services Authority (CIALSA) and is the environment with which the author is most familiar. The CIALSA jurisdiction is actually a dynamic mix of city, suburb, small town, and farmland. It may serve as an example of the complexities facing urban cooperatives. These include the setting of geographic boundaries, the spanning of political jurisdictions, the bringing together of public and private sectors in meaningful, working relationships, and the provision of legal bases and funding alternatives for multitype cooperatives.

DEFINING GEOGRAPHIC LIMITS

One of the persistent problems of multitype library cooperatives is the definition of geographic limits of service. In continuously expanding urban areas, this problem is accentuated. There are proponents of both open and closed boundaries. Regardless of which philosophy prevails, the matter of boundaries is one that should be decided when the cooperative is established to avoid the political problems that are likely to result in later stages of its development. This may be accomplished by including geographic criteria for membership.

Early in the planning for Indiana's Area Library Service Authorities (ALSA), the state library chose to set the boundaries of the ALSAs to coincide with the state's Economic and Planning Regions.[1] Fortunately for central Indiana, the CIALSA region also coincided with the Indianapolis SMSA. Although this is an excellent arrangement, two drawbacks over which the library community has no control have emerged so far: the state altered some of its own regional designations and the ALSAs can be linked psychologically with other regional planning efforts, notably those mandated by the federal government. In some parts of Indiana, regional planning agencies are quite unpopular, primarily because they are viewed as an intrusion by the federal government, complete with unnecessary rules and regulations.

In other states, some multitype cooperatives have identified themselves with, or have been initiated by, regional planning agencies. One such group has operated very effectively for a number of years as the Librarians Technical Committee of the Metropolitan Washington Council of Governments.[2] The Central Colorado Public Library System, now a multitype cooperative, functioned within the Denver Regional Council of Governments for several years. Unfortunately, the council evidenced a growing interest in regulating the system and in skimming off more of its operating funds for its own use.[3]

Other bases for setting boundaries have been by political jurisdiction (usually counties), by previously drawn areas for a library system that evolved into a multitype cooperative, and, most often, by the SMSA. Some 38 SMSAs encompass two or more states, which further complicates matters for the library cooperative. Since most are supported with LSCA funds or state aid, the tendency is to draw boundaries at state lines, which often are not where natural library service boundaries lie. Overcoming this problem requires interstate compacts or other specific enabling legislation.

SPANNING POLITICAL JURISDICTIONS

Another problem in multitype library cooperation is the spanning of numerous political jurisdictions. Some portions of the cooperative's area may not have public library service at all, as is true in the CIALSA area where 4 percent of the population is not in a public library district. School corporations with school libraries in these areas may expect to use the cooperative to serve the adult population through the school library, certainly no substitute for local, tax-supported public library service. The cooperative must avoid both the reality and appearance of providing such service. Nonresident fees imposed by public libraries conflict with open-access programs like INFOPASS, if the latter includes borrowing privileges. Heavy users of interlibrary loan located or working near the cooperative's resource library, although not actually a resident of that library's district, find it difficult to understand why they cannot simply select their books and check them out at the lending library rather than go through the interlibrary loan process. Other conflicts in political jurisdictions are created by the failure of school corporation boundaries to coincide with public library districts.

PROVIDING A LEGAL FRAMEWORK AND FUNDING

There is also the problem of bringing the public and private sectors into a closer working relationship. In urban areas where there are many corporate libraries that zealously guard their services from the general public, what programs or compromises can be inaugurated that permit effective interchange? How is it possible to overcome the barrier of the private sector's fear of being overregulated by a government unit, even one as harmless as a multitype library cooperative? The means of achieving symbiosis must be by persuasion and by honoring corporate sanctions rather than by dictation.

The Indiana Library Services Authority Act of 1967 established a legal framework that permits the spanning of the gulf between public and private sectors and between one political jurisdiction and another. It requires the governing body of the library to join the ALSA by official action and to appoint a representative or representatives to participate in the decision-making process of the ALSA. The procedure is the same for all types of libraries, although the nature of the governing bodies varies. An important feature of the ALSA act is that the number of privately supported institutions that are members of the ALSA must never equal or exceed the number of publicly supported ones. Although the act has proved adequate for intrastate cooperation and is the first such legislation to do so effectively, it does not provide a mechanism for cooperation across state lines.[4]

Although the ALSA legislation was passed in 1967, there is still no allocation of state funds. This is certainly a common problem for almost every multitype cooperative. In examining the *ASLA Report on Interlibrary Cooperation*, it is found that only 9 states have statutory funding for multitype library cooperation, while 40 have enabling legislation on their books.[5]

ADVANTAGES TO A METROPOLITAN SETTING

There are many advantages to a metropolitan setting for multitype library cooperation. The most obvious ones are the wealth of resources to be shared, a relatively sophisticated library community, and a large enough cross section of libraries of all types working together to make the concept viable. Favorable urban environmental factors include relatively cheap communication (local telephone), centralized transportation patterns (interstate highways converging on a central point), and high density of library facilities and therefore short distances that facilitate physical access and rapid document delivery. All of these affect the nature of urban multitype library cooperation by allowing for cost-effective delivery systems, reference networks, and other programs.

Although it is possible to distribute publicity about library services to an urban area through a few relatively large and important media, there is much more competition for coverage than in a rural area where a small project might be "big" news. CIALSA contracted with a university advanced motion picture class for the production of eight television spots promoting library service.[6] These have been given extensive airing as public service announcements by Indianapolis stations, including some prime time slots. The Library Council of Greater Cleveland has written radio spots as one of its early cooperative projects.[7]

As noted earlier, the library scene in a metropolitan area is complex. One feature is generally the presence of one or two very large "have" libraries that have traditionally dominated the library community. Patterns of use have been established and are often hard to overcome. Eric Halvorson refers to the "biggest library syndrome" in reporting on his research on INFOPASS referrals to the University of Chicago Library.[8] At the other end of the spectrum are the numerous small libraries—public, school, and special—whose librarians sometimes back off from involvement, believing they have little to offer in joint activities. It is useful for the cooperative to communicate to all types of librarians what their potential role in the cooperative can be. Usually the staff in a small library has more intimate contact with users and can identify their needs more readily. Meeting those needs is the ultimate goal of all library service.

STANDARDS

Businesses, government units, and nonprofit agencies that have collections of books are sometimes definited as libraries. The Library Services Authority Act has a definition of a library that can be applied when these groups express interest in cooperative membership; however, there are still gray areas. In Indiana, standards have been established that libraries of all types must meet in order to belong to an ALSA.[9] In general, these standards are intended to encourage member libraries to maintain local financial effort and to employ qualified staff. Again, it is not always simple to apply these and other standards to very small libraries; nevertheless, some attempt must be made to set minimum service levels so that the cooperative is not used as a substitute for basic library service within the member institution or community.

RELATIONSHIPS BETWEEN COOPERATIVES

Another facet of the urban scene is the presence of other consortia, cooperatives, and networks, often created for a single purpose or limited to one type of library. For instance, in central Indiana there is an academic consortium with a librarians' committee, two health science consortia, and a strong chapter of the Special Libraries Association that functions in some measure as an informal cooperative. Coming into existence concurrently with CIALSA was the Indiana Cooperative Library Services

Authority (InCoLSA), a statewide network linked to OCLC.[10] The AL-SAs and InCoLSA were enabled by the same law. What are the implications of this multitude of library organizations? The first is that new librarians or interested persons outside the library field, including legislators, are thoroughly confused. Some libraries have actually joined the wrong organization. Previously existing organizations feel threatened by newcomers and tend to emphasize the uniqueness or superiority of their member services. Time wasted in conjecturing and politicking can be minimized if, in the organizational stages, relationships with other cooperatives are well planned and the roles of each are defined. Ideally, cooperative planning will ensure that conflicting services are not developed and efforts of similar organizations can be coordinated. A mutual appreciation of the diverse roles of all the organizations involved can then result just as different types of libraries have learned to appreciate each other's diverse roles. If joint planning and coordination are not feasible, the least all the cooperative groups can do is to maintain close communication with one another. Since funding is now being sought for both ALSAs and InCoLSA from the state legislature in an omnibus bill, the precise roles of each and the relationship of these roles are being articulated more clearly.

ROLE OF THE STATE LIBRARY

The state library agency is a key institution in the development of multitype library cooperatives. The design of suitable legislation, the planning of pilot programs, and the coordination and funding of these programs are appropriately done at the state level. The primary disadvantage of this approach is that conditions vary as widely among cooperatives as they do among libraries, and usually policies are applied across the board at the state level. This may be a result of failure to educate the powers that be to the vagaries of tailoring library service to local needs.

Natural tensions between large libraries in metropolitan areas and state agencies do exist and need to be overcome by constant communication. Other tensions result from lack of agreement on the appropriate involvement of the state agency in the policymaking and day-to-day operations of the cooperative. State library agencies may find it desirable at some future time to reorganize in order to accommodate vigorous multitype library development for their whole states. Overall, state agency involvement prevents a piecemeal approach.

The state agency can assist cooperatives in obtaining statutory support when that agency and the library community clearly see the advantages of multitype library cooperation. Without state funding, it is unlikely that the trend toward multitype service will realize its full potential, for it is obvious that no simple uniform method of self-support can be expected. A fear of fee assessment has been the primary reason some libraries have not joined the Central Indiana ALSA. We must define more precisely just what the multitype cooperative can do, and do better than other organizations, before we can expect legislative support. If and when state support is gained, it will be interesting to see what new problems and issues arise.

Another type of organization within the library community to which a multitype cooperative might relate is the library professional association. The multitype director or cooperative will probably belong to all local library groups and to several state associations in addition to the pertinent national ones. The associations can serve a number of functions: provide a forum for discussion of matters relating to cooperative development, coordinate efforts to obtain favorable legislation and funding, and provide a mechanism for communicating the cooperative's program to the larger library community.[11]

Complexity is a given of urban existence, and the library community in an urban setting is no exception. The multitype library cooperative has demonstrated its ability to cope with that complexity in order to mobilize more and more of the resources of the metropolitan area for the benefit of its residents. Despite the day-to-day frustrations of survival, there is reason to believe that the multitype library cooperative will become a more and more pervasive element of the metropolitan library scene.

NOTES

1. Indiana Library and Historical Board, *Rule II: Plan for the Development of Area Library Services Authorities*, effective December 21, 1973.

2. *Information through Cooperative Action; Library Services in the Metropolitan Washington Area* (Washington, D.C.: Metropolitan Washington Council of Governments, 1974).

3. Personal communication, Ed Sayre, coordinator of the Central Colorado Library System.

4. Library Services Authority Act of 1967, IC 20-13-6.

5. ASLA Interlibrary Cooperation Subcommittee, comp. and ed., *ASLA Report on Interlibrary Cooperation* (Chicago: Association of State Library Agencies, 1976).

6. "Proposal to Develop TV Spots Promoting Libraries," *CIALSA Newsletter* 2, no. 10 (October 1975): 3.

7. Molly Glazer, "Public Relations Committee Report," *MLS Newsletter* 2, no. 3 (October 1976): 6–7.

8. Eric Halvorson, *The INFOPASS Program and Misreferrals: The Regenstein Situation* (Chicago: Illinois Regional Library Council, 1975), p. 5.

9. Indiana Library and Historical Board, op. cit.

10. Barbara Markuson, *The Indiana Cooperative Library Services Authority—A Plan for the Future* (Indianapolis: Indiana State Library, 1974).

11. Edward G. Holley, "The Role of Professional Associations in a Network of Library Activity," *Library Trends* 24, no. 2 (October 1975).

INDIANA CASE STUDY 2: THE STONE HILLS AREA, A RURAL EXPERIENCE

Mary Jordan Coe

A rural area presents unique challenges when establishing a multi-type, multipurpose library cooperative. The major difficulty in providing library service to rural populations is getting the resources to the people who are sparsely located. Library services therefore have traditionally been much weaker than in areas with a higher density of population, and the understanding of what libraries are or can be tends to be quite unsophisticated. The population must be educated to use libraries, and the local libraries must be backed up by cooperative resources to answer these new demands if a library cooperative is to succeed.

Indiana's Area Library Services Authorities (ALSAs) are established under the provision of the Library Services Authority Act of 1967.[1] An ALSA may incorporate one or more of Indiana's multicounty planning and development areas. There are currently nine ALSAs in operation, of which seven have areas that are predominantly rural. The Stone Hills Area Library Services Authority (SHALSA) includes four counties in south central Indiana, the largest of which has a population of 85,000 and the smallest a population of 12,000. Although SHALSA has one of the major library resources in the state in Indiana University, it also includes one county in which many of the residents do not have public library service.

THE CHALLENGE OF RURAL MULTITYPE LIBRARY COOPERATION

For generations, country people have asked their neighbors and relatives when they needed information. Even the members of governing boards and town councils are rarely aware of the library as a source of information. While television has made an impact as a major informational source, the public library is generally viewed as that vaguely worthwhile place where the nicer ladies in town go to obtain entertaining reading matter, and the school library is seen as a secondary adjunct to curriculum, competing for funds with the basketball team and occasionally losing. Certainly, few school or public library boards in a rural area would see a library cooperative as a gain to the community if they were asked to pay for such a service, while their metropolitan peers tend toward greater appreciation of the effects of sharing resources. Thus, one of the major goals of a cooperative in a rural area must be to educate the community to use their libraries for informational and educational purposes, while at the same time providing the local libraries with the resources to answer these new demands. Not until this has been done can one expect the community to understand or reap the benefits of a multitype, multipurpose library cooperative.

In Indiana the ALSA program has been federally funded by the Library Services and Construction Act (LSCA), permitting free participation by the libraries. Free membership is probably essential to start such a cooperative in a rural area, due to poverty and the lack of support for library service; but federal funds present another handicap. Rural communities today are quite proud of their identity and are fighting to preserve their autonomy. In the past federal funds frequently have meant restrictions and guidelines that removed responsibility from local control. Communities feel very strongly about *their* library and *their* school. To succeed in a rural area, a library cooperative must not threaten local control or imply in any way that *their* public library may become the branch of the largest library in the area. The American "do-it-yourself" independence can be used in forming a cooperative by emphasizing the need for each unique community and its resources to benefit the other libraries in the area. If this is not done, the spirit of independence, which can become the basis of sharing, will kill the first efforts to create a cooperative endeavor.

The types of libraries in a rural area are not so varied as in a metropolitan community. For example, CIALSA in Indianapolis has eight academic and thirteen special library members, while the four-county area of SHALSA has only one academic and one special library. There are also differences in services offered by the same type of libraries in a rural area. Some school libraries are little more than study halls, while others are active reference centers. Public library members in SHALSA range in per capita expenditure from $1.74 to $6.70, obviously creating large differences in service.

In a rural area, nonprofessionals frequently have full responsibility for libraries and may feel insecure when joining professional librarians in a cooperative. This factor influences the kind of continuing education program a rural cooperative develops. The SHALSA continuing education segment has centered on training library staff to utilize better the cooperative services offered, concentrating on such subjects as orientation to the interlibrary loan and reference referral center, the reference interview, basic book selection, and other basic functions. In contrast, metropolitan continuing education programs may lean toward such relatively esoteric topics as government documents and videotape production. A similar contrast is found when comparing the resource support needed by metropolitan and rural areas. A metropolitan group may compile a union list of reference titles that cost more than $100, but a rural cooperative may need to purchase multiple subscriptions to basic selection aids, such as *Library Journal* and *Publishers Weekly*, to share among those members who do not have access to them. A rural cooperative may discover an entire facet of library service that has not been provided well in its area due to lack of funds or facilities, such as children's services or business reference.

A problem of multitype cooperatives identified by Susan Cady in the preceding article is defining the geographic limits of the service area. She notes that metropolitan areas are continuously expanding and may well include two or more states. The economic, planning, and development regions, which define the ALSAs' geographic limits in Indiana, present yet another problematical aspect. Rural communities tend to rely on the nearest city for their needs, and local libraries reflect this pattern. The communities in SHALSA use primarily three cities, none of which is actually in the SHALSA area: Louisville, Terre Haute, and Indianapolis. Most of the communities involved would be much more comfortable in a cooperative based in their nearest city rather than one centered in a town within the area. Other states now creating multicounty cooperatives should give careful consideration to the design of their service areas and incorporate, if possible, already existing geographic patterns made by the population. Any service area definition, however, will probably be arbitrary to some degree.

SIMILARITIES BETWEEN RURAL AND URBAN COOPERATIVES

Having noted some of the differences between urban and rural cooperatives, it would be useful also to mention some of their similarities. There are many shared problems and services, although the solutions may vary because of the rural and metropolitan setting. Most librarians and library boards have a natural fear of their own collections being "wiped out" by heavy use from other libraries. Two tactics can be used simultaneously when this situation occurs (please note the "when" not "if"), for this attitude is always present. The first approach is assurance that a participating library always has first call on its own materials and that the whole *raison d'être* of a cooperative is to share resources rather than rely totally on one library. Indeed, it is beneficial to encourage member libraries to write a policy that, for example, limits the number of titles a library will loan in any one subject area. Out of fairness to all of its members, a library cooperative must make an effort not to create unreasonable demands by asking for material that all of the members need at the same time, such as leaf identification and tree guides in the fall.

The second tactic has been best demonstrated by Dorothy Sinclair[2] of the Library Council of Greater Cleveland. She conducted a study of the holdings of member libraries in comparing them to the *Choice* listings in one issue. The study demonstrated the great range of materials available in the different Cleveland libraries, proving even to the largest members that the smaller participants owned many more unique titles than might have been expected. This study was facilitated by the fact that the majority of the libraries are also members of the Ohio College Library Center (OCLC) so that most of the searching was done at a computer terminal rather than at card catalogs. Another means of doing this for rural cooperatives with few OCLC members is to keep statistics on all loaning between members and to document the exchange.

Any rural multitype cooperative that includes school libraries in an interlibrary loan service will have to train school library staff to use the service effectively. Most school corporations have not even experienced interlibrary borrowing between their own schools. This new service may require some preparation. A procedures manual may well suffice for a metropolitan community; however, in a rural area more effort must go into this. SHALSA has combined a procedures manual, orientation workshops at the interlibrary loan and reference referral center, an interlibrary loan form designed for the schools, and talks to the teachers at each school. The last has been most important, because introduction to a new service by an outsider appears to make more impact than an in-house treatment of the same subject.

Basic services may be handled very differently by metropolitan and rural cooperatives. Interlibrary loan and reference referral in rural SHALSA is contracted to the largest public library, paying for a professional assigned to this function and a half-time clerk. In contrast, Indianapolis-based CIALSA has two contracts, one for the public and school members with a public library and one primarily for the academic and special library members with a university; both contracts are for services rendered by existing reference department staff, rather than by paying the salaries of one or two professionals who would perform CIALSA work exclusively.

Delivery of materials has also been handled in a variety of ways. Metropolitan CIALSA chose United Parcel Service and rural SHALSA a leased delivery van for the same purpose—to allow the small, scattered libraries to participate. The difference in solution was created not by the rural or urban setting in this case but by the size of the areas and the number of potential members. CIALSA's potential membership is so large that it might require several delivery vans to provide service equal to that of UPS, whereas SHALSA's potential membership is small and will not create a demand for more than one delivery van. CIALSA's physical size is almost double that of SHALSA, and when the problems of city traffic are added to the greater number of miles to be traveled, it becomes quite clear that a dedicated delivery system for the Indianapolis area libraries would be extremely expensive. The difficulty of deciding upon a means of delivery is to create cost effectiveness so that the delivery cost goes down as the number of materials delivered increases.

Several of the ALSAs in Indiana now offer film services, and again this has been managed in different ways. A metropolitan ALSA was able to contract with a large public library to pay for the use of its film collection by the other members, but a rural ALSA that did not have the resources in its area has decided to rent a collection of films for its members.

When advertising library services generally or the services of a library cooperative, a metropolitan group must compete for press coverage with a multitude of news. A rural public relations campaign, in contrast, can succeed if it is aimed at the local level; this means a separate press release to each town's newspaper describing how the library cooperative affects that community specifically. Television spots may not be as useful in a rural area because the people may watch stations from a variety of cities outside the service area and from other states, but local radio stations are very popular and are an excellent means of reaching the public.

COOPERATIVES COOPERATING

Metropolitan and rural multitype library cooperatives can also work together in many endeavors. The most obvious area of cooperation is the sharing of experiences and techniques for producing services and products. The rural cooperative may learn from its city neighbor how to attract the one or two large resource libraries into its membership, while the urban cooperative may learn from the rural group the appeal that most influences the very small libraries in its area. Continuing education priorities are frequently different, as noted earlier; however, the rural cooperative will produce workshops that interest a few of the metropolitan organization's members and vice versa. If geography permits, a cooperative may open its programs and workshops to another group and happily satisfy the needs of more members in both areas.

Products may also be most beneficially shared. CIALSA produced a slide-tape program to introduce basic library skills to the new staff of its urban libraries, and this has been heavily used by the rural ALSAs. Television and radio spots to advertise libraries generally and to get the public into the library may also be shared when the format appeals to both rural and metropolitan communities.

The most crucial area of cooperation is, of course, the search for financial support. If metropolitan and rural library cooperatives are eventually to create an efficient state network, they must pool their resources and efforts when seeking financial support, whether from private foundations, the state legislature, or the state agency responsible for federal funds distribution. In Indiana, the ALSAs are attempting to achieve state funding for long-range support. This means that together rural and metropolitan ALSAs have helped formulate the legislation and are supporting the lobbying effort necessary to provide passage. The individual legislator must know from experience that the local library has information he or she needs, before being expected to understand the benefits of library cooperation. Directors of multitype library organizations must work closely with the librarians in their geographic areas to influence the public image of the library.

STATE AGENCY COORDINATION

The Indiana State Library created the concept of area library services authorities and has provided the financial backing for the start of ALSAs from LSCA monies. An ALSA advisory committee and a LSCA advisory council were created from members of the library community throughout the state to provide a broad perspective in developing guidelines for ALSAs and applying LSCA funds to cooperative endeavors. Emphasis has been placed upon treating each ALSA according to its needs, and the ALSAs have been free to develop unique programs to ameliorate local problems. Differences between metropolitan and rural cooperatives have been acknowledged, but not studied, in Indiana. An examination of these differences may prove to be necessary before the ALSAs can effectively be joined to create a state network. If, as in Indiana, the long-range objective of a multitype, multipurpose library cooperative is to upgrade and to equalize library service to the entire population, it should be made obvious to all concerned that this process may take extra time for public and professional education and resource development in rural areas that lag far behind the cities in library services. There may be, however, other priorities for multitype, multipurpose cooperatives that would not be affected by metropolitan or rural setting.

The major role for state agencies in the planning and growth of cooperatives is that of establishing guidelines and standards. The time is fast approaching for a new look at state agency coordination of these efforts in light of how well local cooperatives interact with each other and with interstate and national networks. Multicounty library cooperatives like the ALSAs in Indiana will meet the needs of the future only if they become efficient nodes of a state network, which, in turn, plugs into a national network. State agencies are in a unique position to become the centralized interface for network development of the future.

NOTES

1. *Library Services Authority Act of 1967, IC 1971, 20-13-6.*
2. Dorothy Sinclair, "CAMLS: A New Species among Ohio's Cooperatives," *Ohio Library Association Bulletin* 47, no. 1 (January 1977): 29–35.

MILWAUKEE CASE STUDY: AN EMERGING FEDERATED PUBLIC LIBRARY SYSTEM

Henry E. Bates, Jr.

The first public library systems to be officially certified under Chapter 43 of the Wisconsin Statutes did not begin operation until January 1, 1973. Within three years, eleven federated systems had been formed, covering 65 percent of the state. A requirement of the Wisconsin Administrative Code is that the public library systems develop formal agreements with other types of libraries by the end of their second year of operation. Fulfillment of this requirement may be facilitated by the existence of multitype library councils that existed in four areas—Madison, Green Bay, Milwaukee, and Kenosha—prior to the establishment of the public library systems. This paper is concerned with the Milwaukee County Federated Library System's early operation and with the system's relationship to its local multitype library council, the Library Council of Metropolitan Milwaukee.

SERVICES OF THE SYSTEM

The Milwaukee County Federated Library System began operating early in 1973 with six suburban libraries and eight communities without libraries as members. Since then, two other suburban libraries have joined the system. The Milwaukee Public Library, of course, with its 12 neighborhood libraries, is a member, and its central library serves as the headquarters library for the system, which is wholly supported by state funds. The system's board chose to focus on several areas in its 1974 plan:

1. Centralized electronic circulation control system for all member libraries
2. Prime emphasis on the purchase of nonprint materials with special focus on the development of a film service for the system
3. Daily delivery service from the headquarters library to member libraries
4. Centralized processing of federated system materials
5. A telephone intercommunication network for all member libraries
6. A grant to each member library to be used to support system services

7. A credit grant to each member library for the purchase of nonprint materials for each library and the centralized processing of such materials

8. The creation of a systemwide borrowers' card

The 1974 plan committed the system to the maintenance of the long-term goals inherent in the original plan. The following year, the board felt that there was a lack of direct service programs to the public and consequently added a component that provides special library service to people in all the member communities who are over 60 years of age.

Before the Milwaukee County Federated Library System began functioning, all Milwaukee County libraries went their own way in handling the circulation of materials. There were different loan periods, overdue charges, and methods of checking books in and out. Under the federated system's guidance, the member libraries joined together and agreed to centralize all of their circulation activities through an electronic circulation control system. This centralization and standardization also made it possible for the system to implement almost completely a reciprocal borrowing contract between libraries.

Other activities with system funds have made possible an extensive collection of videotapes (over 600 titles) with playback equipment in all libraries. Also, close to 700 16mm films, 446 Super-8mm titles, 221 standard 8mm films, and 2,301 audiocassettes, kits, and filmstrips are now federated library system property being shared by the member libraries. Individual libraries have increased their capacity in the area of nonprint material by using their allotment of federated system money for this purpose.

All member libraries are now connected by telephone communication, and a daily delivery service between all libraries helps provide quick access to all library materials.

The other component of the system is the very successful Over 60 Service. Bookmobiles and a staff move about the county to places where the elderly are, including nursing homes, residential areas, rest homes, day centers, and other facilities. Shut-in service and canvassing are also important parts of the Over 60 Service, and there are no fines for overdue materials.

PROBLEMS OF THE SYSTEM

What, then, are the problems? The greatest one could be the erratic level of funding by the state. Being a little philosophical, other more nebulous concerns assume primary importance.

The long-touted belief "that the success of a larger unit depends not so much on the number of smaller libraries which have agreed to cooperate, consolidate, or federate, but rather on the size and quality of the strongest library within the larger unit of service"[1] has to be examined. In Milwaukee County, where over 80 percent of the local individual library funds are expended within the city of Milwaukee library system, its dominance can seem frightening; its credibility and sophistication can be suspect. When the staffing of one city neighborhood library often equals the whole staff of a suburban library, there are fears of largeness dominating. An example of this apprehension: When, at its monthly meeting, the systems analyst for the electronic data services operation asked the Technical Advisory Committee (TAC), composed of all the directors of member libraries, for approval to increase the telecommunications lines to 4,800 baud, discomfort and fear were sensed on the part of TAC that the central headquarters library was purchasing something that would benefit the city library. The reservations actually expressed pertained to the lag in telecommunications response time; however, the administration was not sure that was really the issue. Rather, TAC might have felt threatened by the lack of comprehension of the computer language.

Before 1973, only one or two libraries in the system had developed any kind of a collection in the area of nonprint material, that is, videotape, 16mm films, audiocassettes, framed art prints, filmstrips, and phonograph records. The computer hardware decisions, the development of individual videotape playback units, and the difficult decisions resulting from a new, untested service, at least in this area of the state, again caused some credibility gaps.

Gregory and Stoffel state: "To the uninitiated, cooperative efforts within a system may give rise to the fear of losing the right to independent action. Rules and procedures seriously affecting the local libraries are determined democratically, that is, by majority vote."[2]

This isn't necessarily so! One of our member libraries, for example, used federated system acquisitions money to supplement its own 16mm film collection. This library had maintained its same circulation procedures (loan periods) for federated system films as for its locally purchased collection, making it terribly inconvenient for the other member libraries. In order to work within the delivery system to other libraries, the loan period would have had to be extended. The majority of TAC wanted this change, as did the federated library board, but this local library's board did not want to alter its circulation procedures for this first film collection in the system, which did, in fact, precede the federated system. The federated system board backed off from demanding a change due to the fear of the image of big-city dominance. Democracy rules? Or helpless giant?

HISTORY OF CONTRACTUAL COOPERATION IN MILWAUKEE COUNTY

Contractual cooperation in Milwaukee County dates back to 1915, when individual suburban libraries contracted with the city of Milwaukee library for book service, delivery and a per circulation charge for their residents' use of the city's central library. A reference and research contract, by which the county reimburses the city of Milwaukee for reference and in-library use, dates back to 1965. As stated in the beginning of this article, the Milwaukee County Federated Library System actually became operational in January 1973, with six cooperating suburban libraries and the city of Milwaukee library system; two other suburban libraries have joined since then. Eight other suburban communities without libraries agreed to participate in the system, with the hope that they would eventually establish their own libraries. Two fairly large southside suburban libraries, South Milwaukee (population 23,297; collection, 69,000 volumes; and over $200,000 budget) and Cudahy (population 22,078; collection, 52,000 volumes; and over $170,000 budget), did not wish to participate in a federated library system. To this day, they have not joined, although each is part of the suburban contract with the city of Milwaukee library. It is in the true democratic spirit when one of the trustees of the South Milwaukee Library Board serves on the federated library board (which is composed of seven members appointed by the county executive). This trustee keeps us on our toes and brings a nonmember's perspective. He rightly concerns himself with any decisions that would lead to direct benefits to the city library; he carefully questions the adding of personnel to the system; and in many ways is our local general accounting office.

FEAR OF BIG-CITY DOMINANCE

There are only three city representatives on this seven-member board, which ideally should mitigate the fear of big-city dominance. The Wisconsin state law specifically protects the local community and its autonomy: "A federated public library system board shall have the powers of a library board under S. 43.58 to 43.62 with respect to system-wide functions and services. The local library boards shall retain responsibility for their libraries in all other areas."

The credibility factor comes into play in these two nonmember communities, as well as to a lesser extent in the eight member suburban libraries. A contractual arrangement is clear and less threatening than a federated library system where, again, Milwaukee's size, coupled with the fear that this is the start of metro government, makes these communities reject the system.

Stoffel speaks about "a persistent fear among the decision makers in communities that have supported the library well enough to allow for good collection building in that they will be over-burdened and undercompensated by affiliation with weaker neighbors."[3] This is a definite factor in Milwaukee County. There is one reluctant library board of a member library that is hesitating to sign the reciprocal borrowing contract (the only holdout) because of this undercompensation notion and fear of being "raided" by adjoining member communities without libraries.

There has recently been a change of directors in one of the non-member libraries, and her latest annual report pointed out the necessity of getting into the audiovisual business. She knows the federated system, with its expertise (sophistication?), is there. Still another nonmember library thinks its library is good, feels it serves its community's needs (supplemented by the suburban contract), but has no room for AV materials.

Serious attempts have been made to bring these two libraries into the system. There have been meetings with their trustees that have been conducted with some of the objectivity of a new director coming into an already established system. Despite this, and despite the great enthusiasm shown by the system proponents, they have not been brought into the system. Perhaps their real concerns are the size of the central headquarters operation; its staff's sophistication; the fear of metropolitan government (sneaked in the back door by an innocuous library system, but perhaps leading them to being part of a racial desegregation plan?); and a strong conviction that they are doing just as well alone, without those outside dollars that never should have been taken from their pockets in the first place.

REPRESENTATION BEYOND THE PUBLIC LIBRARY SYSTEM

The Milwaukee County Federated Library System is prospering, but there are always a few problems, and they are important ones.

On a larger front, I could say that, in general, most public library systems in Wisconsin have not implemented the Wisconsin administrative Code that requires that "a public library system shall by the end of the second year of its operation develop formal agreements with other types of libraries in the system area, providing for appropriate sharing of library resources to benefit the clientele of all libraries."

Perhaps the biggest reason for this nonimplementation is the lack of consistent or dependable sources of funding throughout the system's brief history. It is difficult and frustrating to develop a long-range plan of service and then have the budget allocation reduced by 50 or 25 percent.

An even more important factor is the absence of other representation on most of the federated library system boards. Without representation from special, academic, and school libraries, there will never be any significant sharing and cooperation. In Milwaukee County, the Library Council of Metropolitan Milwaukee was developing at the same time and has become successful, partly because of its board representation. The Milwaukee Public Library and the Milwaukee County Federated Library System showed their support very early. The city library supplied a room, heat, light, and maintenance service without charge; routed periodicals and other materials through the office; and helped in many general ways. The Milwaukee County Federated Library System came to LCOMM's financial rescue last year by granting $4,000 for the fiscal year. Another library system in Wisconsin has also given financial support to its intertype council.

One of LCOMM's most successful ventures was the development of the Coordinated Collections Committee, which brought together the libraries of Marquette University, University of Wisconsin-Milwaukee, and Milwaukee Public Library into a coordinated collection development plan. In keeping with the Wisconsin tradition, the LCOMM long-range plan, "A Plan for Cooperative Action," placed major emphasis on the autonomy and freedom of choice of its member libraries. (Significantly, the two communities not in the Milwaukee County Federated Library System are members of LCOMM.)

Statewide cooperation became a big issue during 1976. Under the excellent leadership of the Division for Library Services, a Task Force on Interlibrary Cooperation and Resource Sharing was formed. It became evident very early that public library systems were not the best vehicle for interlibrary cooperation. Broader representation was needed, and after much discussion, and sometimes heated debate, the final report recommended, among many other things, the formation of multitype organizations that would be the vehicle for cooperation among areas in the state. Some felt that the formation of these councils could lead to the further development of library systems in Wisconsin; in a nonthreatening way, libraries could begin to share their resources and to cooperate in more meaningful ways. The task force members agreed that one type of library or library network should dominate the structure for planning and implementing intertype activities. Hence, the area multitype organizations could include total membership of libraries within the area or be made up of a smaller group of representatives of the various types of libraries. Some of the functions of these organizations as recommended by the task force are:

Present recommendations for statewide programs and policies to the state council

When necessary, arrange for contracts to carry out cooperative programs

Plan area programs when development is needed to supplement state-level programs.

Finally, the librarians within the state are aggressively seeking significant ways to cooperate.

NOTES

1. Roberta Bowler, ed., *Local Public Library Administration* (Chicago: International City Managers' Association, 1964).

2. Ruth Gregory and Lester L. Stoffel, *Public Libraries in Cooperative Systems: Administrative Patterns for Service* (Chicago: American Library Association, 1971).

3. Ibid.

NEW YORK CASE STUDY 1: ROCHESTER—A RURAL/URBAN MIX

Evaline B. Neff

U.S. citizens are notoriously mobile. They change jobs and residences frequently, choosing to live in the country and work in the city and vice versa, pursuing their education through formal and independent study programs, and being creative in many settings. The lines between rural and urban tend to become increasingly blurred. It is no longer possible to package people into rural and urban, because it is no longer true that all those who live in rural areas have interests and information needs that are limited to agricultural and/or very simple concerns, nor is it necessarily true that most urban dwellers have more sophisticated needs than their country-dwelling counterparts.

It is more germane to speak of types and levels of needs, and to consider the tiers of services required to meet them. This layered approach is the one used in the Rochester Regional Research Library Council microuniverse. It allows a person with a variety of requirements to plug into a great selection of outlets. Available services are mostly free of charge for those services that the state of New York chooses to subsidize. For persons whose needs are not met with services subsidized publicly or privately, the only present alternative is to pay for them. It is preferable to offer services for a fee, rather than not to offer them at all.

To illustrate how the New York layered scheme works, imagine a creative person developing a private invention in the basement of his home in the rural hills overlooking Canandaigua Lake. Several small public libraries are available to him for his and his family's recreational and nontechnical information needs. Virtually all of the materials and services from these outlets are available without direct charge, including an interlibrary loan network that will forward his request through a local network of public, academic, and special libraries on to a statewide network that queries the major research collections in the state. When he has a requirement for the technical information needed to refine his invention, he may find that the so-called "free service" no longer satisfies his needs.

For so long as he knows exactly which book, article, technical report, or patent he needs, it is a simple matter for the local public library to pass the request on to the next layer of libraries (large public, academic, and special). If some of the requested material, however, is in a foreign language unknown to him, the material is of no value until it has been translated, a service not presently available to him without a substantial charge. In the event he is not sure that he has a complete list of the publications dealing with the subject of his invention, he has a number of options. He can travel to a nearby academic or special library, search catalogs and indexes, and then request each item on interlibrary loan through his local public library outlet or borrow some items through his regional borrower's card. He can pay for the services of a literature searcher, since in-depth literature searches are not subsidized. As he seeks to refine his invention further by determining its patentability, he discovers that a patent search service is also not available on a subsidized basis, only on a very stiff fee basis. Our fictitious library user does indeed have a mixed experience because of a somewhat mixed-up funding system that subsidizes some services completely and others not at all.

THE ROCHESTER MICROUNIVERSE

The Rochester Regional Research Library Council (RRRLC) microuniverse is that of an urban-suburban county, surrounded by four rural counties (3,168 square miles) in the metropolitan Rochester, New York, area. Demographically, the general population is concentrated in the urban county of Monroe, where the city of Rochester is located, as is the population of users of research level and specialized information publications. Census Bureau sources show that of a total of 964,689 general population users, 711,917 live in Monroe County. The number of users of specialized information in the RRRLC region are estimated to be 113,648, of which 11,675 are school teachers, 70,381 are academic faculty and students, 10,553 are in the health services, 17,503 are scientific and technical personnel, and 3,836 are from other professions. The area is characterized by a higher than average level of education influenced by the presence of a university and 11 other institutions of higher education, and by R&D-oriented industries and research organizations that require a high proportion of Ph.D.-caliber personnel.

PIONEER FEDERATED LIBRARY SYSTEM AND RRRLC

The library needs of area residents are served by two separately funded library cooperatives: the Pioneer Library System and the Rochester Regional Research Library Council. Pioneer is a federation of five county (Monroe, Wayne, Livingston, Ontario, Wyoming) and one city (Rochester) public library systems, with 77 outlets. RRRLC is a multitype library cooperative with 50 member libraries: the 6 Pioneer systems, 12 academic institutions, 17 company libraries, 10 health sciences libraries, 3 museum, and 2 other special libraries. The council is one of the nine multitype library councils in New York chartered under the State Education Department's Reference and Research Resources (3 R's) library program. The statewide aspect of 3 R's is the New York State Interlibrary Loan (NYSILL) network, which links nine major research libraries, each of which is reimbursed for supplying materials to users across the state. NYSILL also includes three public library systems that are reimbursed for filling requests on a statewide basis.

RRRLC and the six public library systems are each governed by their own boards of trustees; in each case, the board is composed primarily of laypersons who are trustees of a member library. Each of the public library systems receives statutory state aid through a reimbursal formula based on square miles and population served, and expenditures for library materials. Aggregate 1976 state aid to Pioneer for public library services was $1,207,832. Public libraries pay no membership fees to their county library systems, though some of the counties contribute to their respective systems. RRRLC receives state aid from an appropriation in the New York State Executive Budget; the sum was $92,000 in 1976. Additional income was derived from membership fees, service fees, and grants from foundations and the federal government.

The summary of services each type of cooperative offers its members is provided in Tables 1 and 2. The public library systems were established between 1952 and 1960 and had a full program of services long before RRRLC was founded in 1966. The programs offered by each are complementary rather than duplicative, although by necessity there is some overlap.

Generally speaking, public library systems receive state aid to provide public library services to the general public through their member library outlets. Concurrently, 3 R's Councils receive state aid to provide services to persons needing research level materials through their member library outlets. Where services cross system lines, contractual arrangements between the Rochester Council and the systems are developed. Neither type of cooperative normally offers library services directly to individuals. RRRLC does offer three: translation, literature searching, and fast patent copying.

SERVICES TO LIBRARIES

Interlibrary loan service is provided through a combination of state funding, contractual reimbursal arrangements, and exchange at no charge. The area's central public library collection is the Rochester Public Library. The Monroe County Library System Interlibrary Loan staff uti-

Table 1   Summary of *Similar* Services Each Type of Cooperative Offers Its Members

Service	Pioneer System	Rochester Council
Delivery	All members	10 largest only
Interlibrary loan	All members	All members
Regional library borrowing card	All members	Partial only
Continuing education programs	Extensive	Limited
Media materials	All types	16mm film only
Centralized processing	Complete	None
Publications	Numerous	Few

Table 2   Summary of *Different* Services Each Type of Cooperative Offers Its Members

Service	Pioneer System	Rochester Council
Book and film programs	Many	None
Bookmobile	As needed	None
Translations	None	By referral
Union list of serials	None	Most libraries included
Patent copying service	None	Fee service
Technical and business information (literature search service)	None	Arranged through free-lance searchers

lizes that collection to fill requests from all of the public library outlets in Pioneer. Each of the four rural county library systems pays Monroe Library System on a transaction basis of $1.35 for service to its member libraries. Monroe County Interlibrary Loan staff also fills requests from academic and special libraries on a reimbursal basis of $1.30 per transaction, charged to the Research Library Council. Academic and special libraries that are not members of the council are charged $5 per interlibrary loan transaction by the council. All types of libraries also exchange materials at no charge to one another, except for photocopying in some cases. The "central" library collection for academic and special libraries is the University of Rochester library system. The university is reimbursed on a search ($1 per transaction) and supply ($3 per transaction) basis under the terms of its contract with the State Education Department.

A selective compilation of the 1975 Interlibrary Loan statistics in Table 3 illustrates the extent to which academic and special libraries borrowed from public libraries and vice versa.

RRRLC's Media Center was established in 1973 in a member library, the State University of New York College at Brockport. Its purpose is to

Table 3   Rochester Area Interlibrary Loan Statistics—Calendar 1975

Total Loan Requests	Number	Percentage
From public library outlets	73,857	100.0
Filled by public libraries	65,559	88.7
Filled by RRRLC (academic–special) libraries[a]	1,857	2.5
Filled by NYSILL statewide network	4,487	6.1
Requests not filled[b]	1,954	2.7
From academic-special libraries	34,793	100.0
Filled by public libraries	2,527	7.3
Filled by RRRLC academic–special libraries	22,360	64.2
Filled by NYSILL statewide network	4,284	12.3
Filled by NLM network	290	0.9
Requests not filled[b]	5,332	15.3

[a]Of a total of 3,811 requests channeled into the RRRLC network, 1,857, or 48.7 percent were filled.

[b]Not filled: materials not available or requests were not referred to supplying libraries because of user deadlines.

assist members in securing *audiovisual materials* for higher education instruction. To date, only 170 16mm films have been purchased. They are available to the members on a $5 per booking handling charge—a token fee when compared with the $15 to $100 booking fees charged by other distributors. Through this regional pooling of expensive films, the member institutions achieved aggregate savings of $22,377 in rental fees during fiscal 1975/76. Income from bookings during fiscal 1975/76 was $3,135. Thus, shared use of expensive materials is among the most cost-effective benefits of a multitype council.

The Reynolds Audio Visual Department (RAVD), established in 1948, is located in the Rochester Public Library and is funded separately at the $150,000+ level. The collection serves a wide range of user needs with the following assets: 5,000 16mm-film titles, 4,000 8mm-film titles, 150 videotapes, and 2,000 filmstrips. The first 50 films are free; thereafter booking charges are $2 for 10 minutes for color and $1 for 10 minutes for black-and-white films.

Rochester Library Council's OCLC Shared Terminal Project has a twofold purpose. It provides individual member librarians with the opportunity to learn how to use an on-line cataloging system. It also documents information on modes and costs for the sharing of one terminal by two or more small libraries, neither of which can justify the cost of subscribing to OCLC singly. One experiment in sharing between Hobart and William Smith College and the Community College of the Finger Lakes demonstrated that it was possible for two libraries to share one terminal effectively, and that it was cost effective to do so.

Centralized *technical processing* is provided by the public library systems to their member libraries at no cost to the member library.

A *union list of serials* that is updated periodically is a basic necessity in a resource-sharing network that is involved in interlibrary loan and photocopying services. RRRLC's list has been expanded and updated three times between 1970 and 1975. The third edition contains 29,235 unique titles and costs $15,301 for 125 copies.

RRRLC's *continuing education* seminars and workshops are attended by some 300 persons each year. They cover a wide range of topics, reflecting the great variety of users and services in a mixed multitype cooperative. Some of the offerings have been 1970 Census Data, Conservation and Restoration of Printed Materials, Government Documents (federal, state, United Nations, and local), Personnel Management, Library Orientation Programs, A Series on All Aspects of Serials, Medical Clinical Librarianship, The Use of Chemical Abstracts, and many others. The public library systems conduct in-service training, orientation, book review, and continuing education programs tailored to public library services.

SERVICES TO INDIVIDUALS

Technical and Business Information (TABI) is designed for the person who needs in-depth specialized information. It utilizes free-lance librarians who have degrees in the fields of the topic to be searched, i.e., given a customer with a requirement in the field of chemistry, a chemist who is an experienced searcher is assigned to him. The searcher conducts an interview, usually in person, to determine search parameters and terms and to arrive at a cost estimate. The client then sends a written purchase order to the council, and the searcher proceeds with the order up to the limit authorized by the client. If the search turns out to be more complex and time consuming than foreseen, the searcher reports on the work accomplished, and is either instructed to terminate the search and provide all data found up to that point or is authorized to complete the search.

Both the searcher and the council share in the income from TABI fees. The council charges $15 per hour to persons associated with not-for-profit institutions and $25 per hour to those in profit institutions. Additional expenses incurred by the searcher, such as photocopying or arranging for interlibrary loans, are passed on to the client. RRRLC receives $3.50 or $8.50 per hour and the searcher $10 or $15, depending on whether the search is done at the $15 or $25 per hour rate. Costs to the clients have ranged from $25 to $380.

Search topics have covered a diverse range of fields, from criteria for establishing an executive incentive system to antiblock additives for polyethylene resin systems. TABI users are primarily R&D personnel associated with small companies that do not have in-house library services. Persons in both larger companies and not-for-profit institutions have used the service also. It is usually the one-and-a-fraction person operated library that finds TABI helpful. In this type of situation, the librarian is fully occupied with the day-to-day management of the library, with reference questions, and with short searches. He or she usually cannot find the time to perform a medium to long search, and thus finds it expedient and economical to use an on-demand service.

Translation service is offered on a referral basis, using free-lance translators. The council identifies and tests persons with a combination of educational achievements and language proficiency. Those wishing to be referred by the council as translators are asked to fill in an application form that details their capabilities and gives several references. Following application, a test is sent to the applicant with the request that it be returned when completed. The test is several paragraphs of a text in the field and language in which the applicant claims proficiency. When the test is returned, it is graded for accuracy, style, format, neatness, and promptness. If the work satisfies the test specifications, the person's name is added to the roster of translators and will be referred to a client whose request requires that translator's subject and language competencies.

The fee for the service is determined by agreement between the client and the translator. Fees range from $2 to $6 per hundred words, depending on the language and the complexity of the subject matter. Western European languages are less expensive than Oriental ones, and business letters cost less than the text of a patent. The council derives no income from this service.

In the case where a needed resource is not available in one council's area, it makes good resource-sharing sense to arrange with a neighbor who has it. The RRRLC's *fast patent copying service* provides copies of U.S. patents in three days instead of three weeks (the time it takes to get a copy of a patent from the U.S. Patent Office in Washington). In this instance, speed, the user's prime requirement, is achieved through the cooperation of two 3 R's Councils and one public library system.

The U.S. patent depository collection nearest Rochester is at the Buffalo and Erie County Public Library, 60 miles away. RRRLC contracts with its counterpart in the Buffalo area, the Western New York Library Resources Council, which is based at the Buffalo and Erie County Public Library. By the terms of the contract, Rochester pays Western New York $1.25 per patent copied (up to a maximum of 50 pages) for the costs of retrieving the patent from the stacks of the Buffalo and Erie County Public Library and photocopying and mailing the patent to the requestor. Individuals purchase a $1.75 coupon that entitles them to one copy of one

U.S. patent. The coupon is a three-part ordering form that gives both the user and the processor in Buffalo a record of the transaction. The service is self-supporting. Transaction volume has averaged 4,000 per year since 1972. Users of this service are primarily patent attorneys in private practice and those in the patent departments of major local corporations.

SUMMARY

The New York mixed experience, better known as the 3 R's, has demonstrated the validity of serving the nation's library needs through cooperative coordination of many types of library collections and services. In the Rochester area it has proved the following:

Librarians from diverse types of libraries are interested in learning together, planning together, and working together to implement their plans.

Small and large libraries can make contributions each at their own levels.

Users are willing to pay for specialized services tailored to their unique needs.

Owners of large collections who act as major suppliers need to be reimbursed for the labor and the materials in a "net supplier" situation.

Inventiveness, imagination, and compromise in devising cooperative arrangements will overcome most impediments.

One of the key ingredients to success is money, in the millions of dollars range at the state and multistate levels. Without realistic funding, participants' enthusiasms wilt, expectations are not fulfilled, and the entire effort is jeopardized.

BIBLIOGRAPHY

1. *Interlibrary Loan in New York State*. New York: Nelson Associates, February 1969.
2. Neff, E. B. "Contracting in Library Networks." *Special Libraries* 67, no. 3, March 1976: 127–130.
3. _____"Fast Patent Copying Service." *The Bookmark* 33, no. 1, Sept.–October 1973: 23–26.
4. _____"Rochester Regional Research Library Council." *The Bookmark* 28, no. 7, April 1969: 214–219.
5. *Regional Interlibrary Loan in New York State: A Comparative Study*. A report prepared for the Division of Library Development of the New York State Library. Washington, D.C.: Checchi and Company, March 1976.
6. *A Reference and Research Library Resources Plan for the Rochester Area: An Analysis of the Proposals of the Commissioner's Committee on Reference and Research Library Resources as Applied to a Selected Region*. New York: Nelson Associates, 1962.

7. *The 3 R's Program: Meeting Industry's Informational Needs.* Cambridge, Mass.: Arthur D. Little, September 1967.

8. University of the State of New York. State Education Department. The New York State Library. Library Extension Division. *Building on Strength: New York's Plan for a Reference and Research Library Program.* 1963.

9. University of the State of New York. State Education Department. Division of Library Development. *Profiles of the Reference and Research Library Resources Systems in New York State.* 1970

10. University of the State of New York. State Education Department. New York State Library. *Report of the Commissioner's Committee on Reference and Research Library Resources.* December 1961.

11. University of the State of New York. State Education Department. *Report of the Commissioner of Education's Committee on Library Development.* 1970.

NEW YORK CASE STUDY 2: THE METRO CONTINUING EDUCATION PROGRAM

Morris A. Gelfand

The central purpose of the continuing education program in a multi-type library cooperative is to instruct and to encourage the staffs of member libraries to make the strongest possible contribution to the goals of the cooperative. These goals can be defined functionally as strengthening library resources and facilitating access to them. By providing educational programs and other participatory activities for the staffs of member libraries, the cooperative helps libraries to raise their effectiveness and their ability to contribute to the common goals. It also supports individual librarians in their efforts toward professional advancement. This is not to deny the validity of the conceptualizations of continuing education and in-service training by Stone,[1] Penland,[2] and others, but rather to establish a sharp focal point for the cooperative.

The multitype library cooperative can offer an attractive and supportive environment for information interchange on a high professional level in discussion groups and committee work. Involvement in such groups is purely voluntary and usually free of the constraints under which individuals may have to meet in their own libraries. The experience of METRO (New York Metropolitan Reference and Research Library Agency)[3] bears this out. In recent years, hundreds of librarians have participated in committee work and other group activities. During the year ending April 1976, 650 volunteers took part in 124 projects.[4]

This massive involvement of volunteers has provided the principal source of ideas and personnel for activities, services, and programs, including continuing education. The volunteers serve on METRO's standing committees, subcommittees, and task forces, and they belong to specialist groups, such as the Small Libraries Discussion Group, the Reference Librarians Discussion Group, and others. The large array of subcommittees and task forces falls into an orderly pattern under the four standing committees: Administrative Services, Public Services, Resources Development, and Technical Services.[5]

METRO'S COMMITMENT TO CONTINUING EDUCATION

METRO's interest in continuing education dates back to its beginning in 1966, when there appeared in the first issue of its newsletter a proposal entitled "Meetings and Lectures for Librarians."[6] In the following year, the Committee on Special Projects was given responsibility for "interlibrary training and discussion programs." Arrangements were made with IBM for the first continuing education program: IBM Computer Concepts Course, conducted September 5–8, 1967, for 35 persons from METRO member libraries. METRO continued to rely on outside organizations until 1970, while it developed its own programming. The first METRO-conceived project, an all-day workshop based on the IBM Computer Concepts Course, took place on March 7, 1968. On October 1, there was a full-day workshop on Personnel—Procedures or People.

The importance of continuing education as a major METRO service was confirmed in 1970, when the committee structure was reorganized. In the new structure, each of the four standing committees was charged with a responsibility for "planning interlibrary training programs." This was a highly significant change of policy from a centralized, general approach to a decentralized, subject-oriented one. METRO continues to operate in this mode.

A highlight of the 1970 program was a lecture-demonstration on the care and repair of books by Carolyn Horton on April 7 before an audience of 135 persons. This program was so successful that it was repeated as part of the three-day Conference on Botanical and Horticultural Libraries at the New York Botanical Garden on April 2, 1971, and it has since been repeated under METRO auspices.

In 1971, the Public Services Committee held a general meeting on orientation of undergraduates. This was followed by a series of three regional workshops in which simulated classroom situations demonstrated individualized approaches to instruction. A meeting on the Problems, Pitfalls, and Possibilities of Automation was sponsored by the Technical Services Committee on May 5.

A variety of new programs, some sponsored jointly by METRO with other organizations, marked 1972 and 1973 activities. A highlight of 1972 was the Friday Seminars, a series of four closed-circuit television programs produced cooperatively by METRO and the City University Mutual Benefit Instructional Network (CUMBIN). These programs were offered live from the City University Graduate Center and remote at Brooklyn, City, Hunter, and Queens colleges. There were provisions for direct dialogue with the Graduate Center audience and interaction by telephone with audiences at the other four campuses. The seminar topics are of some interest: Staff Involvement in Decision Making in Libraries; Total Library Service; A New Look at Library Cooperation; Microform Publication and Use; and Systems Approach to Library Operations and Management. In all, 525 viewers participated in this program. In the subsequent evaluation, about half of those registered for the series responded to a questionnaire. The general conclusions were that the television medium was effective; and that such a program could be made even more effective with more practical presentations.[7]

In June 1972, METRO members were informed through the newsletter[8] about several continuing education programs offered by other organizations. Open to METRO membership, they included a workshop on documents, a symposium on the applications of computer technology, a workshop on materials for the handicapped, and several short courses in library and information science. The widely distributed newsletter has itself been a useful medium of continuing education. It contains not only news about METRO activities but also notices of coming events, new programs offered in the library schools of the metropolitan area, advances in librarianship, and other professional information.

Another 1972 highlight was a program on the international cataloging rules. Sponsored jointly by METRO's Technical Services Committee and the New York Technical Services Librarians, it was presented on December 14 to an audience of 250. The topic was International Cataloging Rules on the Line or Who's Afraid of Chapter 6 and the I.S.B.D.? In preparation for this meeting, seven METRO librarians from a variety of library environments wrote questions that were submitted in advance to the speakers. There was also an informal question period.

GROWTH AND DEVELOPMENT, 1973–1977

In October 1972, a new period of growth and development of continuing education in METRO was initiated by the appointment of METRO's first full-time executive director, Forrest F. Carhart, Jr. The two previous directors could devote only part of their time to METRO while continuing to perform with distinction in their original positions. Although each gave strong leadership to the organization and encouraged some important educational programs, such as the Friday Seminars in 1972, it was not until Carhart's time that the programming could receive continuous leadership and support.

Shortly after Carhart took office, he strengthened the committees and coordinated continuing education activities in a more sustained and orderly way. As a result, he could say in his first quarterly progress report, "Many additional workshops or seminars are in various stages of planning, with a view towards the appointment of sub-committees to plan for details."[9]

In 1973, the Professional Communications Subcommittee of the Administrative Services Committee completed two videotapes to demonstrate how this medium could be employed for staff training. The tapes were shown at the annual meeting of METRO on April 10. The demonstration was followed on May 23 and 24 by a two-day seminar on The

Services of Processing Agencies. The announcement of the seminar brought into sharp focus its objectives, scope, and the audience for whom it was intended:

The objective is to provide librarians with a basic understanding of services offered by processing centers and how they can best be utilized. . . . In terms of the needs of individual libraries, the program will attempt to highlight guidelines for evaluating the advantages and limitations of the services. The seminar is directed toward the concerned administrator as well as individuals directly involved with library support functions, whether they are school, special, public, college or university librarians. The emphasis will be on monographic materials. Services involving both traditional union catalogs and more sophisticated data bases will be discussed.[10]

This strong emphasis on the definition of objectives and the target group would henceforth characterize the germination of possible program topics in the committees and subcommittees and give direction to planning efforts. And the role of the executive director would expand further.

The Executive Director's Role

During 1973 and much of 1974, the executive director gave much of his time to the committees. He took part in their discussions, encouraged the planning of meetings, the recording and distribution of minutes, and the development of a problem-oriented approach. Occasionally, he would suggest an idea for a seminar or workshop, but generally he served as an information resource, adviser, and catalytic agent. Under his guidance, program concepts were examined critically, objectives refined, and the audience to be served clearly envisioned. At this point, a proposal might be drafted in outline for further discussion in the appropriate standing committee. If there were a favorable consensus, a subcommittee or task force would be formed to carry out the proposal. As the planning developed, the executive director and his staff became progressively involved. He advised on budgeting, scheduling the event, and arranging for speakers, and he provided needed clerical support, a place for the seminar, editorial and printing assistance, publicity, mailing, and the collection and disbursement of funds.

Role of the Responsible Committee

Insofar as it was practicable, the committee or task force was expected to plan and carry out the program, to decide on the format (whether it should be a seminar, workshop, lecture, symposium, or some other form), to select and recruit speakers, to conduct the program, to evaluate it, and to report back to the parent committee. The distinctions between the roles of the executive director and the program planning committees have not always been clear-cut, but, in general, the committees are strongly encouraged to represent and to interpret the needs of METRO's constituency and to formulate plans and programs for meeting those needs that can be served best by training and education. The record of METRO's activities in this regard is a tribute to the cooperative attitude of the members.

METRO'S CONTINUING EDUCATION PROGRAMS AFTER 1973

Table 1 illustrates that METRO's activities indeed had expanded in volume and scope after 1973. Most of the programs were offered in cooperation with two other 3 R's Councils, the Long Island Library Resources Council and the Southeastern Library Resources Council. Although METRO's own members continued to constitute the prime audience, the doors were opened to possible participation by METRO's neighbors. METRO also cooperated with local professional associations and avoided unnecessary duplication of programs offered by the local library schools and other professional agencies.

Most of the programs listed in Table 1 were sponsored by the Technical Services Committee and directed to the needs and interests of METRO and its member libraries. The seminars on collection development were aimed toward the larger context of regional needs. Libraries with sound collection development policies and programs were in a strong position to aid in the formulation of a METRO-wide program. The Exhibition Catalogs seminar was a member-oriented conference that drew a large audience of specialists, many from outside the METRO region. The workshops on the Lockheed Dialog system were a result of a beneficial collaboration between Teachers College Library at Columbia University and METRO. METRO agreed to pay part of the basic rental of the system with the understanding that its members could make use of it, paying only for individual searches, but members had to learn how to use the system.

The 1975 program reflected the growing interest in problems of administration and the continuing interest in technical services. The BALLOTS (Bibliographic Automation of Large Library Operations Using a Time-Sharing System) program was offered because of its high potential for library networks in general and for its possible relevance to METRO's needs. The seminar on standards in reference work was designed "as a forum for the exchange of ideas on reference services and the proposed standards that will be voted on during the 1975 American Library Association Conference." The Human Relations Seminar was directed to middle managers and supervisors from METRO libraries. Two groups of workshops on care and repair of library materials attracted much interest. A feature of the workshops was a series of demonstrations in which five or six persons could receive hands-on experience. These programs necessarily had to be limited to small groups, 30 to 32 persons in all.

The emphasis was on reader services in 1976, as Table 1 shows. Library automation continued to be a strong field of interest and interlibrary loan and direct access problems were a concern. There were interesting

Table 1   METRO Continuing Education Programs

Program/Topic	Date	Format	Sponsor(s)
Spring Lectures		Lecture	METRO/New York Technical Services Librarians
Progress Report on Chapter 6 AACR	2/20/74		
Bibliographic Access	3/20/74	Lecture	
The Research Libraries Group	4/17/74		
Conservation of Library Materials		Seminar	METRO Technical Services Committee
Binding	3/29/74		
Microforms	4/19/74		
Preservation and Restoration	5/24/74		
Library Collection Development		Seminar	METRO Resources Development Committee
Collection Policies and Cooperation	4/11/74		
Development of Resources	5/9/74		
Exhibition Catalogs	10/21/74	Seminar	METRO in cooperation with SLA/ARLIS—New York
Lockheed Dialog Retrieval System	10/31/74 11/1,2,3/74 4/10,11/75	Workshop	METRO and Teachers College Library
Care and Repair of Library Materials	3/20,21/75 9/25,26/75	Workshop	METRO Technical Services Committee
Human Relations Seminar for Supervisors/ Managers	10/25/75	Seminar	METRO Administrative Services Committee Middle Management Subcommittee
Library Security	11/12/75	Seminar	Middle Management Subcommittee
Nonprint Media	3/19/76	Seminar	METRO Technical Services Committee
Reading Aids for the Physically Handicapped	4/28/76	Seminar	METRO/Medical Library Association New York Regional Group
Automated Library Systems	5/4,5,7,8, 11,12/76	Workshop	METRO Technical Services Planning Committee
Measuring Reference Service	5/14/76	Workshop	METRO Reference Librarians' Discussion Group

Table 1   METRO Continuing Education Programs, Continued

Program/Topic	Date	Format	Sponsor(s)
Library Service for the Spanish-Speaking User	5/21/76	Workshop	METRO/Hostos College/ CUNY Bilingual Library Service Subcommittee
Volunteers in Libraries	10/14/76	Workshop	METRO Volunteers in Libraries Task Force
Personal Access: Myth or Reality?	10/29/76	Seminar and Workshop	Personal Access Seminar Task Force
Lending and Borrowing— Ways and Means through Interlibrary Loan	11/17/76	Symposium	Public Services Committee

by-products of the continuing education program; for instance, the demand for the pamphlet on Library Service for the Spanish-Speaking User,[11] issued to participants in the seminar on this subject, was large enough to warrant a reprinting.

PLANS FOR 1977

Plans are well advanced for continuing education programs in 1977. The Acquisitions Librarians Discussion Group will hold a meeting on the format options open to serials and monographic collection (librarians);[12] the Public Services Committee will present a workshop on the *New York Times* Index; a seminar on "closing the catalog" is being planned by a special task force under the joint sponsorship of the Technical Services Committee and the Public Services Committee in which alternatives to the card catalog will be examined as well as results of such closings; the Middle Management Task Force is planning two seminars, one on Management of Change and the other on The Problem Employee; the Education and Psychology Librarians Discussion Group will meet; and there will be an all-day workshop on locating census data in printed reports.

FINANCES

METRO's continuing education program is not intended to be self-sustaining. Registration fees are the principal source of income; a secondary and minor source is income from sale of publications resulting from seminars or workshops. A revolving fund of $2,000 finances initial expenses and is replenished with income from the programs. Income and expenses associated with each program are accounted for individually.

For fiscal year June 30, 1976, the net expenditure for 11 programs, after totaling up cash income and expenses for each program, was $690.

Table 2   Income and Expenditures for Four Continuing Education Programs, 1975–1976

Income	Library Security	Nonprint Media	Measuring Reference Service	Spanish Speaking	Total	Per-cent
METRO member attendance	20	67	53	33	173	55
Member registration fees	$200	$1005	$1060	$165	$2430.00	46
Cosponsor members attendance	11	31	28		70	22
Cosponsor registration fees	$110	$465	$560		$1135.00	22
Balance from cosponsor	$55	$155	$140		$350.00	7
Nonmembers attendance	25	7	29	11	72	23
Nonmember registration fees	$375	$140	$725	$82.50	$1322.50	25
Total attend	56	105	110	44	315	100
Total registration fees	$740	$1765	$2485	$247.50	$5237.50	100
Expenditures						
Typing and clerical work	$ 86.00	$335.50	$402.25	$254.00	$1077.75	23
Design and printing	177.85	187.00	215.94	181.14	771.93	17
Publicity	236.25	59.50	278.25	60.25	634.25	14
Materials for distribution	36.00	243.00	70.00	18.75	367.75	8
Luncheon (speakers) coffee	135.44	141.40	63.75	61.12	401.71	9
Honoraria and travel		808.87	388.10		1196.97	26
Rent			100.00		100.00	2
Refunds (registration fees)	15.00	20.00	25.00	7.50	67.50	1
Total expenditures	$686.54	$1795.27	$1543.29	$592.76	$4617.86	100
Difference between income and expenditures	+ $53.46	− $30.27	+$941.71	− $345.26	+ $619.64	

The analysis in Table 2 of the cost figures for four of the programs conducted during this period shows in detail the income from fees and total expenditures, other than the cost of the executive director's services. Expenditures vary with the subject matter and format of the program. For some programs, such as Nonprint Media and Measuring Reference Service, it was necessary to bring in experts from the outside, with a resultant expense for travel and honoraria. A consistently high proportionate expense was for publicity, design, and printing. These functions are, in fact, intertwined. METRO has learned that a good response in terms of attendance is a result of not only a good choice of subject, but also of a professional job of publicity, including good design and printing.

Usually a month is required to produce and mail a brochure/program and another month must be allowed for registration; thus timing becomes important. Materials for free distribution and expendable supplies are provided according to need. At the seminar on Nonprint Media, for example, each participant was given a copy of *Anglo-American Cataloging Rules: Chapter 12 Revised.* In the workshop on Library Service for the Spanish-Speaking User, the participant received a kit, including a 41-page pamphlet. Other customary expenditures are lunch (or, occasionally, breakfast) for the speakers and coffee for the audience. The meal for speakers provides an excellent opportunity for a review of the program and an interchange of ideas. Rent is paid infrequently for the use of a facility, and typically one or two refunds go to persons who find they cannot attend a program.

Some programs produce substantial income above expenses, while others must be subsidized. METRO does not insist that all programs pay their way. Over a year, losses tend to be balanced off by gains. The intrinsic value of a program in the light of METRO's goals is always an important consideration. The attendance and magnitude of the fee can obviously make a big difference. If in the case of the program on the Spanish-Speaking User, a member fee of $15 and a nonmember fee of $20 had been charged, an income of $715 would have been brought in by the 44 attendees, or $122 more than the expenditures. The decision to charge $5 and $7.50 to members and nonmembers, respectively, was deliberate. The Bilingual Library Service Subcommittee planned the event with a view to attracting up to 200 persons. Perhaps the timing was bad, but there was no lack of interest in the subject. It is significant that since the workshop was offered, some 100 copies of the publication issued to the participants have been sold.

In addition to its own members, METRO has attracted to its programs members of the Long Island Library Resources Council and the Southeastern Library Resources Council, which, like METRO, are among the nine 3 R's (Reference and Research Resources) Councils in New York State. Up to 1977, these councils paid part of the nonmember's rate to encourage their own members to attend at the METRO member rate. Nonmembers, including persons from these two neighboring councils, account for 45 percent of the total attendance, as reported in Table 2. There are also some invited guests—students—at each seminar and at some workshops. METRO has made it a practice to invite two students from each of the five (now six) library schools in the region.

EVALUATION

In a broad sense, the continuing education programs have effectively contributed to METRO's goals. Membership support and satisfaction are generally high. Library directors encourage their staffs to participate both actively as well as passively. The board of trustees does not doubt the validity of METRO's commitment.

Many of the individual programs have been evaluated by the participants. There is no uniform procedure as yet; each sponsoring group, interested in learning the opinion of the participants, has prepared a distinctive evaluation form. The Task Force on the Services of Processing Agencies Seminar, a two-day program, distributed a brief, single-page questionnaire with six questions at the close of the seminar. The responses were generally favorable and were subsequently reviewed by the task force and reported with recommendations to the METRO staff.

The participants in the Human Relations Seminar for Supervisors/ Managers, held October 25, 1975, received a questionnaire two months later from the program planning committee for this event. Most of the questions called for value judgments, as in the question, "What are your opinions of the learning technique used in the seminar for library manager training?" Eventually, the planning committee made a comprehensive analysis of the responses to guide its future work, and sent a summary to the participants. There was general agreement that the seminar was successful and that the participants wanted more such experiences. Encouraged by these responses, the Middle Management Subcommittee of the Administrative Services Committee decided to continue its activities with plans for two new seminars.

The Task Force on the Personal Access Seminar, held on October 29, 1976, took still another approach to evaluation. In a series of groups convened after the formal morning program, participants were invited to discuss critically the papers presented in the morning and to formulate recommendations. These recommendations were later considered in the task force, grouped according to their central theme, and forwarded to three of the standing committees for further action. As an outcome, several new task forces have been formed to deal with the recommendations.

Evaluation is not solely an insiders process or prerogative; it is also invited from outside observers. Recently, the library press has become interested in METRO events. Reports have been published on the workshops on Volunteers[13] and Personal Access[14] and the seminar on Lending and Borrowing.[15]

ANOTHER CONTINUING EDUCATION ACTIVITY: DISCUSSION GROUPS

Continuing education is not necessarily a formal activity that takes place in seminars, workshops, or library school classes. Active and meaningful participation in professional associations and in the committees of a library council can be most beneficial and, in some ways, even more effective. METRO can now offer still another avenue of professional activity and development—the discussion group. Since 1974, five such groups have been formed. These are free associations of specialists: acquisitions, reference, science-technology, education, and psychology librarians and representatives from small libraries. These groups meet to discuss common problems and to find ways to improve their libraries and to promote individual professional development.

The Small Libraries Discussion Group was organized in 1974 as the Ad Hoc Committee on Small Libraries. Its charge at that time was "to examine the role of the smaller library in a cooperative organization. . . ." This committee subsequently became the Small Libraries Round Table and, in the fall of 1976, it emerged as the METRO Small Libraries Discussion Group. Among topics the group has considered, the following are representative: The New METRO Cooperative Acquisitions Program Guidelines for Small Libraries and The Computer and the Small Library.

The Acquisitions Librarians Discussion Group held its first meeting on December 6, 1974, and shortly thereafter got under way with a program of meetings. Topics included Acquisition of Latin American Materials, Gift and Exchange Problems, Effects of Recent Budget Cuts on Acquisitions Programs, and Book Production and Manufacturing. This group has produced a list of jobbers that will soon be published.

During 1976, in rapid succession, the Science-Technology Librarians Discussion Group, the Education and Psychology Librarians Discussion Group, and the Reference Librarians Discussion Group were organized.

All of the discussion groups have been lively and productive. They have added a new dimension to METRO by encouraging more effective support on interlibrary cooperative efforts through better understanding of METRO's goals and more effective utilization of the individual expertise of their peers.

CONCLUSION

METRO's early commitment to continuing education has been confirmed and strengthened by direct experience, particularly since 1973. The voluntary participation of hundreds of librarians from member libraries in planning, conducting, and evaluating continuing education programs has been invaluable. It has led to a fuller understanding of METRO's goals and objectives and increasingly stronger support of its programs and services. Leadership and assistance from the METRO staff, particularly in the person of the executive director, have greatly contributed to the success of continuing education.

NOTES

1. For a comprehensive view of continuing education in the context of the information needs of the public and those of the library profession, see Elizabeth W. Stone, ed., *Continuing Library and Information Science Education. Final Report to the National Commission on Libraries and Information Science* Washington, D.C.: GPO, 1974.

2. In-service training is discussed within the framework of a systems approach to continuing education in Patrick R. Penland, "Inservice Training," *Encyclopedia of Library and Information Science*, vol. 12, pp. 46–79.

3. METRO is one of the nine regional Reference and Research Resources (3 R's) Councils operating under the New York State Library. It was chartered in 1964 and began to function as a cooperative in 1966. METRO serves a population of 9 million residents in New York City and Westchester County.

4. METRO, *Progress Report—January 1, 1977*, p. 11.

5. For a full description of METRO's organization, see Morris A. Gelfand, "Metropolitan Reference and Research Library Agency (METRO)," *Encyclopedia of Library and Information Science*, vol. 17, pp. 491–508.

6. METRO, *For Reference*, no. 1 (October 1966): 3.

7. METRO, *For Reference*, no. 25 (June 1972): 2.

8. Ibid., p. 5.

9. METRO, *Progress Report—January 1, 1973*, p. 2.

10. METRO, *The Services of Processing Agencies*, p. 1.

11. Daniel Davila, ed., *Library Service for the Spanish-Speaking User: A Source Guide for Librarians* (New York: Metro and Hostos Community College, City University of New York, 1976), mimeographed.

12. METRO, *For Reference*, no. 63 (February 1977): 2.

13. Noel Savage, "Volunteers in Libraries," *Library Journal* 101 (December 1, 1976): 2431–2433.

14. Noel Savage, "Metro Meet on Access: Curse or Cure?" *Library Journal* 101 (December 15, 1976): 2532–2535.

15. Noel Savage, "Interlibrary Loan: New Constraints & Fees," *Library Journal* 102 (January 1, 1977): 24–25.

NEW YORK CASE STUDY 3: THE METRO COOPERATIVE ACQUISITIONS PROGRAM

David O. Lane

The New York Metropolitan Reference and Research Library Agency (METRO), one of nine reference and research library agencies that blanket the state, was chartered by the state of New York in 1964. It was established to promote better cooperation among libraries of all types, and was charged with developing resources and improving access to all area library resources. METRO serves the five boroughs (counties) of New York City plus Westchester County, and provision has been made for admitting nonvoting members from nearby New Jersey.

In 1971, the Resources Development Committee, one of four METRO standing committees, decided, after several years of inconclusive discussions, to charge a subcommittee with the writing of a plan for a practical cooperative acquisitions program. Within weeks, a proposal was produced and approved with some modifications by the Resources Development Committee and then it was endorsed by the trustees of METRO.

In early 1972, an appeal was made to all types of member libraries of METRO to contribute to the new cooperative acquisitions project fund. Those participating, initially, were expected to contribute one-quarter of 1 percent of their total acquisitions budgets, with a lower limit of $50 and an upper of $1,000. A deadline for participation was established and a rather elaborate system was formulated by which a steering committee was elected. The original concept was that the project would not only increase the library resources of the area but would also promote cooperation among libraries of various types and sizes. The project was also envisioned as a means of opening library doors to a wider clientele. The steering committee was charged with selecting expensive items not available in the region but that had been recommended by project participants. The items purchased were to be deposited in appropriate participating libraries, thus building on existing collection strengths. Any library accepting a deposit was required to make the material available to any patron of any METRO member library on the same basis that access was afforded to its own primary user group. A qualified user of a public library in Westchester County, for example, might gain access to a private college library in Brooklyn.

The original rules asked that suggestions for purchases be limited to items costing more than $500. Ultimately, suggestions in hand, the steering committee began the difficult task of deciding the following: were the various titles, indeed, not available or on order in the area; were they available for immediate purchase in complete form; and, finally, where should each ideally be deposited?

A further problem developed later. METRO applied for a Higher Education Act, Title II-A, Special Purpose Type C Grant in the name of its academic member libraries, and was awarded $50,000. A second selection committee representing the academic libraries was then formed. The Resources Development Committee soon decided that both groups should function together on a one-member, one-vote basis. So, from the beginning, the Cooperative Acquisitions Fund Steering Committee had a dual purpose: to expend the contributed funds on expensive research items and, at the same time, to spend the Type C federal grant in an appropriate manner. In following years, the amount of federal funds available to the steering committee was much smaller and the committee tended to consider the federal monies as another contribution to the Cooperative Acquisition Fund sources, albeit funds that did have to be expended in a different manner.

In its first year of operation, the Cooperative Acquisitions Fund project was considered quite successful. Twenty-seven libraries donated $12,000, a sum that was successfully expended upon appropriate research titles.

In 1973, the METRO board of trustees voted to continue the Cooperative Acquisitions Fund project. The Resources Development Committee voted some small but very important changes in procedures; the contribution requested was one-third of 1 percent of the institution's budget for library materials and the upper limit was raised to $1,500. The time-consuming practice of electing the steering committee was dropped. The METRO Committee on Committees appointed the committee and its chairperson from the staffs of participating libraries. That year it was requested that suggested items "should probably cost more than $1,000, certainly no less than $500." A Special Purpose Type C Grant was sought and again awarded, this time in the amount of $50,000, plus a basic grant of $4,235. Thirty of METRO's approximately 75 members participated.

CATALOGING PROBLEMS

Several problems associated with the program began to come into focus. As initially conceived, the libraries agreeing to accept the deposits were required to catalog the items fully, all too often complex collections of related materials, such as "Great Britain, Government Publications Relating to Uganda." As a result, cataloging copy was sometimes very slow in reaching the METRO office and not always of uniform quality. It had been agreed that the directorate would disseminate data concerning the cooperative purchases in two ways: by including it along with the appropriate locations symbols in the published book catalog of the New York Public Library Research Libraries and, additionally, by the distribution to all members of a complete set of catalog cards for all titles purchased. By the second year of the program, it was obvious that this procedure, with its delays and extra steps resulting from the necessity of editing member-produced catalog copy to the New York Public Library standards, was not only quite expensive but it also did not meet the program's goals of getting information concerning all purchases to members promptly. Something would have to be done.

ISSUE OF GEOGRAPHIC DISTRIBUTION

The steering committee faced still another problem. Some members began to feel that there should be a more or less rigorous parity in the geographic distribution of deposit locations. It was argued, for example, that the deposit of three items in Brooklyn required the deposit of three in Queens, three in Staten Island, and three in Westchester County. Several meetings and numerous discussions were necessary to produce a new consensus that the purpose of the program was, indeed, to build the research resources of the entire region, and to do so by building on existing strengths.

THIRD YEAR CHANGES

1974 was the third year of the cooperative effort. The program, approved as an ongoing activity of METRO, was retitled Cooperative Acquisitions Program, or CAP. The requested contribution was changed to one-half of 1 percent of book funds, with upper and lower limits of $2,000 and $50, respectively. The Resources Development Committee decided to attack the cataloging problem by having METRO hire a cataloger who would handle the work for all purchases centrally before the items were actually distributed for deposit. It was hoped that this would speed the production of cataloging copy, copy that also would be in accordance with the New York Public Library practices. Before the year was out, all concerned agreed that METRO would cease the increasingly expensive practice of distributing complete sets of cards to all members. The production, collation, and distribution of card sets for the 1974–1975 purchases would cost in the neighborhood of $12,000. For $5,000, it would be possible to produce a cumulative book catalog for all purchases for the first three years. As all titles were from the beginning included in the New York Public Library Research Libraries computer-produced book catalog, it was a comparatively simple matter to pull out the METRO entries and to set up a separate METRO publication. The executive director arranged with the New York Public Library for the production of the volume. When it appeared in 1975 (delayed somewhat due to problems in obtaining complete catalog copy even when centrally produced), it was a publication of 149 pages containing 6,500 entries, describing the 1,800 titles that had been cooperatively purchased up till then.* Copies were distributed to all members. Up to that time, $167,000 had been expended for cooperative purchases.

Meanwhile, the 1974–1975 steering committee struggled with another problem. The generously funded Special Purpose Type C Grants for the first years had been expended quite properly on items of direct interest to METRO's academic members, many of which were and are rather small liberal arts or specialized colleges. By 1974, the grant had shrunk to only $4,200. As a result, fewer items of a "reference" nature (to use the jargon adopted by the steering committee) were purchased. The majority of both the steering committee and the parent Resources Development Committee felt the member-contributed funds should continue to be expended on "research" materials; that is, for example, the 261 reels of microfilm containing the archives of the American Missionary Association. A minority of members, aware of the frequent purchase of college reference materials in the first several years, came to feel the program held no benefits for their library users. When would an undergraduate student need to consult a file copy of the "Registers of the Archbishop of Canterbury" deposited by METRO at the Fordham University Library? This divergence of opinion had no simple solution. Throughout the year, the steering committee continued to discuss the problems, as did the Resources Development Committee and the METRO directorate.

CHANGES RELEVANT TO SMALLER LIBRARIES

As a result of the many meetings and discussions in 1974–1975 concerning the relevance of CAP to smaller libraries, it was decided at the beginning of the 1975–1976 program that a new effort would be made to make the project more immediately attractive. It was agreed that all funds donated to the program by small libraries ("small" defined as those libraries holding less than 200,000 volumes) would be kept in a separate pocket and used to purchase more modest items. It had been agreed by the groups involved with CAP that, indeed, the purchase, say of a specific index for deposit in a college library in Queens, was as much a contribution to the library resources of the METRO region as was the purchase of a microfilm copy of a Tokyo newspaper deposited at a university library in Manhattan.

*METRO CAP Catalog, Cooperative Acquisitions Program (New York: New York Metropolitan Reference and Research Library Agency, 1976).

Due to this redefinition, the METRO Committee on Small Libraries actively supported this program. In that year, the number of participants in CAP rose to 31, a new high, though the funds available to the steering committee decreased somewhat, reflecting, no doubt, the decrease in book funds at many member libraries.

CAMPAIGN TO ATTRACT PURCHASE SUGGESTIONS

Realizing that the program was valuable only in proportion to the quality and desirability of the titles purchased, the 1975–1976 steering committee began a campaign to attract more purchase suggestions from the METRO membership. Many concerned with the program felt that there had been a falling off in the potential usefulness of some of the more recent suggestions. From the inception of CAP, the steering committees, through their procedures, had attempted to require requesting libraries to verify holding locations in the METRO area of purchase suggestions. Its success in this varied. It seems possible that some librarians may have stopped making suggestions because previous recommendations had not been purchased. Perhaps a poor initial location check had resulted in recommendations to the steering committee of items that were ultimately located in a number of local libraries and were, therefore, not ordered. In any case, for whatever causes, the committee sensed a falling off in the quality of suggestions. A publicity campaign waged in the *METRO Newsletter* and by a direct mailing attempted, with some success, to counter this trend.

In 1975 METRO published an attractive pamphlet "Reverse the Recession—Expand Your Book Budget with CAP." It was designed by METRO's public relations consultant and explained why CAP was of value (expands services, builds on strengths, and saves money) and how it worked (members' suggestions, central purchase and processing, deposit in cooperating libraries). Its wide distribution might account for the number of participants reaching a new high. A memo, issued in January 1976, showed that up to that time, 26 member libraries (from the New York Public Library to the Engineering Societies Library, from Columbia University to Iona College) had received deposits of CAP materials.

The fall of 1976 saw the beginning of the fifth CAP year. Examples 1–4 show the general premises, purchase policies, procedures, and depository agreement pertaining to the 1976–1977 Cooperative Acquisitions Program. The previous year's steering committee had expended $19,000 on about 20 titles, a fact noted in the publicity concerning the beginning of yet another year of cooperative activity. METRO membership now stood at 80. By late autumn, another steering committee had been appointed, chosen from the early pledging libraries, and broadly representative of METRO's member institutions. Pledges and funds are continuing to come in. It is too early to say how successful this fifth year of CAP will be. One could guess at least as successful as last year. At the close of the 1976–1977 year, hopefully a five-year METRO CAP catalog will be accumulated and published.

Example 1   METRO Cooperative Acquisitions Program: General Premises

1. All members of METRO are invited to participate in the Cooperative Acquisitions Program.
2. The annual participation fee is one-half of 1 percent of the member institution's budget for library materials (not including binding). Minimum fee: $50. Maximum fee: $2,000.
3. The expenditure of the Cooperative Acquisitions Fund is the duty of the METRO Cooperative Acquisitions Program Steering Committee that is made up of representatives of the participants and appointed by the METRO Committee on Committees. The Cooperative Acquisitions Program Steering Committee is a subcommittee of the Resources Development Committee.
4. Each year, the METRO secretariat requests from all members suggestions for materials to be purchased and placed on indefinite deposit in appropriate cooperating METRO institutions.
5. Acceptance by a member institution of materials obtained through the Cooperative Acquisitions Program carries with it the responsibility for making such material available to all METRO members on the same basis as to its own community. Such institutions may relinquish materials to METRO. Alternatively, METRO may withdraw custody of deposited materials.
6. Purchases are made in such a way as to contribute to the goal of building on existing strengths wherever they exist in METRO.* The major emphasis is on the acquisition of expensive items needed in the METRO area but beyond the resources of any appropriate institution to obtain. In addition, the program is administered in such a way that the strengths and emphases of smaller institutions are noted and deposits added to their collections as appropriate. Participating libraries are eligible for deposit.
7. METRO members who participate in the acquisitions program receive priority in the determination of materials to be purchased.

*Such purchases are considered a supplement to, not a substitute for, each library's own responsibility to support properly its instructional or other community programs.

Example 2   METRO Cooperative Acquisitions Program: Purchase Policies 1976–1977

The following statements guide the Cooperative Acquisitions Program Steering Committee in its consideration of suggestions for purchase:

1. The goal of the Cooperative Acquisitions Program is to increase the reference and research resources of libraries in the METRO area. It seeks to build upon existing strengths among the libraries. CAP acquisitions are distributed (deposited) among the participants both large and small.
2. Selection conforms to current federal guidelines when federal funds are involved.

3. Series, serials, or incomplete sets that require updating are not usually considered for purchase with CAP funds.
4. Under normal circumstances items costing less than $200 will not be considered for purchase.
5. No consideration is given to collections created by publishers when the individual titles in the collection cannot be identified. Reprint collections are not normally considered if the individual titles of the collections are already available in the area. An exception might be made if, for example, the collection is very superior and would be desirable for use in an additional METRO library.
6. Materials that will create inordinate cataloging problems are not normally considered for purchase.
7. The steering committee may consider suggestions other than those submitted by METRO member libraries.
8. Up to 25 percent of contributed funds will be used for the purchase of reference-oriented rather than research-oriented materials.

Example 3   METRO Cooperative Acquisitions Program: Procedures

Libraries making suggestions for CAP purchases should observe the following:
1. Type citations on 3″ × 5″ cards. Include the identification of the library making the suggestion. Attach the card to either the original or a photocopy of the citation (publisher's flier, *Books in Print* citation, or other evidence of the actual, not proposed, existence of the item). Unsupported citations will not be considered by the committee.
2. Recommended items must be available *in their entirety* for prompt delivery by the publisher. This should be verified by the library making the suggestion.
3. Indicate a suggested deposit location for the item.
4. Record as an attachment to the suggestion card the justification for the purchase, for example, what strengths in the library suggested for deposit would urge the purchase of this item?
5. Usually, any research item suggested for purchase should not now be held in the METRO area. The library making the suggestion must make every effort to determine the present holdings of appropriate METRO libraries (including checking with the METRO Clearinghouse for the Acquisition of Expensive Library Materials) before making the suggestions. Libraries so queried will be noted and any holdings discovered in the METRO area will be listed. Justification for the purchase must be given.

Example 4   METRO Cooperative Acquisitions Program—Depository Agreement

The Cooperative Acquisitions Program Steering Committee is now receiving the items selected by it for purchase this year. Libraries have been identified as depositories in accordance with the guidelines adopted at the start of the program. Your institution has been selected as the depository for the item(s) listed on the attached sheet.

Although you have previously signed an agreement relative to the Cooperative Acquisitions Program, one specific stipulation has been made and must now be agreed to in relation to the item listed.

Access to all items purchased with Cooperative Acquisitions Program funds must be provided to all readers from METRO member libraries on the same basis as the items are made available to members of your own community.

Under this condition, are you willing to accept deposit of the item(s) listed? Your signature on the copy of this letter returned to this office will be sufficient indication for us to arrange the deposit.

Failing to hear from you within four weeks of the date of this letter, a similar offer will be made to the alternate depository.

Sincerely yours,

Forrest F. Carhart, Jr.
Executive Director

FFC/atw
Enc.
Agreed to:

_____

(Signature)

FUTURE POSSIBILITIES

What of the future? CAP is now a valuable part of the METRO program. Though 100 percent of METRO's members may never participate in CAP, there will undoubtedly be a slow, steady increase in numbers. Nor will CAP ever please all the librarians who make up METRO's constituency. Comments, such as "Why are you wasting perfectly good money on such obscure material?" will continue to be voiced. Interlibrary cooperation between various types of libraries will become increasingly important, and CAP is an outstanding example of such cooperation. Some of the problems dealt with in the past will return, possibly in modified form: the tendency to split between larger and smaller library interest groups, the "what's in it for me" attitude, and a lack of imagination that can tend to depress the quality and quantity of suggested purchases. CAP steering committees of the future will have to grapple with problems no one has foreseen, but the program will continue, if only because it has been quite successful in meeting its two main objectives: CAP *has* opened library doors to people who would once have been considered outsiders and it *has* increased the library resources of this area.

If METRO and the other eight New York State 3 R's regions are ever funded at the level envisioned by the founding legislation, many more dollars will become available, some of which will be expended on regional resources development. With this possibility in mind, the Resources Development Committee has already drafted (and the METRO board of trustees approved in principle) a greatly expanded big brother to CAP, known as the Coordinated Acquisitions Program. All that is needed now are the funds.

CLEVELAND CASE STUDY: YEAR ONE OF A COOPERATIVE

Dorothy Sinclair

The Cleveland Area Metropolitan Library System (CAMLS) was officially one year old on July 15, 1976. It is not entirely accurate, however, to describe CAMLS as a one-year-old, since its parent body, the Library Council of Greater Cleveland, has existed for a number of years. There are, as of July 1976, twenty members, including ten public, seven academic, and two special libraries and one library school. The council, an informal organization of library directors, had undertaken a number of cooperative projects, using committees of staff members of the various libraries for interlibrary loan, for collection study, and for public relations activity. What is one year old is the funding made available under LSCA Title III, which has provided, for the first time, an office and regular staff. This past year, the office staff had the full-time equivalent of one and two-thirds persons.

The LSCA grant was essentially for planning, but since committees and some experience with cooperation already existed, it was decided that the council would not merely commission a study but would establish an office in order to test in action various policies, procedures, and projects. CAMLS is preparing a plan, therefore, based on actual experience gained through a number of activities in practice, working through existing committees, new committees, or the office staff, as appropriate. A few highly pragmatic studies have also been made. In addition, the office has taken on characteristics that some other cooperatives will recognize—coordinating, stimulating, troubleshooting, and, even on occasion, applying an invisible brake.

One of the characteristics of any multitype cooperative is that it tends to be multieverything, including multimotivated and multiopinioned. This is normal for a group of autonomous agencies, especially when different types, sizes, and goals are represented. One of the major discoveries made by the executive secretary during an early round of visits was the fact that CAMLS membership is small enough to undertake projects that involve directors and staffs closely. The extent of commitment to CAMLS varied widely. Those who had spearheaded the request for funds were naturally enthusiastic. Some were much more guarded, willing to give it a try but requiring proof that CAMLS would benefit their individual libraries. Others were uncertain of the reaction of boards and other governing bodies. From some, rightly or wrongly, one got the impression that their attitude was "Oh, well, it's only for a year!"

At that time, it looked very much as though it were indeed only for a year. Ohio's meager state aid goes to one public library cooperative in Appalachia, and there was, and is, no more than a faint hope that Ohio's rather cautious legislative body would miraculously become more generous immediately. CAMLS's current funding was made possible by release of impounded LSCA monies; never again, perhaps, would Title III have so much available. All these factors made the executive secretary feel strongly that the first objective must be to prove the value of CAMLS to its members during this one year, and prove it to the extent that they would be willing to fund a continuation from their own budgets. This meant developing services, not merely making paper plans. CAMLS has not, therefore, come up with a handsome and detailed long-range plan. It is working on one, and a preliminary model has been prepared for the State Library for metropolitan library systems in Ohio.

The first year has been devoted to services—testing new ones, changing old ones, studying them in order to identify problems, and undertaking other studies designed to demonstrate the need for CAMLS. Some of these activities and studies may best be illustrated by statistics prepared for use at the annual meeting in April 1976.

In the planning model is a diagram, as shown in Example 1, which is basic to CAMLS's service objective, the effective sharing of resources. The vertical columns divide access to materials in terms of the user's inquiry for an object or for a message. By "object" is meant a specific item wanted—book, journal, or film—to which the user has a citation. By "message" is meant information or some other content type of material for which the user does not specify an object. On the horizontal axis, two means of referral are distinguished: referral of the inquiry to another li-

Example 1   CAMLS Planning Model

	ACCESS TO	
REFERRAL OF	OBJECT	MESSAGE
INQUIRY	A Interlibrary loan	B Cooperative reference
INQUIRER	C User sent for a specific request	D User sent to a collection

brary with the response coming back to the user's library or referral of the inquirer to another library for direct use. The four quadrants, then, are these: A—referral of inquiry for an object (the familiar interlibrary loan); B—referral of inquiry for a message (or cooperative reference); C—referral of inquirer for an object; and D—referral of inquirer for a message. Most of what has been done and is planned for the future to improve access to collections fits into one of these four categories.

INTERLIBRARY LOAN

Interlibrary loan is to many libraries the chief reason for cooperation. It was important to revitalize this function, active a few years before but more recently fallen into a kind of hit-or-miss telephoning, with neither efficient communication nor delivery. With no money in the planning budget for either of these procedures, it was necessary to assess the members, first for commercial daily delivery and second for an inexpensive facsimile transmission system to be used chiefly for communicating interlibrary loan requests.

CAMLS had the choice of two means of locating materials: an old regional union catalog, which was no longer complete nor accurate, or OCLC, which was still too new to carry many of the system's holdings, although ten of the member libraries were OCLC members and another has since joined. It is clear, therefore, what direction CAMLS should take in the future. It is indeed foolish to embark today on more than simple and specialized union listing. For the interim, CAMLS needed some way of locating the bulk of the interlibrary loans among members. It was determined, therefore, to use a relay system as both communicator and locator, an experiment that has worked fairly well and has provided a body of data for November and December 1975, during which all libraries kept detailed records.

Examples 2 through 5 show the type of information recorded and counted. The relay method merely passes along requests according to a regular route from library to library. CAMLS has two loops, one for academic and special libraries and the other for public libraries. The Cleveland Public Library acts as interface and switching center between the loops. The value of the telecopier in this process is that the same message can be sent several times without being recopied. There is no direct correlation between the communication and delivery systems; the commercial delivery service stops at regular pickup points daily and delivers packages to any addressee, which may include a branch library. Of 636 interlibrary loans made in November and December 1975, 41 percent were found on the first node of the relay system, 57.8 percent were found by the second node, and 64 percent by the third node queried.

As with any experiment, there was some resistance. One question that came frequently from the larger libraries was, what was the use in their sending requests around the loops, since smaller libraries were unlikely to be able to supply their needs; and, therefore, why not send all requests directly to the large libraries? Two small studies were undertaken to examine this premise. One study, an actual check of a small sample of interlibrary loan requests sent outside the CAMLS membership by a large academic library, showed that 40 percent could have been borrowed within the group. The second study was a determination of the extent of holdings of current imprints by CAMLS libraries. A current rather than retrospective bibliography was chosen since most of the checking could be done on OCLC. For this reason, the April 1975 issue of *Choice* was selected for this study. There is no suggestion, of course, that any library ought to have everything in *Choice*, but it does appear reasonable that in the Cleveland area one should be able to find a majority of the titles listed.

Example 2   Effectiveness of CAMLS Interlibrary Loan Relay System for Member Libraries*

Public Libraries	Number Requested	Number Received	Percent Received
Cleveland Heights-University Heights	130	87	67
Euclid	130	77	59
East Cleveland	15	12	80
Shaker Heights	132	82	62
Willoughby-Eastlake	134	89	66
Lakewood	55	32	58
Porter	25	17	68
Rocky River	60	47	78
Cuyahoga County	188	77	41
Cleveland	27	13	48
Total	896	533	59.5
Academic Libraries			
Baldwin-Wallace	34	23	67.6
Cleveland State	59	33	56
John Carroll	4	4	100
Cuyahoga Community	31	25	80.6
Cleveland Health Sciences	9	6	66.7
Case-Western Reserve	18	12	66.7
Total	155	103	66.45
Grand Total	1,051	636	60.5

*Seventy-five percent of requests were located in system.

The study showed that CAMLS as a whole owned 466 of the sample of 585 titles, or about 80 percent. The libraries holding the greatest number were Cleveland State University and Cleveland Public Library, with

Example 3   *Choice* Check for Holdings in CAMLS Libraries

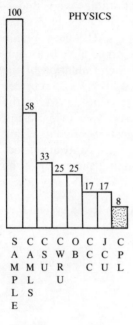

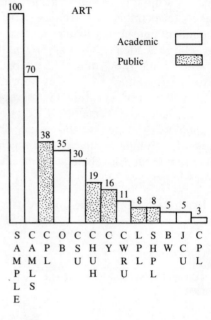

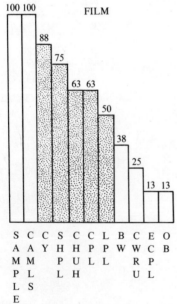

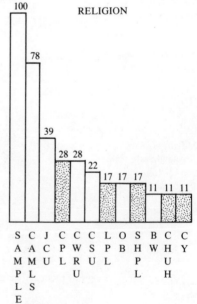

32 and 31 percent of the items listed. Academic libraries together held 690 titles; public libraries, 638. When one looks at the various subject divisions within *Choice*, one finds interesting variations, as illustrated by Example 3. In subjects like Physics, academic libraries predominate; in books on Film, the public libraries hold the most. Libraries varied in strength of holdings from subject to subject—in Political Science, Oberlin; in Religion, John Carroll; in Physics, Cleveland State University; in Arts, Cleveland Public Library.

The point of interdependency was made, insofar as a sample of approximately 600 current titles could be relied upon. CAMLS as a whole is greater than any one of its parts. The member libraries do need each other. A second independent piece of evidence bore out, to some extent, the findings of the first. A total of 421 actual requests that had been filled by member libraries, other than the Cleveland Public Library, were checked in that library's catalog and on its shelves to determine how many it could have filled. When those actually found at CPL were added to those it could have filled, the total approximated 40 percent of the sample. Since CAMLS has no funds for reimbursement of net lenders (those who lend more than they borrow), it continues to use the relay arrangement. Later studies and experience may suggest a change that would send all requests first to larger holders, but it seems more probable that direct requests to holders identified via OCLC will supersede the relay system.

COOPERATIVE REFERENCE SERVICE

The second quadrant of the square in the planning diagram refers to cooperative reference service. CAMLS has not yet moved into a full program, that is scheduled for 1976–1977. It did, in the first year, negotiate a consortium contract for the New York Times Information Bank. (A change in the Information Bank service offered reduced costs of telephone lines and equipment, and eliminated the need for the consortium contract in mid-1976, but the opportunity for all members to use this service, with separate identification numbers and billings, and with incentive payment of one-third of the cost of data base time, is still available to nonterminal members.) Three terminals began operating in April 1976. CAMLS is not paying for this service, but does make small incentive payments to encourage the use of the bank by libraries without terminals. An ID number has been reserved for each CAMLS member, so that each can have searches made for and charged to it.

IDENTIFICATION OF COLLECTION STRENGTHS

Quadrants C and D of the planning diagram involve referral of the inquirer to another library. To accomplish an effective referral requires knowledge of collection strengths and locations, and presupposes mutually developed procedures and service agreements. CAMLS has developed a few specialized finding tools but does not plan to compile elaborate union lists. The Resources Committee recently completed its *Union List of Business Services*, and a subcommittee is updating an old one of journals in the field of education. This last project is a spinoff of the collection study. Called Safari, it is an effort toward satisfying Quadrant D, which requires identification of collections.

"Safari," originally a nickname for a plan developed for collection study, is now also an acronym for Site Appraisal for Area Resources Inventory. Behind Safari lies the conviction that a directory of resources that depends on the libraries' own appraisals of subject strengths leaves something to be desired. Through the Safari method, libraries believed to have subject strengths are identified, and each contributes its most expert staff member for the actual expedition. Academic libraries are encouraged to send faculty members as well as librarians. The team visits each library in turn and examines its collection in the special subject field according to a plan. At a later meeting the team arrives at consensus and prepares a report. CAMLS's first Safari, in the field of education, divided its report into two parts, Subject Access and Library Profiles. Example 4 shows a page from a subject section and Example 5 shows a sample profile from the education Safari.

Example 4   Education Safari: Subject Access Section

Library Strengths by Subject
    Administration and organization—CSU, JCU
    Adult education opportunity file—CPL
    Alumni magazines—CPL
    Bibliographic tools—CSU, CWRU
    Camps, Summer—CPL
    Career information—CCC, CPL
    Catalogs—CCPL-MH, CHUH, CPL, CWRU
    Catalogs, foreign—CPL, CWRU
    Catalogs, retrospective—CPL

Key to abbreviations: BW: Baldwin-Wallace College; CCC: Cuyahoga Community College, Metro Campus; CHUH: Cleveland Heights-University Heights Public Library; CCPL-MH: Cuyahoga County Public Library-Maple Heights; CPL: Cleveland Public Library, downtown; CSU: Cleveland State University; CWRU: Case Western Reserve University-Freiberger Library; ILL: Interlibrary Loan; JCU: John Carroll University; Micromedia: May include microfilm, microfiche, microcards; ND: Notre Dame College.

The education librarians and faculty were all enthusiastic about this experiment, even though this Safari took place in a howling blizzard. They enjoyed the opportunity to meet with one another, to see each other's collections, and to discuss holdings and methods of cooperation. As a delightful fringe benefit, a faculty member reported that she had come away from the experience with a greatly enhanced respect for libraries and librarians.

Example 5   Education Safari: Sample Library Profile

Cleveland State University (CSU)

Collection	Circulating 22,000
	Reference 750
	Journals 202
Lends to	Public, students, and faculty
AV	Micromedia, reader-printer, cassettes, film-strips, records
CAIN	Yes
Classification	LC
Depository	Partial-integrated
ERIC	Yes
OCLC	Yes
Subject specialties	Administration and organization
	Bibliographic tools
	Curriculum materials
	Education psychology
	Elementary education
	Higher education
	Newsletters
	Secondary education
Notes	

The Safari on music took place in June, and that group was also enthusiastic. Their report is more elaborate than that on education, because of the many varieties of materials covered.

The Safari method, coupled with some of the techniques tested in the *Choice* check, such as use of OCLC, forms the basis for a special project to be undertaken in 1976–1977 under a grant from the U.S. Office of Education under Higher Education Act Title II-B, Research and Demonstration. To the factual data found through OCLC checking of a sizable sample, plus the Safari technique, CAMLS hopes to add a further element: agreements among libraries to accept systemwide responsibility for collection in depth in special subject areas. Including faculty members and other major users in Safari teams is an essential component in this program, since in some universities and colleges, it is they who must be convinced of the need for and value of such a plan. If the attempt is successful, a manual of procedure will be prepared so that other groups that might like to try the method can have the benefits of this trial-and-error planning.

USE OF RECIPROCAL RETURN PRIVILEGES

Another small contribution to Quadrants C and D was a study made of the use of reciprocal return privileges among members. It showed, to some extent, user patterns as they related to multilibrary use. Books owned by the Cleveland Public Library were returned to many County Library branches over a very wide geographic spread. Books belonging to Lakewood Public Library, in a western suburb, were returned almost exclusively to other west suburban libraries. This pattern always brings a laugh among Clevelanders, for it reinforces the notorious east-west cleavage of the area so badly that it is claimed that one really needs a passport to cross the Cuyahoga River.

SERVICE IN THE HOME OF THE USER

One last service project does not fit neatly into the planning diagram. It involves taking service into the home of the user, and it is CAMLS's method of cooperating with the Cleveland Society for the Blind. The society's Radio Reading Program, broadcast only to the blind and partially sighted, includes one hour daily from member libraries. Topics have varied. Book talks have been used, children's stories have been told, recordings have been played, and a few patron discussion groups have been taped. Faculty members of academic institutions have helped with this effort, as they also have with the CAMLS weekly five-minute radio program, a project of the Public Relations Committee.

Since this article is about services, little space has been given to the history, organization, and budget of CAMLS. These important matters probably do not differ significantly from those of other multitype library cooperatives with a background of informal cooperation and a first year of experience with outside funding. CAMLS has had, and will have, its growing pains, and it has a long way to go. However, it also has had a busy, lively, and, on the whole, rewarding first year.

ROCKY MOUNTAIN REGION CASE STUDY: A STATE-BASED NETWORK

Donald B. Simpson

The first question one might ask is just what is BCR? Why is the name BCR suddenly cropping up in lists of long established networks that include NELINET, SOLINET, and others? BCR is the Bibliographical Center for Research, Rocky Mountain Region, Inc. It is a relatively new network, but it has some features that make it unique among networks in the library community. BCR has a strong role to perform in the improvement of library services for its member states and contracting libraries.

BCR is a regional service center. It is not clear who coined that phrase or that concept, but it seems to have appeared first in literature from the Western Interstate Commission on Higher Education (WICHE) in its bid for network development in the western states. A regional service center is one that operates on a single state or multistate basis to provide a number of library networking services. Principally these are often a mixture of direct, in-house centralized activities and indirect on-site activities at the libraries. The regional service center is certain to be a major component of a national network as it emerges. There are only a few states across this country that can support the operation of a regional service center for a single state. Most states need to take their interlibrary cooperation dollars received from whatever sources and pool them to obtain an economy-of-scale effect.

BCR is a broker. "Broker" is also a recent term in library literature that parallels the brokerage concept in the stocks-and-bonds world and with the business world's concept of a wholesaler or distributor. Simply, a broker is an agency that buys a service or product from one source, enhances it, and distributes that service or product to others.

BCR is one of some 16 or 17 Ohio College Library Center (OCLC) network offices. Borrowing on the concept of a broker outlined a moment ago, it follows that BCR acts as a broker for OCLC services and OCLC becomes one of those products provided by the regional service center to its participants. That BCR provides the liaison between libraries and OCLC is healthy for both libraries, as well as for OCLC and of course for BCR.

BCR is also becoming a major network office for BALLOTS, the Stanford University library automation system, which has just recently announced a number of networking activities. Until recently, BALLOTS had been primarily a system at Stanford University and certain California libraries. BALLOTS will soon be using a new full-face shared cataloging system to expand BALLOTS into other areas of the country.

BCR also acts as a communications center in that it has been and is today the hub of a teletypewriter (TWX) interlibrary loan network throughout the Mountain-Plains region of the United States. BCR has recently taken on several contract-grant projects that are enhancing communications networks with new services, new functions, and new technology.

BCR is a research and development center that seeks grants to perform research in librarianship and to develop new programs or to enhance present ones. BCR's research and development program provides technical consulting both from BCR staff and from technical staff brought in on a contract basis.

Above all, however, BCR is state based. A number of networks in today's library community are not state based; rather, they are institution based. BCR feels a strong commitment to the role of the state library agency as the basic coordinating vehicle for a state's library program. With headquarters in Denver, members are all libraries in the primary member states of Colorado, Iowa, Kansas, South Dakota, Utah, and Wyoming, and select institutions within North Dakota, Texas, Nebraska, Oklahoma, Illinois, Arizona, and Missouri.

THE HISTORY OF BCR

BCR was founded in 1935 by Malcolm Glen Wyer, then Denver City librarian and president of the American Library Association, for some six to eight Front-Range libraries in Colorado. Wyer was a man ahead of his time. He had a vision that a day would come in which library budgets would begin to decline and in which libraries must turn to interlibrary cooperation and the sharing of resources in order to do a better job of providing library services to their publics. He suggested, therefore, to his colleagues in Colorado's major libraries, that rather than having all of them buy copies of the same expensive bibliographical works, perhaps one set could be bought with pooled money, to be housed in one location but accessible to all. In this way, the first portion of the Bibliographical Center for Research, the bibliographical collection, was born.

This became a most satisfactory experience for the Front-Range librarians when they were able to ascertain correct bibliographical information concerning a number of materials. It then became necessary to know where one might find these items. In 1937, a Carnegie Foundation grant was sought to provide a modest amount of monies to develop a regional union catalog. First, a process was designed. A number of libraries were selected for inclusion in the initial compilation of the union catalog. A copy of the Northwestern University Library catalog was purchased and became the basis for the union catalog. Second, teams of microfilmers were dispatched to a number of key libraries in the area. These libraries' catalogs were filmed and the film processed. One might expect at this point that one of the first microfilm union catalogs would have been established; however, in the 1930s technology for microfilm was not so advanced as it is today. Innumerable typists sat down, therefore, and transcribed from microfilm readers onto cards for a card catalog.

In 1942, it was determined that the center should be independent and it was incorporated under the Colorado Non-Profit Corporation Act. What followed was roughly 20 years of modest growth in services. BCR staff took an active part in the development of revisions of the national interlibrary loan code and in the establishment of communications networks for interlibrary loan. In 1962, Phoebe F. Hayes, a noted interlibrary loan expert, became director of BCR and established a teletypewriter network throughout the region with the hub at Denver in the Bibliographical Center.

The transition from the inflationary 1960s into the rocky 1970s was one that was most difficult for the center to undertake. Libraries are highly labor-intensive activities. Major problems were caused for BCR because it was a bibliographical center with a collection of high-cost bibliographical tools and a practitioner of one of the most labor-intensive activities in libraries, that is, filing in manual card catalogs.

BCR, like most nonprofit corporations, and particularly those in the library community, is governed by a board of trustees. At present, there are ten trustees, six of whom are the state librarians from the primary member states. The additional board members are at-large trustees, who are appointed by the entire board as a result of nominations from an advisory council and interested parties. The center's bylaws vest the responsibilities for the affairs of BCR in the board of trustees.

The advisory council is a group of up to 13 members, who are appointed by the board of trustees to provide input, counsel, and evaluation on BCR. At one time in its history, BCR was made up of some 850 individual voting members. This became quite cumbersome because some business items could only be accomplished once a year; oftentimes over the years, a significant board position or policy decision was made by a substantial minority of the eligible voters.

Finally, each program has a series of advisory committees to discuss the development of new systems and activities. Most of this activity has been in the area of OCLC development up to this point.

SERVICE PROGRAMS

To best understand BCR's activities, one must understand the concept of the integrated library system, which states very simply that a library should be able to perform a maximum number of functions, using the least amount of equipment, to save the most dollars rather than using less efficient means to accomplish the same ends. The four functions of the integrated library system are technical services, communications, resource sharing, and information retrieval.

The first BCR program was begun 42 years ago, and is now called INTERLOAN. INTERLOAN is the interlibrary loan clearinghouse through which state libraries or individual libraries may send interlibrary loan requests for locations to BCR by a variety of communications means. If unable to locate the materials in local or regional resources, the BCR staff then circulates these requests on up to the Library of Congress. The Regional Union Catalog, currently consisting of 6.5 million titles, is still in its nonmachine-readable form. Roughly 16 percent of the catalog is only in rough filing order and because of the pressures of finances in the late 1960s and early 1970s, nothing has been done to correct the situation.

The next program, developed in January 1976, was BIBLIO. BIBLIO is basically the broker for the Ohio College Library Center's services. The Stanford University BALLOTS system has also become a vendor under the BIBLIO brokerage concept.

METRO Program

The third program at BCR is METRO.* METRO was established first as a Colorado program at BCR in July 1975, through a $26,000 LSCA Title III grant from the Colorado State Library. The grant project set up BCR as a broker of information retrieval services from the New York Times Information Bank, the data files of the System Development Corporation, the Lockheed Missiles and Space Corporation Information Systems Division, and the Bibliographic Retrieval Services, Inc. These data files, of course, provide computerized reference services that complement traditional reference services. Some informal testing on the ERIC data file has shown that eight hours of manual ERIC searching can be done in one hour of machine searching at less cost when one considers the labor of the searchers.

The first installations in Colorado were on-site installations in which the equipment was placed by BCR and training in the use of the systems was performed by BCR. The on-site installation is still a regular option for METRO services throughout the region.

*Not to be confused with the New York Metropolitan Reference and Research Library Agency known as METRO.

Following the advent of information retrieval services, it was found that there were still many libraries that were, and would for some time be, unable to afford the cost of the computer terminal and the expertise needed to perform an adequate job of information retrieval; therefore, Central Access on METRO was created. Central Access allows libraries to communicate their requests by a variety of means to BCR, where the searches are performed and the results returned to the library. This is particularly good for small-volume users who can afford the cost of a search now and then, but cannot afford either the on-site installation or highly regular use.

A third mechanism, the Self Search, was established for libraries in the Denver metropolitan area. Searchers are certified by BCR trainers, and then by appointment may rent equipment at BCR to perform searches to their own satisfaction rather than having a third party do them.

BCR recently received an $84,890 grant from the Colorado State Library to develop the Colorado Information and Communications Network, which is an outgrowth of METRO activity. Colorado is divided into multicounty library systems. The libraries in the systems are able to channel their requests into the system where a computer terminal with communications capability and cassette tape capability forwards the searches to BCR in Denver where the searching is done. The search results are sent back over the same devices. In addition, the same circuits will be used for the processing of interlibrary loan requests, thus reducing what was formerly two circuits to one. It is evident that some costs savings will be effected by this program.

Finally, METRO provides large-scale basic and continuing education. In addition to the basic training on the use of information retrieval systems and the theory behind information retrieval systems, BCR has a series of informational workshops on particular data bases and files, plus advanced training in the use of information retrieval systems.

Acting as a network service agency, BCR's METRO enhances services originated by the data base publishers (e.g., Chemical Abstracts) and distributed by the data base vendors (e.g., SDC Search Service). This enhancement occurs both to the benefit of the vendors, who can save on labor-intensive activities, such as marketing, sales, training, promotion, and direct contact with the clientele, and to the benefit of the using libraries, who gain by having local or regional contact with the network service agency and by receiving reduced rates, established under network-group contracts with the vendors.

Networks are often caught up in a circular argument that is self-defeating. Unless the network service agency can raise volume and perform certain functions often accomplished by the vendor better than the vendor (and thus save the vendor dollars), the vendors may be unwilling to lend credibility to the network service agency. At the same time, unless the network service agency can provide better services at a cheaper cost than by the customer going directly to the vendor, the using libraries are unwilling to add their searching volume to that of the network service agency and therefore reduce prices. One can thus witness a never-ending circular argument with price chasing volume chasing price chasing volume and so forth ad infinitum.

BCR attempts to price its METRO services using the following formula:

$$X < Y < Z$$

where X is the cost to BCR, Y is the cost to the library participating with BCR, and Z is the cost to libraries not participating in BCR. The formula works to everyone's benefit once the "circle" is broken.

Under the original METRO project funded with LSCA monies from the Colorado State Library, a careful evaluation of the project was done using as measures user satisfaction,[1] a marketing study,[2] and a participating searcher survey.[3] The user satisfaction study found that among 45 percent of the respondents, 40 percent found the service to be excellent; 100 percent felt the service was one libraries should offer. In the second study, 81 percent of the 54 respondents stated that word-of-mouth recommendations were the most influential factor in making the decision to use METRO.[4] The third study found that personal contact was the most effective means of marketing the services.

The conclusions drawn about METRO are that the information retrieval services are useful and effective for libraries to offer and that METRO, as the network service agency, improves the provision of these services. METRO will continue to expand and grow as a BCR program. There is little doubt that on-line retrieval services have had significant impact on the people of the Mountain-Plains region. Continued efforts to create improved networking applications will aid in the future development of library services.

NOTES

1. Michele Brandt and Nancy Peterson, *A User Satisfaction Study of the METRO Information Retrieval Network* (Denver: University of Denver Graduate School of Librarianship, May 1976).

2. Bibliographical Center for Research, *METRO Information Retrieval Network Final Report to the Colorado State Library on LSCA Project 75-III-1*, BCR, December 1976.

3. Donald B. Simpson and Mary Grush, *Networking for On-line Information Retrieval Services—METRO Information Retrieval Network*, BCR, June 1976.

4. Bibliographical Center for Research, op. cit.

PARTICIPATION OF SCHOOL LIBRARIES

Anne Marie Falsone

The question is often asked why school libraries do not participate more fully in multitype library cooperatives. The implications seem to be that schools do not want to participate in networks or that they have little to contribute to a network if they do join. From the perspective of the assistant commissioner of education in charge of the Colorado State Library, it is apparent that schools can make a real contribution to multitype networks and are interested in joining them.

LIMITS TO SCHOOL PARTICIPATION

Schools are often prevented from participating in multitype library cooperatives, or limited in their participation, because of a variety of factors:

1. Schools are usually open only during the school day, which may not correspond with hours kept by other types of libraries. Thus, cooperative transactions can only be handled during certain times of the day, and often not at all during the summer months.

2. The school library's collection is chosen to support the curriculum. It may not meet the needs of other types of libraries in the community; hence, the school library may not be able to make a large contribution in materials to an interlibrary loan network.

3. The interjurisdictional loan of school library materials or equipment is sometimes prohibited by school district policy. In addition, a significant part of the materials and equipment in schools has been purchased with federal funds, which often prohibit the use of such items by anyone but the students and teachers.

4. Sometimes schools are prevented from cooperating with other types of libraries because of a lack of the most basic communication tools, such as a telephone located within the school library.

5. Students and teachers often have an "immediacy of need" for materials that inhibits interlibrary loan from two angles. First, since students and teachers often want materials "now" in order to answer a question that has arisen in class, they do not look kindly upon discovering that the material is out of the school on loan to another library. Second, this

133

same problem of "immediacy of need" means that interlibrary loan from another library is often not a viable alternative to having the materials located in the school library, where they can be accessed at a moment's notice.

Despite the limitations that school libraries face in participating in cooperative ventures with other types of libraries, they have unique strengths to bring to multitype cooperatives. By looking at the positive rather than the negative aspects of participation of school libraries, we can discover ways in which they can become part of the growing number of interjurisdictional library cooperatives on the local, state, and regional levels.

STRENGTHS OF SCHOOL LIBRARIES

What are some of the strengths that school libraries can contribute to multitype library cooperatives?

1. Many school libraries have fine collections of children's or young adult literature. These collections are often larger and more extensive than those found in neighboring public library branches or in the demonstration libraries of teacher-training institutions.

2. School library personnel or school district employees frequently have advanced knowledge in the selection of audiovisual equipment. This may include expertise in writing bid specifications, equipment repair data (including cost comparisons of various brands and models), and knowledge of the various selection tools that should be consulted before purchasing expensive audiovisual equipment.

3. As a rule, school districts have personnel with training and experience in cataloging, handling, and delivering audiovisual software; in addition, many school districts have conducted cost-effectiveness studies of centralized versus building-level collections of audiovisual materials. The larger school districts have special nonprint catalogers who can share their expertise with catalogers in other types of libraries who are grappling with the problems involved in handling nonprint media.

4. Many school librarians have had specialized training in production of audiovisual materials. These skills may be as elementary as basic photography techniques, facility in using a dry mount press, or experience in producing a slide-tape presentation, or as highly technical as the operation of an educational television studio, the production of 8 or 16mm motion pictures, or the preparation of complicated multiscreen presentations utilizing a variety of media formats.

5. Many school district offices already have computer terminals or teletype machines that could be used for communication within a multitype library network. Some employ computer programmers, keypunch

operators, and data base management specialists, all of whom might be called upon to assist in handling networking problems.

6. The greatest strength of school libraries in rural areas may be that they often employ the only person with professional library training within that community. Public and academic libraries tend to be clustered in urban and suburban areas, whereas schools reach into every nook and cranny of rural America. In Colorado, it is possible for the school library and its librarian to form the nucleus of library services for the entire community by serving as the coordinating agent of a joint school-public library. The concern is often expressed that the school librarian may find it difficult to serve adult as well as student needs. This fear is usually unfounded and even if the school librarian lacks in-depth skills in reader services to adults, or sophistication in answering reference questions, many rural communities are quite willing to overlook these minor inconveniences in exchange for expanded hours of service and access to a larger collection than the average bookmobile can provide.

SCHOOL MEMBERS OF MULTITYPE SYSTEMS IN COLORADO

Colorado passed legislation creating multitype regional library service systems in the spring of 1975. The purpose of this act was to make the existing public systems legal entities and to permit other types of publicly supported libraries to join systems. The significant action concerning regional library systems in Colorado is contained in rules and regulations that control the formation, operation, and governance of these regional cooperatives. The rules, which were approved by the State Board of Education in 1976, called for a planning period during which all potential system members could be involved in deciding how the system would be organized. By September 30, 1976, all public library system boards had to vote to disband, and, in their place, the new multitype systems' boards were formed after October 1, 1976.

The new regional library systems in Colorado are truly multitype. Their governing boards are composed of at least one representative from each type of library—academic, public, school, and special. Through the use of a needs assessment, system boards are able to develop programs that meet their unique regional requirements. The services offered by urban and suburban systems are often different from those provided by rural systems. In fact, the only programs that all seven systems share in common are administration and interlibrary cooperation, which includes interlibrary loan and computerized search services.

School members of the regional library systems in Colorado have become vocal, contributing members of their cooperatives. They have discovered that they share many problems with their colleagues in public and academic libraries, and have often been surprised to learn that they have as great a rapport with the concerns of small academic libraries as with those of public libraries.

What contributions have school libraries been able to make since joining the regional library systems? They have been the nucleus for formation of 16mm-film cooperatives, audiovisual equipment repair services, and continuing education programs related to the use or production of nonprint media. Thus far, their requests for interloan of materials have been low, and surrounding public and academic libraries have not been overwhelmed with the volume of interlibrary loan requests that they had anticipated. Obviously, as the interlibrary loan program becomes more familiar to school librarians, teachers, and students, the number of requests will increase. It appears, however, that the "immediacy of need" factor will prevent interlibrary loan from growing to the proportions that public and academic librarians feared.

More and more rural communities are examining the feasibility of joining separate public and school libraries into one community library, serving all members of the community. Since more and more schools are opening their doors at night and during the summer, the concept of a community library becomes increasingly practical. Obviously, a joint school-public library is not the answer for every rural area. There are a variety of factors that must be considered, such as the personalities involved (both on the library staffs and on their governing boards), the existing physical facilities or plans for new facilities, the public opinion toward the school or the public library, and many others.

As more school districts join regional library systems, there will probably be an increasing number of requests for information concerning the formation of joint school-public libraries. This will stem from the fact that the systems' structure demonstrates that different types of libraries can cooperate to their mutual benefit. The interaction between librarians from various types of library agencies will also serve to allay the fears that are often felt toward personnel from another type of library.

Have the regional library service systems in Colorado truly become multitype systems? A look at the officers of the systems' governing boards serves to illustrate how well the integration has taken place. After less than six months in operation, the following types of libraries are represented among chairpersons of the seven governing boards: one academic, five public, one school, and no special. Vice-chairpersons of the governing boards represent the following library agencies: three academic, no public, two school, and one special (one system does not have a vice-chairperson).

Multitype library cooperatives in Colorado are healthy and growing and working to meet the needs of all their members. Many fears expressed concerning the participation of schools in systems have proved to be unfounded. Focusing on the strengths to be gained by schools joining systems rather than on the problems that their membership might create, one discovers that school libraries can become full-scale participants in interlibrary cooperation. As school libraries begin to work more closely with other types of libraries, the cooperative may learn ways to eliminate some impediments, such as restrictive local policies, and may learn to live with other limitations, such as the curricular focus of school library collections. Certainly, much more is gained by directing attention to the strengths that school libraries can contribute rather than by spending time lamenting the limitations that often inhibit interlibrary cooperation with schools.

THE ILLINOIS EXPERIENCE: SPECIAL LIBRARIES

Edward G. Strable

"Special librarians have a long tradition of involvement in informal library cooperation. In recent years, they have recognized the fast-paced development of formal cooperation/resource sharing/networking organizations and have become convinced that formal networking is a necessity."[1] This is the first statement in the Introduction to *Getting into Networking: Guidelines for Special Libraries*, published in the spring of 1977 by the Special Libraries Association (SLA), and it serves quite well as a minute state of the art. A well-documented, timely, and unified nationwide picture of special library participation in cooperatives and networks is now in preparation,[2] and there is no question but that special librarians across the country are not only extremely interested in networks but are also participating in many of them. A recent survey included a partial look at the networking practices of special libraries and reported that there had been a sharp increase in participation between 1974 and 1976.[3] Another indication of interest was the well-attended and well-received 1975 SLA conference in Chicago that examined Systems and Networks: The Synergistic Imperative from a number of angles in the general sessions, the contributed papers, and the meetings of the SLA divisions.[4]

This article is not, however, an attempt to describe the national-special library-networking picture even in its present amorphous form. Rather, the point of concentration is on the issues, concerns, and experiences, now evident from the participation of special libraries in the two multitype networks that have bloomed and flourished in the Chicago area. One network is the Illinois Regional Libary Council (IRLC), a multitype, multipurpose cooperative organized in 1971 to serve the six Illinois counties of the Chicago Standard Metropolitan Statistical Area.[5 & 6] The other is the Chicago Library System (CLS), which serves the city of Chicago and is a unit of ILLINET, the Illinois Library and Information Network,[7] which covers the entire state of Illinois. The CLS Interlibrary Cooperation Project got under way in October 1975. Special libraries have had considerable influence in bringing both of these organizations into being and have been forceful both in planning activities and in participation. Now, with a number of years of experience behind us, it is possible to make some preliminary judgments about the role of special libraries in multitype networks in the Chicago area.

NETWORK MEMBERSHIP

To begin, more special libraries are participating in these two networks than had once been expected. As of the middle of 1976, IRLC had 84 special libraries among its 199 voting members. That is 42 percent of all member libraries and the largest type of library represented. CLS had 77 special library affiliates of a total of 144, or 67 percent. Both organizations continue to attract special library members, and the potential for continued growth is very good.

NETWORK USE

More to the point is that special libraries are benefiting from such membership in a very fundamental way; they are using their networks. For some time now, the special libraries have, in fact, not just in theory, been gaining access to additional and needed valuable resources for the users of their libraries. All of this has come about because networking has opened up many library resources that were impossible or difficult to reach before the advent of formalized resource sharing.

The networking activities have produced some extremely useful products; some of the most valuable are the directories of network members and member resources.[8] These describe resources in such a way that the user can pinpoint quickly just what is available from other libraries in the network. Members are also discovering that these documents have an indirect value. They not only identify for the information-voracious special librarian, often working under time pressures, who is committed to cooperation and who will share but also, by omission, who will not share and is, therefore, not worth wasting time on, when a search for a document or a piece of information is under way.

By and large, Chicago area special librarians believe this newly developed state of affairs is very fine indeed because their library users are benefiting, the special librarians themselves are looking better than ever to their managements, and they are able to accomplish this in the righteous atmosphere of a good cause—that of helping IRLC and CLS member libraries reach their prime objectives of "providing better resources for all users." Thus, it can be said that many Chicago area special libraries have worked their way to the very foundation of multitype library cooperation in a very short time.

CONTRIBUTING TO NETWORKS AND COOPERATIVES

Special libraries in the Chicago area are also beginning to contribute to their cooperatives and networks. Special librarians have always had the reputation of being aggressive in gaining access to the information they need to do their jobs. All the articles in library literature about special librarians as parasites long ago made this point clear, but the same articles usually underlined the point that the parasites are also pragmatists.

Back in 1970, Illinois special librarians held an institute entitled It's Time to Get Ready: What Special Librarians Need to Know about Library Cooperation,[9] and they even acquired an LSCA Title III grant from the Illinois State Library to support it. Right off the bat, special libraries learned that networking is a two-way street; that quid pro quo is more than a familiar-sounding Latin phrase; that there must eventually be as much give as take in networking.

It has taken a little while, and a certain amount of learning, but Chicago area special librarians are now contributing to networking in some relatively significant ways. The massive, 30,000-entry *Union List of Serial Holdings in Illinois Special Libraries*,[10] which will be published this year by the Illinois Regional Library Council for use by all the libraries in the state, is a union list of serials in Illinois special libraries. One of the interesting information spinoffs of this project is learning that a considerable number of the titles held by the special libraries are not represented in the renowned academic collections in the area. CLS has been collecting current periodical lists from special libraries and using them to facilitate resource sharing among all affiliates. INFOPASS is a very successful IRLC program that facilitates physical access among the member libraries. Statistics kept since the program began in 1973 show that about 11 percent of the referrals have been from academic and public libraries to special libraries. Eleven percent only becomes a significant statistic when it is remembered that the figure was probably .11 percent before INFOPASS came into existence.

It is the expectation in many multitype cooperatives that special libraries will serve as "specialized subject centers." There is some indication that this is now occurring, on occasion, within IRLC and CLS. For example, when a government library in Chicago recently asked its nongovernment users to register, the first user was from Harvard and the second from the University of Chicago. Perhaps these two students were seeking material not available in those two great research libraries, or perhaps they found the material in this special library more readily accessible because of the special way in which it was organized. Of the 22 INFOPASSes that an advertising-marketing information center in a profit-making organization received during the first six months of 1976, 13 came in the hands of users seeking detailed marketing information on specific consumer products and services, exactly the area in which this information center member of IRLC has specialized strength in the Chicago area. Filling the needs of these information seekers for market information on microwave ovens, hair coloring, water softeners, laundry detergents, baby food, chewing gum, ice cream, air conditioners, insurance, and pantyhose was clear proof that this information center can function as a specialized subject center in the IRLC.

TAKING FROM NETWORKS AND COOPERATIVES

Nonetheless, special libraries, on balance, are undoubtedly taking more from Chicago area networks than they are contributing. The chief reason for this might be that special librarians are more accustomed to going beyond their own resources. An equally important and concomitant factor is that special libraries are not being used as resources by their colleagues in other types of libraries as often as they might be. Some special librarians believe they must find some way to demonstrate to other members of the cooperatives that moving to a smaller unit of service can also be effective in solving an information problem. There is a need for all libraries, and particularly the large ones, to learn to access down as well as up the collection-size ladder, because there is good information down there, and because it is an important way to help solve part of the problem of overuse of the large libraries in the network.[11]

At the same time, as special librarians get deeper into cooperation, and get to know their colleagues better, they have been heard to wonder (very quietly, of course) whether their colleagues in other types of libraries are as tenacious in the pursuit of information as they might be, or at least as tenacious as their patrons. Good students, for example, have always managed to find their way to the specialized collections in special libraries. Special librarians are finding out that more often than not the students are being directed to the special libraries, not by their college and university and public librarians, but by their professors and fellow students.

TRADITIONAL PATTERNS ARE UNCHANGED

Formal networking has not really changed traditional informal cooperation within the Chicago special library community. Neither the concept nor the practice of cooperation, which underlies networking, is new or strange to special libraries. There have always been large measures of informal cooperation among them—even those in competitive organizations—one of the reasons for the introversion of special librarians.

In Chicago, there was considerable conjecture about how the long-standing patterns of informal cooperation might be affected by special library participation in formal networks. Experience has shown that the answer is hardly at all. Special libraries have one set of practices—the old-fashioned ones—for working among themselves. The formal networks supplement these relationships rather than substitute for them.

Some Chicago special librarians were network holdouts because they were fearful of having to give up these friendly, comfortable, "old-boy" relationships. A good number, however, have decided their fears were groundless and have now joined IRLC or CLS or both. Others are still convinced that there are not sufficient reasons for joining formal networks when the old informal ones work so well.

It is very possible that this attitude, both in Chicago and elsewhere in the country, is now, and will continue to be, the chief barrier to widespread special library participation in networks. Robert Lane, chairperson of the SLA Committee on Networking, last year wrote over 80 personal letters to special librarians in an attempt to identify barriers to networking. He summarized the two main barriers resulting from his investigation: special librarians are satisfied with the service they presently offer; and special librarians already belong to "old-boy" networks and do not see good reasons for joining formal ones.[12]

SOME BARRIERS ARE FLIMSY

Other often-cited barriers to network participation by special libraries are turning out to be rather flimsy, at least in the Chicago area. Just about every discussion of special library participation in multitype library cooperation includes certain barriers that supposedly prevent special libraries from being full and free partners in networking. The ones mentioned most often are that special libraries consist largely of collections of confidential and proprietary information that cannot be shared; that since they are small they are likely to be overwhelmed by requests from outsiders; that special librarians can't possibly convince their managements that resource sharing is a good thing; and that managements will cut back on special library support once they know about the rich resources freely available through networks.

By and large, it has been the Chicago experience that these barriers are paper barriers, or at the very most, cardboard. In fact, they have not been nearly the stumbling blocks they were expected to be. Most materials in special libraries that are wanted by others are published materials, not proprietary materials. The small special libraries in IRLC and CLS have not been inundated by rapacious information seekers. On the contrary, some special librarians say that, networkingwise, they feel like unconsummated bridepersons. It also turns out that executives are smart enough to see the same economic and service advantages of networking that their librarians see. We know of only one instance in the Chicago area where a special librarian tended to substitute networking for collection building—until the error of the subject's ways were clearly pointed out by special library colleagues.

NEW BARRIERS

A couple of new barriers appear to be surfacing. The first is the exclusion of special libraries in profit-making organizations from certain networks and/or network activities, particularly where public funds are involved. This has not been a problem in the Chicago situation, or, more accurately, it is a problem that has been surmounted. Rumblings have come, however, from special libraries in other parts of the country. The problem is likely to surface more often as new programs call for more intensive resource sharing by larger and more specialized special libraries.

A second new barrier is more subtle and philosophical. It is inherent in those aspects of networking that emphasize concepts of coordination and common standards. It must be remembered that a sizable proportion of special libraries spring from, and are a part of, the capitalistic system, which emphasizes competition and individuality and other characteristics in opposition to commonality of goals and standards and activities. All special libraries, whether or not in the profit-making sector, have long followed traditions based on nonstandardization, unalikeness, and unique methods of operation—traditions that are ever present and important elements in the special librarians' self-image. Consequently, if the formalities of networking begin to require too much in the way of deliberateness and red tape and overorganization and big brotherness, it is likely that a barrier will be created that will cause special libraries to shy away from networking. This has not yet become a significant barrier among the special libraries that are committed to the Chicago networks, but has surfaced as a barrier in other places. It is also a barrier that has kept some special librarians out of networks from the beginning. There is much to be said for keeping our networks free, loose, flexible, and democratic.

Fortunately, positive attitudes have far outweighed the negative ones in the Chicago experience. Perhaps the most important salutary effect has been the almost imperceptible melding of special libraries and special librarians into the greater Chicago library community. Beth Hamilton, executive director of the Illinois Regional Library Council, states the case well:

> To most of the Chicago area special libraries, informal cooperation was a way of life long before the Council was founded. Now an even larger group of dynamic librarians is determined to make formal cooperation work. Some members have devoted untold hours on the board, in committees, and individually. They have spent time drafting by-laws, formulating objectives, identifying needs, writing papers, giving speeches, verifying serials entries, developing guidelines, planning, preparing posters, arranging meetings, attending meetings, studying budgets, driving to the state capitol, presenting ideas, communicating problems, and proclaiming successes. On the bal-

ance, the response of the Chicago library community to this cooperative has been the vital spark in whatever success it has attained.[13]

NOTES

1. SLA Committee on Networking, Guidelines Subcommittee, *Getting into Networking: Guidelines for Special Libraries* (New York: Special Libraries Association, 1977).

2. Barbara Evans Markuson, *Special Libraries in Networking: A State of the Art* (New York: Special Libraries Association, in progress).

3. Marcy Murphy, "Networking Practices and Priorities of Special and Academic Libraries: A Comparison," *Occasional Paper no. 126* (Urbana: University of Illinois Graduate School of Library Science, December 1976).

4. "66th SLA Conference, 1975, Chicago," *Special Libraries* 66 (September 1975): 445–497.

5. Joseph Benson, "Why Special Library Participation in a Metropolitan Network?" *Special Libraries* 67 (January 1976): 18, 20–22.

6. Beth A. Hamilton, "Principles, Programs, and Problems of a Metropolitan Multitype Library Cooperative," *Special Libraries* 67 (January 1976): 19, 23–29.

7. "Library Development in Illinois," *Illinois Libraries* 58 (October 1976): 575–672.

8. Joel M. Lee and Hillis L. Griffin, eds., *Libraries and Information Centers in the Chicago Metropolitan Area*, 2nd ed. (Chicago: Illinois Regional Library Council, 1976).

9. This institute was not covered in any depth in library literature. A brief description with a list of recommendations resulting from the institute was prepared by the committee and is available from the author.

10. Beth A. Hamilton, et al., *Union List of Serial Holdings in Illinois Special Libraries* (Chicago: Illinois Regional Library Council, 1977).

11. Eric H. Halvorson, *The Infopass Program and Misreferrals: The Regenstein Situation*, Publication no. 1 (Chicago: Illinois Regional Library Council, 1975).

12. Special Libraries Association, Committee on Networking, minutes of the July 8, 1976 meeting, unpublished.

13. Hamilton, "Principles, Programs, and Problems," p. 29.

LARGE ACADEMIC LIBRARIES

Kenneth E. Toombs

Library cooperation presumes that there is an interchange of services and collections for the mutual benefit of the parties to the agreement. The idea of cooperative networking presupposes that everyone will contribute and benefit, if not equally, then certainly to a degree that makes it worthwhile to participate. "The two most serious barriers to the development of library systems, cooperatives, and networks are fear and funding—in that order," according to Alphonse F. Trezza, executive director of the National Commission on Libraries and Information Science. The fear is loss of autonomy and the funding is whether or not a library receives as much from the network as it contributes.[1]

BURDENS ON THE LARGE ACADEMIC LIBRARY

The large academic library is likely to come up short on both counts in many networks. In Ohio College Library Center (OCLC)-type networks, there is a tendency to rely on democratic governance, which, of course, can lead to policies resulting in increasingly heavy burdens on the large library. If the network is made up of different types of libraries, the burden on the large academic library is likely to be somewhat greater than if only academic libraries are involved.

An example of this problem is the Southeast Louisiana Library Network Cooperative (SEALLINC), a multitype library network. SEALLINC has eighteen member libraries: four special, nine academic, and five public. Yet, during a typical month, February 1976, 76 percent of the requests were from the five public libraries, 20 percent from the nine academic, and only 4 percent from the four special libraries. With the exception of the New Orleans Public Library, the public libraries in this network have few materials that the academic libraries need. The reverse is not true. A large academic library in the network gets more than five times as many requests from the network as it asks of other members. This large private institution gets no reimbursement for its contribution to the network.

REMEDIAL MEASURES

To offset the inequities faced by the larger libraries, several measures have been introduced to make network membership involving various types and sizes of libraries more palatable to the large academic library. Fees are often established so that the lending library is repaid, at least in part, for lending its books to other libraries. Sometimes the fees extend to other services, such as reference service and photocopying.

In cataloging networks, such as OCLC, charges are not made for the input of original cataloging. Occasionally grants are made to rebate costs for staff, office space, telephone, teletype, and equipment.

Governance is sometimes affected. For example, in the Southeastern Library Network (SOLINET), the board has five directors elected from the 25 Association of Southeastern Research Libraries (ASERL) members and only four who represent the hundred or so smaller libraries. This plan of governance was mandated by the ASERL libraries that founded the network and contribute more than half of the income, while constituting only one-fifth of the network membership. They also account for more than one-half of the bibliographic resources of the network. In the general membership meetings, however, where the constitution and by-laws are written and policy decisions are made, each member has one vote.

After all remedial measures have been taken, are the larger academic libraries satisfied? Hardly. They often go along for the ride in order to maintain peaceful coexistence. The larger libraries realize the importance of their collections and actively seek more equitable solutions. It is obvious that they will continue to be the last resort—and often the first resort—in any cooperative network involving smaller libraries.

The payment of fees is an attempt to reimburse the large library and to equalize costs. Unfortunately, the use of reimbursal fees is sporadic and very uneven throughout the country. Generally, in state networks, the state library agency controls the federal and often the state funds that are obtained for operating the network. Sometimes the larger academic library gets little, if any, of these funds; in the South Carolina network, the large academic libraries receive no funds for their participation.

INTERLIBRARY LOAN FEES

In the networks in which the lending libraries receive a fee, the fee usually covers only a portion of the cost. An example of this is in Illinois where $2.20 is paid to a research library for each item it sends to members of ILLINET.[2] Even though a basic grant is paid annually to the large libraries in addition to the current fee, it is doubtful that the full costs are reimbursed to the participating libraries. A recent estimate of $6.39 as the cost per transaction in interlibrary loan is probably conservative.[3] A recent memorandum from Harvard states that "on July 1, 1976 . . . The Harvard University Library will begin charging a fee of $8.00 for . . . [each title] loaned to other libraries."[4]

Most of the larger academic libraries in Canada charge a fee similar to that now in effect at Harvard. Yale and Princeton have recently introduced a $5 charge for lending books to other libraries. It is obvious that the larger academic libraries will soon attempt to establish a national system of charging for interlibrary loans and photo services. The Harvard memorandum states that "We all hope that the charges now being imposed for interlibrary loans by individual libraries will be superseded by a uniform, adequately supported, national plan for interlibrary loan activity."[5] Certainly a national system of reimbursement should be established for interlibrary lending. Perhaps a realistic charge should be about $5 per item sent to other libraries.

One of the most frustrating aspects of library service is the obtaining of an item at great time and expense and then having it remain unused. Certainly this happens more often than we would care to admit. Another wasteful use of interlibrary loans is items for which the sole criterion for the request is based upon the title. Such indiscriminate requests are frequently received by large libraries. Perhaps more responsibility would be instilled in both the borrower and the borrowing library if each had to pay at least a nominal charge of $1. The remainder of the cost of the loan could be charged to the funding agency. There is a tendency to abuse privileges that are free and without responsibility. These suggestions will certainly be met with the prevalent cry of free access to everyone. It should be remembered, however, that someone is paying for the service and perhaps if the responsibility were more evenly spread, there would be less abuse of the privileges.

Libraries throughout the country receive constant requests to grant extensive privileges to patrons other than their own. Most large academic libraries allow materials to be used within the library by any adult. Interlibrary access, as opposed to interlibrary loan, offers many advantages to the library as well as to the user. In fact, this is often encouraged, because the user has far better access to the materials needed with lower costs to the library involved.[6]

INFOPASS is a multitype library cooperative program, inaugurated by the Illinois Regional Library Council in January 1963, to serve member libraries in the Chicago metropolitan area. This program now involves approximately 300 libraries in the Chicago area as well as those in other areas of the United States. This voluntary program is aimed at solving the problems of library users who need access to resources that would otherwise be unavailable to them. It has worked well in areas where there are many privately supported research libraries that need to have control over the use of their collections. Library patrons are carefully screened before being granted an INFOPASS to use in a cooperating library. The screening process minimizes abuse of the privileges. The INFOPASS arrangement is much less expensive to all concerned than interlibrary loan. [7]

GOVERNANCE

The governance of cooperative networks is a problem that will grow as the number of networks increases. The more dissimilar the libraries in size and purpose, the greater the problem will become. OCLC is carefully studying its governance because the affiliated networks and libraries have no voice as to how OCLC is operated.

We have already seen that the larger libraries in SOLINET, as represented by membership in ASERL, have worked out a compromise on governance. The strong tendency to have strictly democratic governance in all types of networks creates obvious problems.

It is highly improbable that the larger libraries will yield to policies formulated by the smaller members if these policies are overly expensive either in funds or services. The problem of the large versus the small library in networks and other cooperative groups will continue until some reasonable governance alternatives are developed and accepted. Perhaps the most equitable application of governance would be a voice equal to the amount of participation either in terms of funds, services, or bibliographic contributions.

The OCLC-type networks are becoming increasingly multitype cooperatives involving libraries of all sizes. The large OCLC data base is available to all members and gives the location of the books listed. As a result of this information, many libraries are requesting books from outside their area and, in many cases, even their region. It is not uncommon for a large library to get requests from small libraries halfway across the nation. This practice needs to be checked by adoption of some national guidelines.

On the other hand, many smaller libraries that are members of the network can more readily borrow from each other. This type of cooperation should flourish once sufficient input has been made into the data bases by the smaller members. If interlibrary loan between the smaller libraries can be developed to a greater degree, it will do much to prevent the interlibrary loan situation from getting out of hand.

There is always the possibility of the larger libraries withdrawing from the present networks and forming their own national or even international network. Unless equitable arrangements are made in the cooperative process, this could very well happen. The Research Libraries Group (Harvard, Yale, Columbia, and New York Public Library) is doing this to a degree. Under the present funding and service systems, it is better for the large libraries to band together in all forms of cooperation than to be a part of a system in which they are much larger than the other members. As John McDonald said so well:

> Although we recognize the various elements required and have the technology to allow these elements to work together, many complex problems remain. Some of these problems are institutional, some of them are organizational, most of them are political in the sense that they require the attention of the nation's leaders and demand a share of the nation's financial resources. All of them underscore the continuing need for planning if we are to create a more effective national system of information and literature access. The need exists, as the Congress affirmed in establishing the National Commission on Libraries and Information Science. Library and information services adequate to meet the needs of the people of the U.S. are essential to achieve national goals and to utilize most effectively the nation's educational resources.[8]

NOTES

1. Alphonse F. Trezza, "Fear and Funding," *Library Journal* 99 (December 15, 1974): 3174.
2. "Introducing ILLINET . . . The Beginnings of a Statewide Network," *Illinois Libraries* 57, no. 6 (June 1975): 369.
3. Rolland E. Stevens, "A Study of Interlibrary Loan," *College and Research Libraries* 35, no. 5 (September 1974): 342.
4. Louis E. Martin, librarian of Harvard College, memorandum to "Libraries Which Have Borrowed Titles on Interlibrary Loan from the Harvard College Library," May 28, 1976.
5. Ibid.
6. David Kaser, "Library Access and the Mobility of Users," *College and Research Libraries* 35, no. 3 (July 1974): 282.
7. "Infopass" (Milwaukee: Library Council of Metropolitan Milwaukee, 1975).
8. John P. McDonald, *National Planning and Academic Libraries* (Washington, D.C.: Association of Research Libraries, 1974), p. 18.

SMALL ACADEMIC LIBRARIES

Melvin R. George

Library cooperation among types of libraries is not a new idea. Forty years ago, an ALA committee recognized the need for the coordination of library resources on a regional and national scale, so that publicly supported school and academic libraries might assist public libraries in serving the public.[1] Stenstrom listed 383 items on the subject in his annotated bibliography, *Cooperation among Types of Libraries, 1940–1968*,[2] and Gilluly and Wert in their supplement for 1969–1971[3] listed another 87 titles. Yet substantive cooperative library activity among types of libraries has yet to touch the working lives of many librarians. True, there have been a number of pockets of vigorous activity, particularly where the local school and college and public librarians knew one another. And there has been a rapid increase in such activity in states where multitype library activity has been sponsored and funded by the state or some state agency. This growth was stimulated to a high degree when the Library Services and Construction Act was amended in 1966 to include the new Title III on Interlibrary Cooperation.

INTERLIBRARY LOAN AND THE LARGE COLLECTION

Except in areas where they are the largest library resource in the region, the small or medium-sized academic library has not been so assiduously courted for interlibrary cooperation purposes as have their bigger brothers, the large university libraries. Given the state of the art of bibliographic control of the collections in smaller institutions, concentration upon the largest library resource in a region made sense. There were relatively few alternatives to the "largest library" syndrome. If a librarian or a library user wished to find material not held in his local library, he had the best chance, statistically, of locating the material in the largest library available, and the larger the library, the better the chance of meeting the need.

Those responsible for networking reinforced the dependence upon large collections because they saw few alternatives. Short of developing manually updated union card catalogs at enormous expense, there seemed little hope of finding a way to identify specific items located in the smaller collections. Guides to library collections within a region or state like the Downs' *Guide to Illinois Library Resources*[4] and the Illinois Regional Library Council's *Libraries and Information Centers in the Chicago Metropolitan Area*,[5] which describe subject collections and strengths, complete with carefully defined descriptors and indexing, somewhat reduced the odds in locating materials. They were never so specific, however, as interlibrary loan staff members needed them to be. It was not possible to determine whether a specific title had been overlooked for some reason by the library that maintained such a collection or—and just as important—whether a nearby library that usually did not specialize in the subject area had by some chance acquired the material.

Lacking any other options, the large interlibrary loan networks concentrated upon strengthening the largest libraries. In Illinois, four large regional collections were identified as R&R (Research and Reference) Centers. Since 1967, each has received a basic annual grant to underwrite collection development and interlibrary loan costs. Each center also receives a payment for each search in connection with an interlibrary loan request; an additional sum is paid if the request is filled. This kind of activity made, and continues to make, good sense. It opened large collections to easy public availability for the first time, and, for the first time, demonstrates a public intent to support the financial burden of large lending libraries.

Other developments, especially technological ones, are making us realize, however, that this concentration upon the large libraries is only the first step in interlibrary loan networking. Preliminary studies are beginning to reveal that other libraries in a region, similar in size and function to the requesting library, can supply a surprisingly large percentage of total interlibrary loan requests when interlibrary loan staff can identify the presence of specific holdings.

INTERLIBRARY LOAN AND THE SMALL COLLEGE LIBRARY

LIBRAS, a consortium of ten private college libraries in the Chicago suburbs, shows the pattern. LIBRAS supports a union author card catalog of all acquisitions since 1967, so that member libraries have increasingly good bibliographic access to one another's holdings. Thus, when library staff members identify needed material, they call Wheaton College Library, which houses the union catalog, to determine whether the title is listed among the 175,000 titles in the file. To be absolutely sure, however, whether new LIBRAS libraries hold the needed item, it is necessary to call each of the libraries involved because new members have not provided cards for acquisitions made before they joined nor have most LIBRAS libraries provided cards for material purchased before 1967.

As an example of the interlibrary loan activity in the small college library involved in both a single-type library consortium and a multitype library cooperative, a look at Elmhurst College's interlibrary loan record for the period from July 1, 1975 to June 30, 1976 provides some interesting data. Table 1 reveals interlibrary loan activity for both books and photocopies using the Northeastern Illinois Delivery Service (NEIDS), an integrated delivery service coordinated by the Illinois Regional Library Council and subsidized by the five public library systems—Bur Oak, Chicago, DuPage, North Suburban, and Suburban Library System.

Several observations about these statistics seem appropriate: A small academic library need not be merely a parasite on other larger libraries. Elmhurst College actually loaned five more items than it borrowed. Of the total of 595 borrowed items, slightly more than 68 percent were provided by other similar libraries in the same geographic area. If no local interlibrary agreement had existed within LIBRAS, most of these requests would have been channeled through the local library systems where they would have added to the overhead costs of both the system and the R&R Center searching the requests and providing the materials.

In addition, it should be noted that these figures do not reflect items exchanged through a direct reciprocal borrowing program. In the same year, Elmhurst College loaned 463 books (there's no easy way to count photocopies) to students and faculty associated with LIBRAS's institutions and 286 books to local high school students.

Of course, the advent of automated systems will make the manually updated union catalog a thing of the past. It will allow interlibrary loan personnel to search the holdings of related libraries quickly and accurately. Many libraries are already feeling the impact of OCLC upon their interlibrary loan procedures. All of the LIBRAS libraries will soon enter the OCLC system with the help of a Kellogg Foundation grant. This grant will cover OCLC terminal, training, and related costs for academic libraries eligible to participate in the Illinois State Library's contractual arrange-

**Table 1   Elmhurst College Library Interlibrary
Loan Statistics (July 1, 1975 to June 30, 1976)**

To/From	Elmhurst Loaned	Elmhurst Borrowed
LIBRAS's libraries	575	407
Local library system and state network	4	127
Other Illinois libraries	21	48
Libraries outside Illinois	0	13
Total	600	595

Source: Carol Barry, *Interlibrary Loan Statistics—July 1, 1975 through June 30, 1976* (Elmhurst, Ill.: Elmhurst College, 1976), typescript.

ment with OCLC. It will be interesting to follow the changes resulting in interlibrary loan patterns as this program develops.

Some member libraries of the Illinois library systems have installed CLSI LIBS 100 circulation systems. The Illinois State Library has been carrying out studies in interfacing these separate systems and using them to generate information for interlibrary loan. The advantage here is that a potential borrower can learn not only whether a library in the vicinity has a book but also whether or not it is checked out. Preliminary evidence once more reveals that similar libraries in the vicinity can fill a large number of requests which have been forwarded to one of the R&R Centers in the past.[6]

Yet another component that requires more localized emphasis in networking is speed, as identified by Arthur Miller, college librarian, Lake Forest College. Miller studied the source of photocopies furnished at the request of the Lake Forest College Library and the speed with which they were delivered. Table 2 is a comparison of time required to receive photocopies from three sources: ILLINET, the ACM (Associated Colleges of the Midwest) Periodical Bank, and the LIBRAS's libraries.

There are clear advantages in making requests locally. All of the LIBRAS's requests were filled within two weeks, while the system and state network took the longest time to respond. The figures do not show that statewide networks are unnecessary, only that they are slower to respond, partly, to be sure, because they are being asked to supply material that is more difficult to locate. LIBRAS's libraries were able to supply only 25 percent of the total requests; however, without LIBRAS or some local source, the 126 requests would have been added to the work load of the system and the R&R Centers.

The import of these data, then, is not that statewide systems are unnecessary. More complete bibliographic access to local collections is likely to lead toward more dependence upon the local sources of a total

Table 2   Source and Delivery Time for Lake Forest College Library Photocopy Requests, February through April 1976

Source	1–5 Days	6–10 Days	11–15 Days	16–20 Days	21–120 Days
ILLINET local system and Central Serials	34	56	13	6	54
ACM Periodical Bank	47	93	44	12	11
LIBRAS's libraries	100	26	0	0	0

Source: Arthur H. Miller, Jr., *A Comparative Study of Periodical Interlibrary Loan, February through April 1976* (Lake Forest, Ill.: Lake Forest College, 1976), ditto copy.

interlibrary loan network. This has real implications for the smaller academic library, which is then recognized as a valuable regional resource. In the past, networking money was spent to strengthen larger collections. Now, as technology makes better information available, we must ask some questions: Should basic grants be provided to allow retrospective tagging of OCLC files or for conversion of data to CLSI files for some of the smaller libraries? If larger academic libraries continue to be funded for searching interlibrary loan requests and furnishing the material, should local libraries be funded in the same way? Will a concentration upon nearby resources result in more concern for delivery services, and since distance is small, can more interlibrary loan activity be shifted to direct reciprocal borrowing programs?

BENEFITS OF MULTITYPE PARTICIPATION FOR THE SMALL ACADEMIC LIBRARY

Technology will bring about a greater emphasis upon local arrangements that will have major implications for the small academic library. This fact, however, does not disclose the advantage to the small academic library of joining a multitype library network—that of having resources of many libraries easily accessible to meet unusual needs.

Every library has at least two levels of responsibility. It serves a limited primary clientele by building collections, organizing them, and arranging user assistance programs. For instance, although nobody can define precisely what a liberal arts college library collection should contain, everybody can agree that it should concentrate upon material for the undergraduate reader involved in a general educational program with some work in the first stage of a subject specialization. The delineation of responsibility cuts out an enormous range of material for which the liberal arts library collection development librarians need not feel responsible. We all know, however, that every library has a secondary responsibility. There are frequently students whose needs go well beyond the undergraduate level; they may be able to handle the most esoteric materials. No single library could anticipate the range of requests it is likely to receive over the course of the years. In the past, the typical college library has attempted to anticipate some of those unusual demands. It had no other alternative because it stood alone, and often failed to meet the needs of the student.

It may be only a matter of perception, but it does seem that library budgets don't go so far as they used to. Probably it is simply that the growth in publishing requires that budgets be stretched farther than in the past. In any event, most small libraries have too little money to supply resources of the range and richness needed to meet their primary responsibilities without attempting to provide esoterica as well. A multitype library cooperative helps relieve this tension. A library can concentrate its efforts upon its primary responsibility while being ensured that the resources of the special library, the school library, the public library, or the large research library will be available to meet the need of the atypical user when it arises. The college library will, in turn, provide the backup for the school or public or special library when their primary clientele makes an atypical request. Of course, nothing in the real world works quite so smoothly as we would wish, but the potential is there. Together we can provide for the needs of a greater percentage of our primary and secondary clienteles than we can by operating alone.

STAFF PARTICIPATION

Working together, however, does not begin or end with physical resources. The small academic library has always realized that its greatest resource is staff. It takes dedicated staff with unusual ingenuity to mine completely a small college collection. A surprising amount of information and cultural enrichment lurks in even the smallest collections, if only someone were available to dig for it. The typical library user is not a digger and unless somebody helps the user exploit a collection, he will pass by a large percentage of any collection's riches.

When it comes to cooperation the library staff continues to play a pivotal role. The library patron who is incapable of using a local collection to fullest advantage is even more unlikely to succeed when several collections become available. Yet, it is quite an adjustment in thinking for the typical library staff member, who is comfortable in his own parochial surroundings, to devote himself to exploiting the resources of a whole group of collections. We are so accustomed to saying, "We don't have it" that it takes time to remember to add, "but I can get it for you." Furthermore, using another collection often means working with someone else in the other library. That takes trust and mutual respect, which develop as a consequence of repeated positive exchanges. Building such a relationship takes time. Most library consortia have discovered that interlibrary loan grows year after year, despite the fact that student bodies remain essentially the same size. Partly, the growth reflects a better understanding of the content of collections among the libraries, but more than anything it reflects the growth of camaraderie, trust, and mutual respect among those who staff the several libraries.

One of the very best investments any library director can make toward greater interlibrary cooperation is in allowing time for staff members to get to know those with whom they will be cooperating. When we involve ourselves in multitype library activity, we must be even more patient. It is hard enough to bridge the gap between two academic library staffs who, because of their involvement in the educational task, at least share a certain mutuality in their experience and goals. It will be even more difficult to ensure that all of us feel comfortable in the hitherto alien territory of another kind of library.

GOVERNANCE OF MULTITYPE LIBRARY COOPERATIVES

Finding a governance mechanism that faithfully reflects the interests and needs of all types of libraries becomes a difficult problem, since all of us are governed so differently. The public libraries have, in a sense, beat the rest of us to the pass. Their previous success and experience in identifying the concerns of the public library through public library systems put the rest of us at a disadvantage. We in academic libraries can be fast learners, and although the task of finding appropriately representative forms of governance causes some difficulties, there must be solutions. We need to find them, for multitype library cooperation is the only way in which we can live up to the highest aspirations of our profession.

NOTES

1. ALA Special Committee on Federal Relations, "Libraries and Federal Aid," *ALA Bulletin* 30 (May 1936): 425.

2. Ralph H. Stenstrom, *Cooperation between Types of Libraries, 1940–1968: An Annotated Bibliography* (Chicago: American Library Association, 1970).

3. Maureen E. Gilluly and Lucille M. Wert, "Cooperation between Types of Libraries: An Annotated Bibliography, 1969–1971 Supplement," *Illinois Libraries* 54 (May 1972): 385–400.

4. Robert B. Downs, ed., *Guide to Illinois Library Resources* (Chicago: American Library Association, 1974).

5. Joel M. Lee and Hillis L. Griffin, eds., *Libraries and Information Centers in the Chicago Metropolitan Area* (Chicago: Illinois Regional Library Council, 1976).

6. William DeJohn, "CLSI Interconnect Program-Update," *Network Memorandum No. 77–84* (Springfield: Illinois State Library, January 3, 1977).

SERVICES OF METROPOLITAN LIBRARY COUNCILS

Susan Keller

Library development in metropolitan areas in the past five years has been multitype development and, more often than not, has been given impetus by the Library Services and Construction Act Title III, which supports projects involving more than one type of library. All councils covered in this article are formally organized, are multitype in that they serve two or more types of libraries, and are multipurpose in that they have been established to provide, or to coordinate, more than one kind of service for their member libraries. It is these services that will be enumerated, with particular attention given to the Library Council of Metropolitan Milwaukee. Typically, metropolitan council services might include publications, union lists, interlibrary use, continuing education, delivery, shared acquisitions, and planning.

BACKGROUND

In order to explore the potential for multitype library council services in metropolitan areas, it is useful to understand what has been done, how it has been done, and why. Much of the data needed to acquire this background are either scattered in the library literature of the past few years or must be culled from publications of the councils themselves. Such publications are generally distributed to individual member libraries, to state library agencies, and to other metropolitan councils, but are not necessarily readily available to the professional community. The ensuing review of council services in major metropolitan areas is based on data gathered by the Illinois Regional Library Council and reported in a paper presented by Beth Hamilton at the 1975 fall seminar of the Chicago Association of Law Librarians.[1]

It is estimated that multitype library cooperation, to the extent we are concerned with here, is being actively pursued in, at most, 15 states.[2] Major metropolitan areas served by cooperative councils and reported in the Hamilton study include Chicago, Cleveland, Indianapolis, Long Island, Milwaukee, New York, Pittsburgh, and Rochester. As reported in detail in several earlier articles in this volume, these councils, nurtured primarily by local planning and LSCA Title III monies, share a number of common attributes:

1. They have members within their geographic areas who have recognized that the needs of their clienteles cannot be met adequately by one single type of library.
2. They have been organized as multitype councils to facilitate efforts at coordinating library services within their areas.
3. They have governing boards representative of their member libraries and small full-time headquarters staffs.
4. They have members joining their organizations and participating in their programs on a voluntary basis.
5. Members meet regularly to discuss problems in serving their specific clienteles; to identify strengths and weaknesses of local collections, personnel, and facilities; to explore methods of solving problems by joint efforts; and to design proposals that provide solutions either by acquiring additional resources or by reassigning responsibility for sharing present resources to meet client needs.[3]

Eligibility for membership in multitype councils varies from council to council, but usually is based on geographic location of the library unit, type of library, and willingness of the library unit to pay annual membership fees. Fees range from as low as $10 per year to as high as $2,500. The federally designated Standard Metropolitan Statistical Areas are often used to determine council borders. Counties or natural service areas can also serve as a geographic base. All the councils studied in the Hamilton sample had academic, public, and nonprofit special library members. In addition, special libraries in profit-making institutions and school libraries are eligible for full membership status in Milwaukee, Indianapolis, and Chicago, and will be in Cleveland according to its plan. Affiliate membership status usually means nonvoting status and is primarily used as a device to bring in as many members as are interested in cooperative programs in the areas being served. In all the New York 3 R's Councils, affiliate status is allowed for special libraries in profit-making institutions; in Milwaukee, for individual libraries; in New York METRO, for New Jersey libraries; and in Chicago, for public libraries that do not pay dues but that are members of public library systems.[4]

The chronology of each council needs to be considered in any discussion of services. Both the New York and Rochester councils were founded in 1966, with staff hired in 1967. Staff was hired in Long Island in 1971, in Chicago and Pittsburgh in 1972, in Milwaukee and Indianapolis in 1974, and in Cleveland in 1975. The councils all had preliminary committees that volunteered for the organizing process, for the development of constitutions and objectives, and for the hiring of staff. It is important to note that considerable time and effort were donated to the establishment of these councils. It was only after staffs were hired, however, that full programs of services were offered.

Publications

Publications are an important service rendered by the multitype councils. Each has published a membership or library resources directory. The directories range from a simple membership listing to detailed guides to collections and services of member libraries. Most are issued not more frequently than once a year and some include entries for nonmember as well as member libraries.

Newsletters to members are also issued by each council, with frequencies of monthly, quarterly, or irregular, and sizes ranging from two to twenty pages. In all newsletters, attention is given to council services, cooperative activities of members, calendars of forthcoming professional events, and continuing education opportunities. Most of the newsletters also announce surplus material, furniture, and library equipment for sale or for free. In Milwaukee and Chicago, the newsletter is available on a subscription basis to nonmember libraries and on an exchange basis with other metropolitan councils.

Both the New York and Chicago councils publish occasional papers covering areas of study related to resource sharing.

Union Lists

A publication particularly common to multitype library councils is the union list, usually of serials or some other frequently used material. Union lists are used not only as locating tools but also as sources of bibliographic information and for the development of coordinated acquisitions programs. Union lists of serials are published in Pittsburgh, Long Island, Rochester, and Chicago. A union list of government documents is offered by the Rochester Council, and one of unusual microforms by New York METRO and the Pittsburgh Regional Library Center. The Chicago list, entitled *Union List of Serial Holdings in Illinois Special Libraries*, was developed under a grant from the Illinois Board of Higher Education and lists approximately 30,000 titles held in 142 special libraries throughout the state. It is not usual for metropolitan councils to command resources sufficient to carry out a project of this size. The Chicago list represents considerable work by council staff and board, as well as the combined efforts of 75 volunteers over a three-year period of time.

Interlibrary Use

The success of most councils is directly proportional to the depth of involvement of its members. One opportunity for involving a maximum number of members is presented by various interlibrary use programs, which can range from full reciprocal borrowing among member libraries to simple physical access. All the councils reviewed have devised programs that attempt to satisfy the clienteles of their areas and the wide range of service philosophies and practices of their members. At the same time, programs have been attempted that accommodate a number of levels of expertise among the participants. Focus oftentimes is on access and flow of materials between member libraries. Bibliographic identification is considered important but often must be less than adequate due to the prohibitive costs involved.

INFOPASS, initially introduced by the Illinois Regional Library Council, is a physical access program that involves the use of, and benefits the users of, all types of libraries. Although the program was aimed at improving physical access, it has been expanded to include borrowing privileges allowed by some libraries. The program has been adopted by councils in Milwaukee, Kenosha, and Peoria and has been reworked to fulfill the needs of each of these areas. In Peoria, it is used as a reciprocal borrowing card. The Wisconsin councils and certain northern Illinois counties outside the Chicago metropolitan area have arranged contractually with the Illinois Regional Library Council to honor INFOPASSes on a reciprocal basis.

Continuing Education

Continuing education programs seem particularly appropriate services for councils that serve many types of libraries. All eight councils studied offer continuing education programs in the form of workshops, seminars, and lectures. CIALSA, one of the Indiana ALSAs, is developing a strong program as mandated by the Indiana Library Services Authority Act of 1967. Two councils are involved in providing OCLC training terminals. The Pittsburgh Center provides this service to students in cataloging classes at the University of Pittsburgh Graduate School of Library Science, while Rochester has arranged to have an OCLC terminal that is shared by two member libraries and is also used for training workshops. What role other councils will have in training and expansion of such programs is not yet known.

A most dazzling array of continuing education programs is offered by New York METRO. Hardly a single possibility has been overlooked. In addition to offering seminars on the BALLOTS system, on OCLC, and on minicomputers, METRO has an interesting videotape demonstration project that allows members to learn to use television cameras and recording equipment and to develop techniques for using this tool in orientation and in-service training programs. The Milwaukee Council has produced a reference training film that has proven to be a best-seller in library circles.

Reference and Referral Service

The reference or referral service offered by multitype cooperatives is dependent, of course, upon the requirements of the community service. Where there are state-supported cooperative reference services available, the metropolitan councils do not duplicate those services. All of the councils studied in the Hamilton sample offer some form of cooperative reference or referral service. The Rochester Council has a fee-based Technical and Business Information Service as well as a translation referral service. New York METRO has its CARE service using the New York Public Library as its backup collection. METRO is also planning a feasibility study to determine the most effective approach for bringing commercially available searching services to the public. The Long Island, Pittsburgh, Chicago, and Milwaukee councils are offering or exploring the feasibility of offering a fee service using commercial data bases. The Chicago Council expects to develop a Datapass program similar in principle to IN-FOPASS and that permits Chicago residents to use search services already available to patrons of some of its member libraries.

Delivery Services

Five councils offer delivery services, either by operating their own, by using United Parcel, or by piggybacking on existing services and making contractual arrangements with the originators of those services for extra volume and mileage. The piggyback arrangement used by the Illinois Regional Library Council and the Rochester Council depends upon the use of the public library systems' vans.

Shared Acquisitions

Although all the councils have interlibrary use programs for the sharing of resources, only New York METRO and the Milwaukee Council have programs aimed at strengthening the resources to be shared. In New York, the Cooperative Acquisitions Program involves the joint purchase and placement of materials needed to fill gaps in area collections. This program was begun with a federal grant and is now self-supporting. Selection and placement of materials are handled by a committee elected for this task. Pittsburgh and New York METRO have coordinated acquisitions information programs and Cleveland and Chicago are planning similar programs. The Cleveland system expects to maintain a file of significant acquisitions and to provide information to its members upon request. The Milwaukee program will be discussed later in this article.

As is obvious from the foregoing, the metropolitan councils under consideration have been involved in many activities that have filled needs unfilled by other library agencies. Their respective library communities have demonstrated their expectations for cooperative programs far beyond the traditional interlibrary loan. In each area, efforts have been made to develop services around existing resources. The first efforts were to identify these resources and the preoccupation is still to describe them precisely. Improved bibliographic access to all resources in any given area has yet to be dealt with effectively. This task, however, will be aided substantially by the use of the OCLC or the BALLOTS system as they become more heavily used as locator tools.

Although the foregoing concentrates on large metropolitan multitype councils, it should not be assumed that such development is limited to metropolitan areas. Similar councils have grown in far less populous areas; they have recognized similar needs and offered similar services, and have experienced problems of the same nature as those confronting their metropolitan counterparts. The multitype council provides a formal channel for making the total library resources of a community, regardless of its size, universally available for appropriate use.

PLANNING

Michael Reynolds views library cooperation as a "social phenomenon by which libraries mutually engage to increase the service capabilities of a single library and by which librarians extend their options to serve clients, including those for whom they actually have no direct responsibility."[5] This practice is subject to many pitfalls. Specific services need to respond to member demand and to be planned and pretested carefully before implementation.

Development of five-year plans is an LSCA requirement for state library agencies, which, in turn, often require projects funded with LSCA money to produce a plan of service. It goes without saying that the local plans of service must be subsets of the overall state plan. Plans of some councils are devised only for the purpose of complying with this requirement; others are actual blueprints for council operation. Planning has not always been done at the outset of a council's operation but is postponed until a full knowledge is gained of the environments in which planned activities will take place. The Illinois Regional Library Council devised a planning procedure that has been used by other councils and that incorporated two means of obtaining member input. First, planning committee members representative of each element of the membership met with their individual constituencies to prepare status reports by types of libraries, following a predetermined discussion schedule. Afterward, a matrix of problems and opportunities for all types of libraries in the council membership was drawn and then solutions were planned for the most obvious and common problems. Second, proposed solutions were then presented to the full membership for revision and ranking in priority order.[6]

The IRLC planning method was used as a basis for the development of the Milwaukee area. Broad areas of interest common to all types of libraries were identified and then investigative subcommittees were formed to report back to the Planning Committee. A comprehensive survey was sent out to all area libraries to test and, if possible, to validate committee findings. Member reaction was received prior to finalization of the report. The Milwaukee long-range plan is presented as a dynamic plan, flexible enough to work with and to take advantage of cooperative programs at all levels as they develop. LCOMM has placed major emphasis on the autonomy and freedom of choice of its member libraries. Again, participation in all programs is strictly on a volunteer basis. Included in the priorities as presented in the plan are the development of the following: an effective coordinated acquisitions program; a direct interloan network; a delivery system; and participation in a bibliographic data base, e.g., OCLC.[7]

One of the problems in long-range planning for multitype councils is in obtaining commitment by members for the planning task in the face of the uncertain future of the councils. In examining the future status of eight councils, Hamilton found that only those in New York and Pittsburgh had any assurance of continued funding. When LSCA funds are turned off, the other councils—in Milwaukee, Chicago, Indianapolis, and Cleveland—must depend on other funding sources. It is unlikely that the operation of offices and programs can be continued with local support. This leaves the four dependent upon funding from private or state sources. Since most private funding sources are not eager to support organizations with such public missions as the councils have, it is a matter then of reliance upon state support. If metropolitan councils are to continue operating, their state agencies must overcome the tendency to try to fit metropolitan library problems into statewide programs that can be justified to legislative bodies. They must find ways to capture funding that will benefit small geographic areas with large populations and they must become articulate in explaining to legislators how such funding will eventually benefit the whole state.[8]

In Wisconsin, a statewide Task Force on Interlibrary Cooperation and Resource Sharing is presently grappling with these very issues. The task force report, scheduled for publication in late 1976, will hopefully outline a plan providing statutory recognition to multitype councils throughout the state. One of the reasons Wisconsin has had to meet this issue head-on is the success experienced by multitype councils over the past few years.

LIBRARY COUNCIL OF METROPOLITAN MILWAUKEE

To illustrate how multitype library cooperation works in one metropolitan area, some description of the Library Council of Metropolitan Milwaukee (LCOMM) operation seems to be appropriate. LCOMM was incorporated in 1973 and became fully operational in September 1974. In the Milwaukee area, the incentive for multitype cooperative activity was not the availability of LSCA or state funding, but rather the responsibility, assumed by professionals in the area, to go beyond interaction with like types of libraries to interaction with all types, with the expectation of improving library service for all library users.

Since its inception in 1973, LCOMM has received LSCA grants ranging from $1,900 to $22,500 with an annual average of slightly more than $13,000. Additional funds have been granted from the local public library system and a private foundation. Membership fees presently are set on a sliding scale from $10 to $35 and account for only a small percentage of the council's income. This extremely low dues schedule was considered essential while the council was in its organizational phase. As it moves into its operational phase of development and is able to offer more services, its dues schedule will increase proportionally. Effective July 1, 1977, dues will increase to a scale of $12 to $150, with an option for libraries to contribute up to $2,000 or more if they are willing and able.

LCOMM is made up of 110 libraries in Milwaukee County and three adjacent, rather rural counties. The LCOMM service area comprises 31.8 percent of the population of the state. During the time LCOMM operated on a volunteer basis, activity was limited to the publication of a bimonthly newsletter, periodic informal get-togethers, and monthly board meetings for planning and brainstorming. In September 1974, LCOMM employed its first paid coordinator and immediately began implementation of a number of programs that had been on the drawing board since 1973.

In searching for a program that could potentially serve all types of libraries and that could achieve the primary objective of improved access to the area's library resources, it seemed logical to begin with a reciprocal privileges program. The INFOPASS concept, first introduced by the Illinois Regional Library Council in 1972, was adopted by LCOMM in 1975. The program has been received enthusiastically by participating libraries, perhaps because it is a voluntary program in which participation is possible on each individual library's own terms and also because it incorporates a number of control features.

A directory of information resources in member libraries was in the process of compilation when INFOPASS was adopted in Milwaukee. The directory, *Libraries and Information Centers in Southeastern Wisconsin*, an essential tool in the new program, was issued in March 1975. It was compiled jointly with the Tri-County Library Council, which serves three rural counties adjacent to the LCOMM area and has been involved with LCOMM programs, on a reciprocal basis, at various stages of development.

Another program of major significance to resource development and sharing has been LCOMM's coordinated acquisitions program. Although this program has been operational only during the past few months, it is already certain that it will have a permanent effect on the development of library service in the metropolitan Milwaukee area. Presently, the program involves the University of Wisconsin-Milwaukee Library, Marquette University Library, and the Milwaukee Public Library in determining areas of collection responsibility. Monthly meetings are held to review systematically all subject areas. At a typical meeting, the acquisitions librarians from these three institutions review only one subject area and invite any interested librarians and faculty to participate. Specific aspects of a particular subject are considered; a library is then chosen to be responsible for collection development on that subject. Primary attention is given to the strengths and weaknesses of existing collections. Some subject areas must, for obvious reasons, be covered by all institutions, especially when dealing with heavily used materials or materials that support undergraduate study. Natural divisions of collection responsibility are emerging as the program develops. Marquette collects heavily in theology and, therefore, will assume major responsibility for that area. Milwaukee Public Library will be responsible in part for government documents, general interest materials, and materials necessary to support the needs of the business community. The University of Wisconsin at Milwaukee will emphasize those disciplines for which doctoral degrees are offered on its campus.

Because of the long-term implications this program has, smaller institutions have not as yet been encouraged to assume sole responsibility for a given subject area. As the program develops, it will expand its parameters. Presently, however, it is in the pilot stage and must be tested with a select number of libraries before LCOMM can determine how others in the area can most effectively interact. Immediate benefits to all area libraries include improved access to the three major institutions in the LCOMM area; sharing of subject expertise with smaller libraries to assist with general collection development; input by special libraries to ensure in-depth coverage of highly specialized areas; coordination of the acquisition and deselection of expensive, seldom-used serials, monographs, and sets to ensure total coverage; and location of seldom-used collections to points in the community where they will be better placed for greater use.

The LCOMM newsletter will serve as the vehicle for keeping members informed of the activities of the Acquisitions Committee. Subjects to be reviewed will be presented to the membership in advance so that all interested parties can participate. As this program develops, the focus of INFOPASS will shift from access to actual loan on a reciprocal basis. This, in turn, will facilitate the need for a delivery service to connect participating institutions.

Continuing education activities play a key role in program development and success. LCOMM does not necessarily involve itself with the creation of continuing education activities but prefers, instead, to monitor all those of other agencies, associations, and library schools and to inform the membership of available programs. If necessary, LCOMM will develop programs where gaps exist. A case in point can best be made with the implementation of INFOPASS. Program components include patron referral as well as interaction between area librarians.

The reference interview is critical to the success of this program. With this in mind, LCOMM produced a 10-minute training film entitled *Reference—More Than an Answer*. This film focused on the reference interview and placed particular emphasis on patron referral to outside agencies. It was used at workshops held in conjunction with the inauguration of INFOPASS. The film's primary purpose was to ensure that area librarians were attuned to the importance of the reference interview and were consciously considering various interviewing techniques. Its secondary purpose was to fill a gap—to our knowledge no film existed on this subject. The availability of the film was announced and presently 12 circulating copies are booked at least 6 to 9 months in advance. All types of libraries are renting and purchasing the film, with copies going as far as Australia and England. The film has thus become a primary source of supplemental funding for LCOMM; hopefully, other continuing education activities the council sponsors will be as valuable to the profession as this effort has been.

SUMMARY

The metropolitan library councils considered were all formally organized, with bylaws, governing bodies, definable geographic boundaries, and member libraries. They were all founded within the past ten years and full programs of services were offered only after headquarters staffs were hired. Services offered included publications, such as directories of library members and library resources, newsletters, union lists, continuing education packets, and occasional papers; physical access and reciprocal borrowing programs; continuing education workshops, seminars, and lectures, using a variety of training tools; reference and referral services; delivery services for speedier document delivery; coordinated acquisitions among member libraries; and identification of opportunities and planning activities to improve library service to users of all types of libraries.

NOTES

1. Beth A. Hamilton, "Metropolitan Library Councils: A Status Report" (Paper presented at the Chicago Association of Law Libraries Fall Seminar, October 9, 1975).

2. ASLA Subcommittee on Interlibrary Cooperation, comp. and ed., *ASLA Report on Interlibrary Cooperation* (Chicago: Association of State Library Agencies, 1976).

3. Beth A. Hamilton, "Principles, Programs and Problems of a Metropolitan Multitype Library Cooperative," *Special Libraries* 67, no. 1 (January 1976): 19–25.

4. Hamilton, "Metropolitan Library Councils."

5. Michael M. Reynolds, "Library Cooperation: The Ideal and the Reality," *College and Research Libraries* 35 (November 1974): 424–431.

6. "The Five-Year Plan of the Illinois Regional Library Council 1974–1979," *Illinois Libraries* 56 (November 1974): 785–819.

7. *A Plan for Cooperative Action: Final Report of the Long-Range Planning Committee of the Library Council of Metropolitan Milwaukee*, 1976.

8. Dorothy A. Kittel, *Trends in State Library Cooperation* (Washington, D.C.: Government Printing Office, 1975).

Four

SUMMARY

POTENTIAL FOR GROWTH IN MULTITYPE LIBRARY COOPERATION

William B. Ernst, Jr

It is obvious that multitype library cooperation has become an integral part of American librarianship. Over the past decade and a half, experiments have taken place across the country. Like the tendrils of a vine, the ideas of sharing and working together toward a common goal have reached into every nook and cranny of the library world. Cooperation comes in many shapes and forms, and there has blossomed forth an infinite variety of ventures embracing all sorts of functions and all types of libraries in an untold number of combinations. Some of these enterprises have borne fruit and others are reaching toward maturity, while a few have withered and dropped away.

All sorts of cooperatives to do all sorts of things have come into existence. Most of the possible combinations of "multi-" and "single-" and "-purpose" and "-type" can be found. They range from the single-purpose organization providing a particular service to a unified group on a regional or state basis to the multipurpose network that seeks to coordinate a broader spectrum of services for a similar group. They include the statewide network emphasizing interlibrary loan and the delivery of materials, the multistate consortium brokering automated bibliographic services, and the multitype, multipurpose council working within the boundaries of a metropolitan area. The philosophy of each is the realization that libraries, if they are to achieve their oft reiterated goal of satisfying all the informational needs of all the people, must work together. It has finally been recognized that no single library can provide complete and universal service, but it may just be possible, though not probable, that this ideal might be approached through joint and concerted effort.

Cooperation has contributed much to the enrichment and enlargement of librarianship and library services. It has broken down many barriers that have grown, or been artificially contrived, among different types of libraries. Librarians have become aware of the problems of their colleagues and have realized that many of these problems are inherent to librarianship in general, no matter what the specific milieu. They have been able to contribute toward the solutions from their store of experience, and, similarly, to draw from the accumulated wisdom of others. The council or consortium or network thus becomes a forum through which ideas can be exchanged and developed and put into practice.

Pooled efforts and pooled funds have made possible many undertakings that would have never been feasible for an individual library. Greater knowledge of the resources, particularly of the specialized materials available within the collections of the cooperative's membership, is one of the benefits that has resulted from an increased interest in sharing. Books, journals, and AV materials are not, as the general public may think, the only important resources; the cumulated staff knowledge and experience forms an highly valuable reservoir to be tapped. The cooperative also provides a medium through which personnel potential can be developed. The ability to cut across function, jurisdictional, and geographic lines is, perhaps, of the greatest import, since it allows the multitype cooperative to serve as a catalyst in bringing about change and as a coordinator in developing new programs.

It is apparent that multitype cooperation is vigorous and flourishing, that it is making worthwhile contributions, and that it is here to stay. There have been some rumblings that the multitype cooperative movement has progressed too rapidly and that it is time to declare a moratorium to avert too rank a growth. These noises come, perhaps, from those who feel a threat to their empires. It may be time to pause for a breathing spell and to take a good look around to see what has been accomplished and what needs yet to be done—a time to assess and to evaluate—but not to stop growth. There are areas within multitype cooperation that need strengthening and possibly those that need supportive remedial attention. A close examination of existing projects and goals and the reordering of future priorities can only be a beneficial exercise, but such would not be the case were a concerted effort made to curtail cooperative activity.

INDIVIDUAL LIBRARY COMMITMENT

One of the strengths of the multitype library cooperative lies in its firm grounding in the basic node, whether single purpose or multipurpose in goal or local, regional, or statewide in geographic spread. It must respond to needs deep in the library community from which it springs. Successful cooperative activity rarely results from an imposition from on high. It must evolve from an expressed need at the lowest level. The director of an individual library may be wholehearted in support of cooperative activities, but unless the staff, they who must do the cooperating, clearly understand the benefits to be derived from such action and can see gain both for the library and their personal growth, there is little chance of making cooperation work. Enthusiasm, commitment, and dedication are all vital ingredients.

With its foundations firmly based on the needs of its membership, the cooperative must be flexible enough to respond to change. It must have the ability to adapt programs and priorities as new membership needs surface and old ones recede. Within a council serving academic, public, school, and special libraries, great suppleness is necessary, since programmatic requirements vary so much. There must be a sensitivity to the interests of the constituency and an ever readiness to assume leadership in projecting new ideas or in reevaluating old ones. A common thread is discernible in the pattern of programs offered by the existing cooperatives, consortia, and systems—directory services, interlibrary loan, delivery service, reciprocal access, reference referral, computer-based informational services, resource evaluation, resource sharing, and continuing education—but there is also a specificity about many of the unique programs that shows they have been tailored to serve an expressed need for that time and that place that attests to their vitality and timeliness.

Staff Participation

It is apparent that good cooperative action springs from strong membership participation. Involvement on a volunteer basis brings with it a commitment to the success of that project and to the work of the organization as a whole. A cooperative is a rather nebulous entity and does not have the tangibility represented by a library or a collection. It must make its presence and its worth felt by projecting an image through its committees and task forces, its workshops and seminars, and the detailed work on directories and union lists that can only be accomplished by countless hours of effort on the part of many people. It must reach beyond the level of the voting member, who represents the institution at annual meetings, or the board member, who helps form policies, down to the assistant reference librarian. It is the staff members who, working on a day-to-day, face-to-face basis with the library user, must have a strong feeling of identity with the cooperative agency if it is to have any success. The working librarian, as opposed to the administrative librarian, must be assured of having a voice, and one that will be heard, in determining the direction the cooperative will take.

GOVERNANCE AND STRUCTURE

Governance and structure then assume an important role. Successful structures are geared to the particular region and the particular mission of the cooperative, and allow for membership input and participation. There is no single pattern, nor are there several, that serve as a model for all cooperatives. What works in an urban setting may perhaps prove to be completely unpalatable in a rural area. Recognition must be made of local pride and the prevailing fears and phobias—the fear, on the part of smaller libraries, of bigness and possible absorption; the fear, on the part of larger libraries, of being overrun and overused without adequate recompense; and the fear, on the part of many, both large and small, of the loss of autonomy and individuality. Governance must be representative so that the interests and concerns of all types of libraries making up the membership of the cooperative will be given equal consideration.

Neither structure nor governance can be mandated from on high except in the most general terms, and then only in terms that allow as much leeway as possible for meeting special conditions. Flexibility is essential so that changing patterns may be reflected in changed governance and organization. Public library systems, for instance, in some areas are changing, or being changed, into library systems that are concerned with total library service within the system boundaries, and are, therefore, involving academic, school, and special libraries in system plans and projects. An eventual revamping of system governance will be needed to allow these libraries a voice in the decision-making process, since they will be affected by the policies that are decided upon. There must be a revision in cooperative structure and governance to reflect the changed roles and relationships, and to acknowledge that the former public library systems are now in themselves multitype library cooperatives.

PROGRAM APPEAL

If a cooperative is to attract membership, it must present an acceptable image that will instill both confidence in its ability to produce and also the desire to participate. This has been a relatively simple task for the multitype cooperative with a regional or interstate base that is concerned with one purpose, such as the implementation and operation of an OCLC network or the provision of data base information searches. Here a single function, albeit one with internal complexities, is being purveyed and usually for a fee. It is one that can be handled in a straightforward manner with good organization and planning.

The multitype council serving a metropolitan or multicounty area has to display a greater versatility in program construction if it is to offer projects with appeal to its diverse membership. Normally, fees are not involved, nor are large budgets available. It becomes necessary to be ingenious in design, artful in presentation, and, above all, skillful in bringing forth just the exact project that will have direct appeal to academic, public, school, and special libraries. Experience has shown that many councils have found the formula that best suits their locale. It cannot be stressed too strongly that this is a highly important element in any success story. The projects that are most successful are simple and direct in conception and operation. They either answer a stated need or a need that becomes visible only after the inception of the project. Above all, they offer some immediate and measurable benefit. If the program can also demonstrate the need for extensive volunteer participation, with a resulting opportunity for professional growth, rather than the infusion of large sums of money, then so much the better. Any number of such projects have been described: IRLC's INFOPASS, Rochester's Fast Patent Copy Service, METRO's CAP, LCOMM's Coordinated Acquisitions Program, Cleveland's Safari Project, and a whole galaxy of continuing education programs. The common denominator of grass-roots involvement with a voice in policy and decision making and a large role in implementation runs through all these examples.

Much has been accomplished and much remains to be done. There are still barriers to be torn down and shibboleths to be demolished. It must be shown that cooperation is not a fearsome thing. Cooperation is at best fragile and the task of exorcising trustees, legislators, administrators, and librarians of the fears that possess them must be approached with diplomacy and tact. Education and discussion, free and open, will help to disabuse some of the false notions that persist and will convince many of the enriching and enlarging potential of multitype cooperation.

RECIPROCAL BENEFITS AND CONTRIBUTIONS

Many librarians may feel that they and their libraries have nothing to contribute to a cooperative group because of their smallness, and, perhaps, because of their very specialized nature and, therefore, limited purpose. This is a fallacy that must be quickly extirpated; the benefits to be received are reciprocal and mutual. It is oftentimes the small and specialized library that has just the very important piece of information needed either through its physical or through its human resources, and very often it can be found with more dispatch and delivered with more speed than would be possible from an hierarchically structured research library. The small libraries must be convinced that while they do not have extensive collections, they do have an expertise that is invaluable when one looks at the totality of information needs. The "old-boy" special library networks have proved this through the years, a reality that has been buttressed by their experience with multitype networking. The academic consortia, such as LIBRAS, have also shown that great resources, ones that can provide speedier delivery, are close at hand and available through cooperation.

Some of the larger libraries, in like manner, must be convinced that multitype cooperation is not a dastardly scheme to overrun them and despoil them of their resources without adequate compensation. Fortunately, most of them are long-time practitioners of the cooperative art through their support of the interlibrary loan network. Many are also integral parts and firm supporters of multitype councils. Many others, however, have to be convinced that sharing goes both ways and that there are rich veins of information in the smaller collections, if they will only take the trouble to mine them.

It must be acknowledged that large research libraries, the "haves," are faced, too, with special problems. The services that are consistently requested from them are a pernicious drain on their dwindling resources. They are the ultimate storehouses of our intellectual heritage, and, as such, present a tempting though monolithic and forbidding front to the general public. There is an insatiable desire to go to the fountainhead, in this case the most prestigious library available, and to be satisfied with nothing less. Yet it would be an overstatement to say that the developing and emerging libraries, the "have-nots," are unwilling to bear part of the cost and effort of finding that one piece of information needed to satisfy a user, if a payment will gain access to richer collections—ones that often sit unused for years on end. The answer to the problem may be controlled access programs, which screen out those users who can be satisfied at a lower level.

Librarians at all levels and in all spheres must be convinced that it is profitable to reach out, both to the small and to the large library, when searching for elusive pieces of information. To do so will require training and effort, but this is what networking is all about. It will mean a heightened awareness of local resources and a greater knowledge of local library personalities; more extensive and repeated use of directories, union lists, and the telephone; a better understanding of the potential of available cooperatives; and a willingness to make referrals.

It is a foregone conclusion that fees for the borrowing of materials on interlibrary loans from the larger libraries are now a permanent fixture. It is just as certain that a more equitable basis of assessing them must be established, hopefully on a uniform national scale. The burden of the cost of such transactions should be shared as equally as possible between the user and the supplier, with a public subsidy where necessary. Normally, fees are charged to recover the cost of providing a given service. There are various ways of figuring these costs, from a simple compilation of staff, equipment, and material expenditures to the more all-inclusive method of pro-rating the expense of removing the dust from under the card catalog and the snow from the sidewalk. A happy medium must be found, combining fees and subsidies that will not be over burdensome to the user, the supplier, or the taxpayer.

The thought of charging fees is anathema to many librarians because the idea of free library service is firmly rooted in the American heritage. Yet the time has come when it is no longer possible to provide the increasingly sophisticated kinds of service that are now available and therefore in demand. Library budgets everywhere are hard-pressed because of inflation and enforced retrenchments to maintain present levels of service without contemplating the addition of new projects. The free provision of books, journals, and reference materials for study, research, and pleasure to all members of the community is a position that is impervious to attack. Is it justifiable, on the other hand, to offer free literature searches in a computer-based information bank or an unlimited number of interlibrary loans from halfway across the country for which the library is assessed a fee? It would, perhaps, be more meaningful and less burdensome to the library if the charges were passed on to the ultimate consumer, the user.

All libraries, no matter what their size, must be coaxed away from attitudes of defeating self-interest, chauvinism, and smugness. A large research library or a small corporate library may each feel that it can supply all the needs of its clientele without reference to other sources. This is a position of lonely eminence that will not stand up under close scrutiny. No one library has ever really been self-sufficient, although vast amounts of money have been spent in attempts to achieve this state. It becomes increasingly impossible to envision any institution ever reaching such euphoria in the future. The pace of publication, the vast quantity of material involved, the huge acquisitions required, the complexity of the organizational problems, the splitting of traditional disciplines, and the emergence of new fields with the resulting demand for more varied and detailed collections and for better means of dissemination all preclude this as a logical development. Improved electronic methods of transmission and the mounting use of computer technology as a method of information storage make it more urgent that libraries abandon any isolationist tendencies that they still may harbor.

Loss of autonomy and fear of absorption loom as large problems in some areas. These arguments may be brought forward as roadblocks to forestall the inevitable day of participation in some form of networking, if only from the necessity to survive rather than from conviction. The basic fear may be that of loss of empire and preeminence. From the formation of the first public library systems, democracy has consistently been the rule. Membership has always been voluntary with equitable representation on the system board, prescribed in the bylaws through rotation or some other mutually agreeable arrangement. The multitype cooperatives have profited from the example set by their predecessors and have followed the tradition. An autocracy, based either on size of budget or collections or the contributions made, has an aura of dictation that has little place in a truly cooperative atmosphere.

How does one measure the value of contributions made by different types of libraries? How many interlibrary loans from a research library equal an answer to a question in a highly technical field, promptly received, from an expert in a special library? How many photocopies of articles from obscure and little used journals equal the assurance that a literature search service, tapping the major data bases, is quickly available? The ability to meet with colleagues at a consortium or system annual meeting on a one-member one-vote parity does not counter the loss, because one is not blessed with bigness, of interaction with some of these same people at the policy setting and decision-making sessions of the governing body. Size alone does not bestow greatness nor denote mediocrity. The manner in which the endowments possessed are used and shared, both with the primary and secondary users group, is the sign of true greatness. It is an outstanding hallmark of American librarianship that the major collections have always been relatively open and accessible.

There is a danger that as the idea of multitype cooperation burgeons and spreads, there will be an outgrowth of agencies that are in competition with, rather than complementary to, each other. It would be self-defeating and a violation of the spirit of cooperation to let such a situation progress too far. Yet it can happen all too readily without careful coordination, but less often in a multitype organization where lines of communication are more direct and easy between the various types of libraries, because of their joint interest in working toward a common goal. A dedication to the precepts of cooperation will do much to obviate any competitive situation. The predominant pronoun used in any cooperative venture must always be "we" rather than "I."

FUNDING

Funding has been and continues to be one of the major problems plaguing multitype cooperatives. The majority of multitype activities are now funded by federal money through LSCA grants administered by state library agencies. While the projects supported in this fashion have become firmly accepted as a way of life on the library scene, the end of each grant period evinces a flurry of uncertainty for the future. It is imperative that the cooperatives subsisting on such temporary support move rapidly toward finding a more permanent source of income. Foundation support has been attracted in some instances, but mainly for pilot projects that are innovative in nature and that can be widely adapted, rather than for the underwriting of administrative expenses. Membership fees in the cooperatives are generally assessed to indicate a commitment to the organization. They are not the means of defraying its basic expenses. Such fees, if they are set too high, tend to drive away those libraries that could benefit most from membership. If a sliding scale is established according to budget or collection size, than a similar governing hierarchy rears its head, with those paying the most feeling that they should have the most to say in the decision-making process. A uniform fee scale, at an affordable level for all, does not bring in much money but it does preserve the democratic and cooperative outlook.

The solution seems to be support from the state level, which then brings the multitype cooperative into apparent conflict with those existing library agencies that draw their funds from tax revenues. It behooves the multitype cooperative, therefore, to clarify its relationships with the state library agency and the public library systems within its geographic boundaries in order to avoid all possible conflict and competition for public funds. In most instances, this should not be an insurmountable task since the systems are generally members of the cooperatives. It is also beneficial that the erstwhile public library systems are drawing more closely toward the multitype concept and are now essentially library systems. The multitype cooperative then assumes a new role by taking on the functions of a coordinating body, cutting across geographic and jurisdictional boundaries to serve as a sounding board, catalytic agent and planning group for new ideas. If this role is well defined and accepted, the cooperative, as a partner with the systems and not as a competitor, can go to the legislature in search of funding that will permit it to continue its crusade for the improvement of library service.

The above presupposes that the necessary educational and publicity campaigns have been mounted to make legislators and library boards aware of the coexistence of the two library bodies, their mutual concerns, their necessity, and their partnership. It also assumes the knowledge, acquiescence, and support of the academic, school, and special libraries and the assurance that they have had a voice in the decisions being taken to obtain such firmly based support. Otherwise, the chances of continued existence seem almost negligible, unless the cooperative hopes to rely solely on volunteers to carry out its programs.

Sound planning, and planning done on an ongoing basis, is a prerequisite. Cooperative agencies living on LSCA funds have become inured to the necessity for detailed planning and periodic evaluation. Indeed, they have found the five-year plan a useful exercise and a helpful document in detailing priorities and goals for the enlightenment of members and funding bodies. This aspect of planning is essential, but a pitfall appears when planning is done for planning's sake and nothing is accomplished because it is time to plan again. Funding will be obtainable, however, only when state officials and legislators have before them a concise and understandable explication of what has been accomplished in the past, how effectively it was done, and what can be expected in the future.

What, then, is the future of multitype library cooperation? It is impossible to predict a pattern simply because the strength of multitype cooperation lies in its spontaneity and its flexibility, in its ability to move quickly in new directions, in its response to membership input through the adoption of new projects, and its willingness to discard programs that have outlived their usefulness. Based on past performance, the outlook is for continued healthy growth.

IMPORTANCE OF THE LOCAL UNIT

The foundation of multitype cooperation is the establishment of close working relationships and the creation and maintenance of functioning channels of communications among the academic, public, school, and special libraries within an area, which, whatever its size—geographic, political, or demographic—forms the logical and workable cooperative unit. It may be urban or rural; it may comprise a single county or a multicounty metropolitan area; it may lie entirely within the confines of one state or spread across the borders of several. Whatever its configuration, it is the local node upon which all other cooperative activity rests. If multitype cooperatives are to grow and develop, then these local nodes must be strong enough in convictions, in organization, in governance, and in programs to serve as the basis of all cooperative activities at succeeding levels—state, regional, national, and international. If the local unit cannot participate in a larger network and bear its share of the load, then the entire network is flawed and the whole cooperative effort suffers.

It has been demonstrated any number of times that the simpler and more manageable in size a program is, the better are its chances to succeed. The programs that are simple in conception and easy to implement and to control are the ones that have had the most lasting impact. If this type of undertaking moves upward from its beginnings at the local level, then the impact is even greater. A directory or union list of statewide magnitude assumes horrendous proportions if data gathering is attempted from the top level down. If, however, the end product is the result of the merger of a number of locally produced lists, then the task becomes more manageable and the results more accurate because of the greater attention paid to detail at the local node.

Small regional and geographically unified consortia or systems can provide speedier reaction and better service than is immediately possible from the larger and more farflung networks. These interlocking systems may serve as the access point to the entire multitype cooperative net, providing greater satisfaction more quickly by circulating requests through the local node and passing those that remain unfilled onward and upward, branching farther and farther afield until what is needed has been found. This would provide the control that seems so essential, and would also allow the larger academic and research libraries to function as last resort centers and to give more attention to those requests that they are best equipped to handle—the difficult and sometimes esoteric ones.

The advent of improved computer technology and its adaption to information processing in libraries have opened many new avenues that will be highly exploited in the years to come. Because of the ease with which information can be stored, retrieved, and manipulated, many tasks can now be accomplished that earlier could only have been achieved manually and with great expenditure of time and money. The possibilities for networking through the application of electronic means seem endless; they will be developed and refined as more and more fertile minds are bent to the task of finding new ways of solving long-standing problems in a non-traditional manner. A simple example of the kind of undertaking that is possible is Interconnect, the developing project between the Illinois State Library and several of the systems that use the CLSI automated circulation system. By setting up an interface between minicomputers, Interconnect will be able to pinpoint the location and status of a given title at any time in any of the participating systems. Were a college or university also using CLSI to join the system, it could tell a student that a badly needed reference for a paper due tomorrow was available right then in his or her local library and perhaps it could place a hold on the title until it could be picked up.

The potential for new cooperative programs is limited only by the variety of needs that are recognized in any given area. The feeling prevalent in some circles that "interlibrary loan" and "multitype cooperative" are synonymous terms must be quashed. There must be a push beyond the traditional toward a greater spread of activity. School libraries, particularly in populous metropolitan areas, must be drawn into closer contact by programs geared to their needs. More attention must be paid to activities that will help staff to grow and develop, especially as active and knowledgeable cooperators. The imaginations of planners will be spurred on constantly by the ever surfacing felt and unfelt needs of users. Librarians, it seems, seek to reach every corner of the community and make everyone ardent library patrons. Until that strongly felt need is satisfied, new and better schemes for reaching nirvana will continue to be developed. The joy of multitype cooperation is in the realization that nothing about it is ever static; there is always something new and different to be done, something of broader scope and wider satisfaction to be accomplished.

APPENDIXES

APPENDIX 1
SELECTED BIBLIOGRAPHY ON
MULTITYPE LIBRARY SERVICE, 1970–1975

BIBLIOGRAPHIES AND DIRECTORIES OF LIBRARY
COOPERATION

Acronyms and Initialisms of Library Networks, 2nd version. Stanford: Stanford University, ERIC Clearinghouse on Information Resources, December 1975. 16 pp. Available from Box E, School of Education, Stanford University, Stanford, Calif. 94305 (check made payable to "Box E" must accompany order; $1.50). ED 114 113.

This second compilation of library network acronyms and initialisms cites 61 networks throughout the United States. Each annotated entry includes the network's acronym or initials, name, and address. A source of further information is cited in many entries, and an ED number is given for references available through the Educational Resources Information Center (ERIC).

ASLA Report on Interlibrary Cooperation. Chicago: Association of State Library Agencies, July 1976. 279 pp. Available from Association of State Library Agencies, 50 E. Huron St., Chicago, Ill. 60611 ($12.50).

This supplement to the 1975 edition of *The State Library Agencies* (Donald B. Simpson, ed., published by ASLA) presents results of a comprehensive survey in the United States conducted by the ASLA Interlibrary Cooperation ad hoc committee, William DeJohn, chairperson. The emphasis is on the role of state library agencies in the area of interlibrary cooperation.

Babcock, Julie. *See* Stenstrom, Ralph H.

Black, Donald W., and Carlos A. Cuadra, comps. *Directory of Academic Library Consortia,* 2nd ed. Santa Monica, Calif.: System Development Corporation, 1976. 437 pp. Available through Baker and Taylor ($25.00).

This revision of a previous directory (Delanoy and Cuadra) includes all library consortia with at least one academic member that compilers were able to locate over a two-year period. Over 400 such consortia are included.

Delanoy, Diana D., and Carlos A. Cuadra, comps. *Directory of Academic Library Consortia.* Santa Monica, Calif.: System Development Corporation, 1972. 308 pp. Available from System Development Corporation, 2500 Colorado Ave., Santa Monica, Calif. 90406 ($12).

Adapted from *A Selected Bibliography on Multitype Library Service 1970–1975.* Jean L. Conner, ed. and comp. Stanford Calif.: ERIC Clearinghouse on Information Resources, 1976, pp. 6–20. (The ERIC Clearinghouse on Information Resources is now located at Syracuse University, School of Education, Syracuse, N.Y. 22210.)

This directory identifies and describes academic library consortia in the continental United States that satisfy the following criteria for inclusion: participating institutions must be autonomous, more than half the members must be academic libraries, two or more libraries must be involved, library consortia must be separate from university consortia with the goal of improving library services, and the consortium must be beyond the exploratory stages and organized so as to benefit the academic participants involved.

Gilluly, Maureen E., and Lucille M. Wert. *See* Stenstrom, Ralph H.

Mantius, Kean. *Supplement to the Directory of Academic Library Consortia.* Santa Monica, Calif.: System Development Corporation, October 1972. 245 pp. Available from System Development Corporation, 2500 Colorado Ave., Santa Monica, Calif. 90406 ($6). ED 072 820.

The decision to produce this supplement came out of a desire to identify and describe a wider range of groups that are participating in the growing movement toward library cooperation. To this end, the criteria for inclusion were significantly relaxed. Cooperatives that were included (1) were not included in the original directory; (2) had at least one academic library member; and (3) were actively engaged in, or actively planning to engage in, cooperative library activities.

Palmini, Cathleen. *See* Stenstrom, Ralph H.

A Selective Annotated Bibliography on Library Networking. Stanford: Stanford University, ERIC Clearinghouse on Information Resources, November 1975. 27 pp. Available from Box E, School of Education, Stanford University, Stanford, Calif. 94305 (check made payable to "Box E" must accompany order; $1.50). ED 115 219.

In response to the increased need for libraries to automate their systems and to share their resources, this bibliography lists some 150 annotated citations, most of which are drawn from the ERIC system, concentrating on library networks. Entries are not categorized.

Stenstrom, Ralph H. *Cooperation between Types of Libraries, 1940–1968: An Annotated Bibliography.* Chicago: American Library Association, 1970. 159 pp. Available from Order Department, American Library Association, 50 E. Huron St., Chicago, Ill. 60611 ($4).

The two requirements for inclusion are that the article deal with cooperation involving more than one type of library and that the program description be in operation. The following are updates to this publication:

Babcock, Julie. *Cooperation between Types of Libraries, 1968–July 1971: An Annotated Bibliography.* Philadelphia: Drexel University, Graduate School of Library Science, September 1971. 32 pp. ED 057 879.

Gilluly, Maureen E., and Lucille M. Wert. "Cooperation between Types of Libraries: An Annotated Bibliography: 1969–1971 Supplement." *Illinois Libraries* 54 (May 1972): 385–400.

Palmini, Cathleen. "Cooperation between Types of Libraries: An Annotated Bibliography: 1971–1972 Supplement." *Illinois Libraries* 55 (May 1973): 358–369.

NATIONAL LEVEL PLANNING AND PROGRAMS

Duggan, Maryann. *Relationship and Involvement of the Multi-State Library and Information Community with the National Program for Library and Information Services. Related Paper No. 16.* Washington, D.C.: National Commission on Libraries and Information Science, National Program for Library and Information Services. In publication. Future availability from ERIC.

Franckowiak, Bernard M. *School Library Media Programs and the National Program for Library and Information Services. Related Paper No. 7.* Washington, D.C.: National Commission on Libraries and Information Science, National Program for Library and Information Services, November 1974. 23 pp. ED 100 393.

The National Program for Library and Information Services could provide substantial improvement in the provision of information services to schools. The national program could provide centralized material processing, automated information retrieval, and staff development opportunities. In return, the school media center could provide expertise in the use of audiovisual technology and open its collection to public use. In order to participate in the national program, a school should meet standards calling for a full range of services in five broad areas: access, reference, production, instruction, and consultation.

Lynch, Beverly P. *National Program of Library and Information Services of NCLIS: Implication for College and Community College Libraries. Related Paper No. 8.* Washington, D.C.: National Commission on Libraries and Information Science, National Program for Library and Information Services, December 1974. 28 pp. ED 100 394.

As educational costs rise and available funds decline, college libraries will be asked to demonstrate that a national plan for sharing library resources and building information networks will be cost beneficial. The resources of many college libraries would be inadequate to meet the standards required for participation in a national program. Financial support would be needed to bring them up to standard.

Martin, Allie Beth. *Role of the Public Library in the National Program. Related Paper No. 2.* Washington, D.C.: National Commission on Libraries and Information Science, National Program for Library and Information Services, October 1974. 31 pp. ED 100 388.

The National Program for Library and Information Services could help overcome some of the barriers to effective public library service. It could aid in financing through increased state and federal funding and in personnel management, selection, and training through programs for library education. It could encourage utilization of technology and accelerate interlibrary and interinstitutional cooperation through a coordinated network of networks.

McDonald, John. *University Libraries and the National Program for Library and Information Services. Related Paper No. 20.* Washington, D.C.: National Commission on Libraries and Information Science, National Program for Library and Information Services. In publication. Future availability from ERIC.

Morton, Elizabeth Homer. *"Cooperation in Canada."* Library Trends 24 (October 1975): 399–416.

Library cooperation in Canada is quite active, and this article mentions only the highlights. Canada has moved through voluntary cooperation, the recommendations of a Royal Commission, and dynamic leadership into an era marked by coordinated cooperation.

Nolting, Orin Frederic. *Mobilizing Total Library Resources for Effective Service.* Chicago: American Library Association, 1969. 20 pp. Out of print.

This pamphlet was prepared as a background paper for a 1969 conference of six divisions of the American Library Association.

Palmour, Vernon E., et al. *Resource and Bibliographic Support for a Nationwide Library Program. Final Report.* Rockville, Md.: Westat Research, Inc., August 1974. 282 pp. ED 095 914.

This study was commissioned to delineate the role of resource and bibliographic centers in the national network of library and information services proposed by the National Commission on Libraries and Information Science. As background material, an overview of existing centers was constructed from earlier interlibrary loan studies; small surveys of public, special, and state library agencies; and staff visits to a number of existing centers and regional networks. To meet the need for improved resource sharing, a recommended structure for the coordination and integration of resource and bibliographic centers into a national network for improved interlibrary loan service was developed.

Strable, Edward G. *The Relationship and Involvement of the Special Library with the National Program. Related Paper No. 3.* Washington, D.C.: National Commission on Libraries and Information Science, National Program for Library and Information Services, November 1974. 26 pp. ED 100 389.

Special libraries can be expected to accept and approve the National Program for Library and Information Services, although certain aspects of the program are antithetical to the nature of the special library. Traditionally independent, special libraries tend to have a local rather than national orientation and to resist standardization. Special libraries are well prepared to accept the national program's emphases on the information function and on the use of new technologies.

Swartz, Roderick G. *"The Need for Cooperation among Libraries in the United States."* Library Trends 24 (October 1975): 215–228.

It is the purpose of this article to take a critical look at the validity of library cooperation based on the recent increase of user need and demand studies and to determine whether cooperation really has been and will continue to be the key to meeting those needs and demands.

Sylvestre, Guy. *"The Developing National Library Network of Canada."* Library Resources and Technical Services 16 (Winter 1972): 48–60.

Discussed are recent library developments in Canada, main problems at the national level, and efforts by the federal government to develop a better integrated national information network.

Toward a National Program for Library and Information Services: Goals for Action. Washington, D.C.: National Commission on Libraries and Information Science, National Program for Library and Information Services, June 1975. 115 pp. Available from Superintendent of Documents, U.S. Government Printing Office, Washington, D.C. 20402 (Stock No. 052-003-00086-5; $1.45). ED 107 312.

The National Commission on Libraries and Information Science presents its goals and plans for a national program of library and information services with the intention of satisfying the nation's information needs to the greatest extent possible. The basic needs and rationale for a national program are stated, and a survey is made of the present situation of public, special, school, university, research, academic, state, and federal libraries and information services.

Trezza, Alphonse F. *Relationship and Involvement of the State Library Agencies with the National Program Proposed by NCLIS. Related Paper No. 1.* Washington, D.C.: National Commission on Libraries and Information Science, National Program for Library and Information Services, November 1974. 11 pp. ED 100 387.

Since the 1960s, state library agencies have been involved in bibliographical systems and networks. In the 1970s, these agencies completed long-range plans to meet each state's library service needs. Because of this experience, the state library agencies are the natural coordinators for carrying out any national program for library and information services.

STATE- AND INTERSTATE-LEVEL PLANNING AND PROGRAMS

Brong, Gerald R. *"The State of Washington's Search for Intrastate Cooperation."* *Library Trends* 24 (October 1975): 257–276.

The goals for this article are to show how cooperative development and operation is the most feasible route to maximize library/information service for a state; to demonstrate that these cooperative efforts are extremely fragile; to provide a strategy to ensure maximized library/information service based on cooperative development and system operation; and to present a model of a cooperative planning strategy, based on current efforts in Washington state, that could lead to the provision of maximized service.

California Public Library Systems: A Comprehensive Review with Guidelines for the Next Decade. Sacramento: California State Library, June 1975. 269 pp. ED 105 906.

An extensive study was conducted to determine if California's Public Library Services Act had succeeded in its goal of improving and extending library service through the establishment and funding of library systems. It was concluded that public library systems in California have demonstrated a limited but constructive value under adverse circumstances. The systems have met substantial public needs for resource sharing, but inadequate funding has prevented optimal service. It was recommended that a top-level consortium of the strongest libraries in the state be created to meet requests that cannot be filled elsewhere.

Casey, Genevieve M. *"Emerging State and Regional Library Networks."* In *Proceedings of the Conference on Interlibrary Communications and Information Networks.* Edited by Joseph Becker. Chicago: American Library Association, 1971.

Available from American Library Association, 50 E. Huron St., Chicago, Ill. 60611 ($15). 36 pp. ED 057 849.

This paper is concerned with the growing edge of librarianship today, that is, with state and regional networks combining resources of several types of libraries. It is based largely upon reports from the states on their administration of the Library Services and Construction Act, filed with the Bureau of Libraries and Education Technology of the U.S. Office of Education, and upon information received directly from state library agencies.

Casey, Genevieve M. *Structuring the Indiana State Library for Interlibrary Coordination. Indiana Library Studies Report 16.* Bloomington: Indiana Library Studies, 1970. 108 pp. ED 044 144.

It was recommended that the Indiana State Library should convene a permanent council for the improvement of library and information services to students and teachers; convene a permanent council for the coordinated building and use of major subject collections: initiate contracts with appropriate major resource libraries to provide 24-hour access to materials, bibliographical searches, and current awareness services to professional groups; and build its collections in fields not covered by other resource libraries.

Chanaud, Jo, ed. *"Interlibrary Cooperation Studied."* Leads 2, October-November 1974. (WICHE, Continuing Education and Library Resources Program, Drawer P, Boulder, Colo. 80302; no longer published.)

This double issue is devoted to a report on an institute, Training the Trainers to Train for Interlibrary Cooperation and Networking, funded by the U.S. Office of Education, July 1974 to June 1975, and conducted by the Western Interstate Commission for Higher Education (WICHE).

Clark, Collin, ed. *Proceedings of the Library Planning Institute, June 23–27, 1975.* Sacramento: California State Library, 1975. 222 pp. Available from Government Publication Section, California State Library, Sacramento, Calif. 95809 (Call number L575 L5P).

The Library Planning Institute brought over 100 participants to San Francisco for a week-long conference, June 23–27, 1975. Included were library trustees, friends, concerned citizens, and librarians representing every type of library. Institute Director Ethel Crockett called upon the group to come up with a statewide plan to provide the best possible library service to Californians over the next decade, at a cost that is acceptable; and begin to shape that plan into a legislative package to give a workable structure and indication of adequate funding at the state level. The institute agenda included talks by state and local government officials, social planners, and eminent visiting librarians, as well as small working sessions involving all participants.

Dejohn, William, and Bridget L. Lamont, eds. *"The Multitype Library Network."* *Illinois Libraries* 57 (June 1975): 1–88. ED 108 692.

This issue of *Illinois Libraries* is devoted to interlibrary cooperation and the multitype library network as exemplified by the Illinois Library and Information Network (ILLINET). The history, geographic coverage, member and affiliate libraries, and the workings of the network at various levels are described. A second section describes the integration of academic, special, and school libraries, along with special resource centers, into a multitype library network. Further activities of ILLINET are outlined in the third section.

Faibisoff, Sylvia G. *Regional Coordination: A Point of View.* Ithaca, N.Y.: South Central Research Library Council, April 1975 (Paper presented at the New York State Library System Conference). 22 pp. ED 108 709.

To provide more adequately for newly perceived user needs, New York State libraries have adopted the philosophy of regionalism through which public, academic, and special libraries can cooperate and share resources. In order to create a statewide network and to communicate with the regions, an administrative unit at the state level could be most responsive if divided by function—a resource section, a collection development section, an interlibrary loan section, a communication and delivery section, and a budget section.

Flaherty, Kevin, et al. *Ohio Library Development and Interlibrary Cooperation. A Background Paper Prepared for the Interlibrary Cooperation Planning Institute at the Ohio State University, October 26–28, 1975.* Columbus: State Library of Ohio, October 1975. 50 pp. Available from State Library of Ohio, 65 S. Front St., Columbus, Ohio 43215 (free).

The Multitype Library Cooperative Experience is among several topics covered in this background paper. Other subjects are Ohio: A Mini-View, Examination of Library Resources and Services, and State and Federal Responsibilities for Library Services.

Hacker, Harold S. *"Implementing Network Plans: Jurisdictional Considerations in the Design of Library Networks."* In *Proceedings of the Conference on Interlibrary Communications and Information Networks.* Edited by Joseph Becker. Chicago: American Library Association, 1971. Available from American Library Association, 50 E. Huron St., Chicago, Ill. 60611 ($15). 79 pp. ED 057 869.

The purpose of this paper is to suggest some steps that must be taken to convert network planning into reality, based upon experiences in New York State.

Interlibrary Cooperation in the Baltimore-Washington Area. Washington, D.C.: Committee on Information Hang-ups, May 1971. 6 pp. ED 053 726.

A survey of interlibrary cooperative projects in the Baltimore-Washington metropolitan area that could be identified during the winter and spring months of 1970–1971 is presented. Cooperative projects included union lists; networks in use; and informal organizations started to fill the need for interlibrary loans among small libraries of similar interests.

Kittel, Dorothy. *"Trends in State Library Cooperation."* *Library Trends* 24 (October 1975): 245–256. A similar article with the same title is available from Superintendent of Documents, U.S. Government Printing Office, Washington, D.C. 20402 (Stock Number 017-080-01467-0; $.40).

This brief review of intertype library cooperative activities makes it apparent that librarians and users of information have devised many strategies and systems to get the information they need. There is great concern about the need for a "national network" and for compatibility among the various state and regional networks. However, it seems clear that networks and other cooperative activities are being developed at the local, state, and regional levels to meet specific needs at those levels. It is doubtful that a "national network" can be designed to meet state and local requirements for all kinds of information transmission.

Library Service, A Statement of Policy and Proposed Action by the Regents of the University of the State of New York. Position Paper 8. Albany: New York State Education Department, October 1970. 32 pp. Available from Gift and Exchange Section, New York State Library, Albany, N.Y. 12224. ED 045 101 (microfiche only).

A plan by which library service and development in New York State can respond to rapid and dynamic changes in society is outlined. The program is based on the principles that all state residents have a right to convenient access to local libraries to meet their needs, that statewide library networks constitute the most efficient means to provide quality user service, and that an integrated library network should be developed.

McClarren, Robert R. *"State Legislation Relating to Library Systems."* Library *Trends* 19 (October 1970): 235–249.

A definition of the term "library system" is followed by a discussion of state legislation relating to library systems.

McCrossan, James A., and Henry O. Marcy. *"Interlibrary Cooperation and Coordination in Vermont."* Catholic Library World 46 (March 1975): 344–345.

The activities of the Vermont Department of Libraries in library cooperation are outlined.

Martin, Harry S. *"Coordination by Compact: A Legal Basis for Interstate Library Cooperation."* Library Trends 24 (October 1975): 191–214.

After a brief survey of the variety of legal devices traditionally used to support library cooperation, this article examines one device, the interstate compact, which holds promise as a coordinating tool. It is advanced that the compact, which has been used in other areas of American federalism, can be applied to the coordination of the nation's information resources.

Master Plan for the Development of Library Services in the State of Maryland, 1976–1980. Baltimore: Maryland State Department of Education, December 1974. Not paginated. Available from Bill Streamer, Maryland State Department of Education, Division of Library Development and Services, Box 8717, Baltimore-Washington International Airport, Baltimore, Md. 21240 (free).

This plan, drawn up at the request of the state governor, was designed to achieve the following: to ensure convenient access to library resources in the state, to provide for the most effective and economic utilization of library and information resources, to provide a policy and program statement for library coordination and development, to delineate state responsibilities and functions, and to provide public information and understanding of library resources and programs. Sections cover Planned Library Service, Maryland's Public Libraries, the State Library Network and Cooperative Library Services, School and Academic Libraries, and Physical Facilities.

The Next Step for North Carolina Libraries: A Libraries Services Network; The Report of a Feasibility Study of the North Carolina Libraries Services Network. Raleigh: North Carolina State Board of Higher Education, January 1971. 26 pp. ED 049 806.

The study finds that North Carolina is only partly prepared to take maximum advantage of the knowledge explosion that is taking place in the United States. It recommends recognition of the North Carolina Libraries Services Network and its expansion to link all information sources with potential users, thus finally achieving a coordinate statewide library service system.

Ohio College Library Center. Annual Report, 1971/1972. Columbus: Ohio College Library Center, 1972. 20 pp. ED 067 118.

The outstanding accomplishment reported in the fifth annual report of the Ohio College Library Center was the implementation, operation, and enhancement of the on-line union catalog and shared cataloging system. Another important development in the history of the center was the decision by the members to extend membership to include nonacademic libraries in Ohio. (The previous four annual reports of OCLC are available as ED 059 730.)

Pennsylvania Library Master Plan Committee Report. Harrisburg: Pennsylvania State Library, 1974. 54 pp. ED 095 866.

The Pennsylvania Master Plan Committee, composed of librarians from all types of libraries and also of other interested citizens, reports on goals, present status, and recommendations for the future of Pennsylvania libraries.

A Plan for a Wisconsin Library and Information Network: Knowledge Network of Wisconsin. Madison: Wisconsin State Department of Instruction, Division of Library Services, 1970. 109 pp. ED 043 358.

This report explores the potential for furthering interlibrary cooperation in Wisconsin by investigating various ways of linking the state's library systems with other information centers into a network. The plan has four main objectives: to promote increased sharing of resources by libraries, to use modern technology in an appropriate and economical manner to facilitate the distribution of information, to equalize the availability of library materials, and to create a comprehensive base of library and information materials with a minimum of duplication and processing.

Report of the Commissioner of Education's Committee on Library Development. Albany: New York State Education Department, 1970. 86 pp. Available from Gift and Exchange Section, New York State Library, Albany N.Y. 12224 ($1). ED 042 482 (microfiche only).

The committee's recommendations cover user access to library services, structure and relationships, special categories of library services, the government of libraries, the resources of libraries, research and evaluation, and finance.

SLICE Office Report for the Period July 1, 1974 to December 31, 1974. Final Report. Dallas: Southwestern Library Interstate Cooperative Endeavor, January 1975. 168 pp. ED 103 003.

The Southwestern Library Interstate Cooperative Endeavor project was an experimental effort to determine the feasibility of a multistate library coordination agency involving the states of Arizona, Arkansas, Louisiana, New Mexico, Oklahoma, and Texas. The success or failure of the project's specific objectives is outlined in this final report. The bulk of the document consists of appendixes containing papers commissioned by SLICE.

Trezza, Alphonse F., and Albert Halcli. *"The Role of Local and State Governments." Library Trends* 23 (October 1974): 229–238.

Local government is not able to bear the burden of financing city libraries. Financial support from the state and federal governments and resource sharing among libraries are necessary.

Young, Heartsill H., et al. *"A Regional Association Launches Cooperative Endeavors." Library Trends* 24 (October 1975): 307–330.

The Southwestern Library Association is examined as a regional association promoting interstate library cooperation. Its history is traced from its beginnings in 1922 through a period of awakening and transformation in the late 1960s and early 1970s. The strategy of this transformation is discussed.

VARIED APPROACHES TO MULTITYPE LIBRARY COOPERATION

Anderson, LeMoyne W., ed. *Networks and the University Library: Proceedings of an Institute Presented by the University Libraries Section, Association of College and Research Libraries, at Las Vegas, Nevada, June 21, 22 & 23, 1973.* Chicago: Association of College and Research Libraries, 1974. 90 pp. Available from Beverly Lynch, ACRL, 50 E. Huron St., Chicago, Ill. 60611 ($3 prepaid, $5 with billing).

This collection of papers presented at the 1973 American Library Association Pre-Conference reports on developments of formal organizational structures, or networks, for library interaction. Over a dozen papers are included, dealing with OCLC, BALLOTS, the MINITEX network, the TIE cooperative, the MARLIN network, and others.

Bird, Warren, and David Skene Melvin, comps. *Library Telecommunications Directory: Canada-United States.* 5th ed., rev. Durham, N.C.: Duke University Medical Center Library, 1973. 35 pp. Available from Duke University Medical Center Library, Durham, N.C. 27706 ($2).

NOTE: The sixth edition of this directory is scheduled for June 1976 publication, with about the same number of pages and price.

Booth, Barry E., ed. *"Intertype Library Cooperation." Illinois Libraries* 54 (May 1972).

This issue contains articles on intertype library cooperation as it relates to the national view, planning by state agencies, nodes beginning to form, and comments of librarians. (This issue's bibliography is cited individually in the first section of this paper.)

————. *"Network Nodes." Illinois Libraries* 55 (May 1973).

This issue contains articles on several aspects of networking, including network synergism, the SLICE project, WICHE, OCLC, and other projects. (This issue's bibliography is cited individually in the first section of this paper.)

Casey, Genevieve M. *The Public Library in the Network Mode: A Preliminary Investigation. Commissioned Papers Project, Teachers College, No. 8.* New York: Columbia University, Teachers College, May 1974. 124 pp. ED 098 990.

The role of the public library within intertype library networks was studied using published reports and information provided by selected state and regional libraries. It was concluded that the intertype network is a rapidly spreading phenomenon and that the public library commonly serves as its nucleus. It was recommended that national coordination, with shared state and federal responsibility, should begin.

Cuadra, Carlos A., and Ruth J. Patrick. *"Survey of Academic Library Consortia in the U.S."* College and Research Libraries 33 (July 1972): 271–283.

This paper discusses the survey methodology, the findings, and two major products of a 1970 nationwide study of academic library consortia. The study involved a questionnaire survey to identify and describe all known consortia and a case-study analysis of 15 selected consortia.

Dagnese, Joseph M. *"Cooperation between Academic and Special Libraries."* Special Libraries 64 (October 1973): 423–432.

The concept of library cooperation is examined generally. The question of the probable future of cooperation between academic and special libraries is addressed and possible support mechanisms for establishing soundly based cooperative undertakings are suggested.

Flynn, M. Elizabeth. *The Community's Educational Resources Centers: Public Libraries/School Media Programs.* June 1972. 7 pp. ED 063 954.

In Massachusetts municipalities there exists the need to develop at the policymaking, fiscal, and administrative levels an awareness, understanding, and knowledge of the functions, objectives, and roles of both the public library and the school media program in relation to children and young adults. Total library media service to the young people of the community presupposes effective working relationships at a decision-making level for both resource centers. The functions of each library program are clearly distinct in the educational scheme of every municipality.

Haycock, Ken. *The School Media Centre and the Public Library: Combination or Co-Operation.* Toronto: Ontario Library Association, School Libraries Division, 1974. 18 pp. Available from Ontario Library Association, 2397 Bloor St. W., Toronto M6S 1P8, Canada ($1 including postage and handling).

In considering possible combinations of public and school library services, thought must be given to the varying roles of the two kinds of libraries, the location of facilities, the collection and circulation of materials, hours of services, qualifications of staff, system services, and community involvement.

Healey, James S. *"Public-Academic Library Cooperation."* College and Research Libraries 32 (March 1971): 121–126.

The legal and structural arrangements for public-academic library cooperation are examined. Rhode Island's program illustrates the problems involved as well as the importance of the role of the state library agency in successfully establishing cooperative programs.

Humphry, John A. *"The Place of Urban Main Libraries in Larger Library Networks."* *Library Trends* 20 (April 1972): 673–692.

Using results of a 1971 survey of the directors of urban main libraries throughout the United States, the author points out that these libraries have much to offer networks and should be given a voice in their operation and funding.

Izard, Anne R. *"Children's Librarians in 1970."* *American Libraries* 2 (October 1971): 973–976.

The article makes a case against the *Report of the Commissioner of Education's Committee on Library Development* (see page 15). Instead of eliminating public library service to children, it recommends total community coordination of planning and budget, including city administrators, public library administrators, school administrators, school librarians, and public librarians serving children.

Josey, E. J., ed. *New Dimensions for Academic Library Service.* Metuchen, N.J.: Scarecrow Press, 1975. 349 pp. Available from Scarecrow Press, Box 656, Metuchen, N.J. 08840 ($12).

The 25 essays written for this compilation focus on a variety of initiatives undertaken by librarians, information scientists, and educators to give increased service with diminished funding. The fourth part focuses upon patterns of library information systems, networks, and consortia.

Kilgour, Frederick G. *"Computer-Based Systems: A New Dimension to Library Cooperation."* *College and Research Libraries* 34 (March 1973): 137–143.

The experiences of the Ohio College Library Center's computer-based cataloging system illustrate how the computer can facilitate interlibrary cooperation. The paper also presents some of the difficult organizational problems in developing a computer-based cooperative system.

Kitchens, James A. *The Olney Venture: An Experiment in Coordination and Merger of School and Public Libraries. Community Service Report No. 4.* Denton, Tex.: North Texas State University, Center for Community Services, School of Community Service, 1975. 55 pp. Available from James A. Kitchens, Department of Sociology, North Texas State University, Denton, Tex. 76203 (free).

Olney, Tex., a town of 4,000 people, reports on a venture of designing a new information and resource center—a single, unified, coordinated community library.

Lindauer, Dinah. *"Regional Coordination—A Modest Proposal."* *The Bookmark. News about Library Services* (May-June 1975): 135–137. Available from R. Edwin Berry, Division of Library Development, 99 Washington Ave., Rm. 1505, Albany, N.Y. 12230 (free).

In a speech given at the First Annual New York State Library Systems Conference in Albany in April 1975, the author discusses how to begin to bring the 500 schools in Nassau County into the existing interloan network.

McNamee, Gill. *Contemporary Trends in Information Delivery. Program for a Workshop. December 11 and 12, 1974, San Francisco Public Library.* San Francisco: San Francisco Public Library, California Bay Area Reference Center, December 1974. 54 pp. ED 101 715.

A workshop, Current Trends in Information Delivery, held in December 1974, was attended by 337 librarians, including Joseph Becker from the National Commission on Libraries and Information Science, who spoke about the national library network that NCLIS is proposing; Gerald Newton of the California State Library, who spoke on library networking in the United States and California; and Gil McNamee, Bay Area Reference Center director, who spoke on the proposed 17-stage Western Regional Library Network.

Miller, Elizabeth K. *"RUIN: A Network for Urban and Regional Studies Libraries."* *Special Libraries* 64 (November 1973): 498–504.

The advantages of network building among small- to medium-sized libraries catering to multi- or interdisciplinary information users are investigated and the practical application of networking being developed by a group of Washington, D.C., area urban studies libraries (tentatively named RUIN—Regional and Urban Information Network) is discussed.

Morris, Effie Lee. *"Library Service to the 'Whole Child.'"* *The Bookmark. News about Library Services* (April 1971): 241–245. Available from R. Edwin Berry, Division of Library Development, 99 Washington Ave., Rm. 1505, Albany, N.Y. 12230 (free).

In a speech given at the Second Conference on School/Public Library Relations held in Syracuse, February 1971, the author presents arguments for retaining and improving children's departments in public libraries, rather than allowing school libraries to assume this role totally.

"Networks: Who, Why, How?" *Wisconsin Library Bulletin* 71 (May–June 1975): 1–52. ED 108 693.

Articles about library cooperative programs and networks cover the following subjects: library network planning and definitions of terms; views on the National Commission on Libraries and Information Science program by school, public, academic, and state librarians; the Midwest Library Network; and school/public library access and cooperation.

Nitecki, Danuta A. *Attitudes towards Interlibrary Cooperation: Summary of a Study.* Philadelphia: Drexel University, Graduate School of Library Science, 1971, 21 pp. ED 066 167.

The participants in the Workshop on Cooperation between Different Types of Libraries, which was held in November 1971 in Philadelphia, were surveyed in an effort to determine their attitudes toward interlibrary cooperation. Followup studies were conducted after the workshop to discover what, if any, effect the workshop had on the participants' attitudes. Generally, the workshop participants favored cooperative efforts among different types of libraries, although some problems were perceived. At the end of the workshop, 70 percent of the respondents agreed that the lack of creative administrative leadership was a significant barrier to interlibrary cooperation, while only 10 percent agreed six months later in followup studies.

Olson, Edwin E. *Interlibrary Cooperation. Final Report.* College Park: Maryland University, School of Library and Information Services, September 1970. 151 pp. ED 046 421.

The major dimensions of interlibrary cooperation that have implications for manpower development in librarianship are identified, categorized, and described. These dimensions include the "power budget" of a cooperative, that is, the capability of a cooperative as represented by its structure, resources, and decision-making processes to accomplish its goals; the "domain" of a cooperative—the current and future claims the cooperative stakes out for itself; and a cooperative's "opportunities and constraints," such as orientation of director, capabilities of the staff, and the perceived barriers to goal achievement that intervene between a cooperative's power budget and its successful establishment and defense of a domain.

Patrick, Ruth A. *Guidelines for Library Cooperation.* Santa Monica, Calif.: System Development Corporation, 1972. 200 pp. Available from System Development Corporation, 2500 Colorado Ave., Santa Monica, Calif. 90406 ($15, photocopy).

This description of a study of academic library consortia provides guidelines on how to form or participate in a consortium. A model of the consortium process and recommendations are outlined.

Reynolds, Michael M., ed. *Reader in Library Cooperation.* Washington, D.C.: NCR Microcard Editions, 1972. 398 pp. $12.95.

Part of the Reader Series in Library and Information Science, this publication contains articles from many sources dealing with behavioral, theoretical, organizational, functional, and operational generalizations about library inter-relationships.

Rowell, John. *"Library Service to the 'Whole Child.' "* The Bookmark. News about Library Services (April 1971): 245–251. Available from R. Edwin Berry, Division of Library Development, 99 Washington St., Rm. 1505, Albany, N.Y. 12230 (free).

In a speech given at the Second Conference on School/Public Library Relations held in Syracuse, February 1971, John Rowell discusses the New York State model library pilot program.

Spicer, Michael W. *A Comparative Analysis of Five Regional and Information Networks.* Columbus: Ohio State Library, August 1972. 36 pp. ED 071 667.

This study of five regional reference networks in the state of Ohio has emerged as an outcome of the cooperation of state and local library personnel. The purpose was to analyze five of the Regional Reference and Information Networks in Ohio from a comparative viewpoint. The study sought to compare the finance, organization, and scope of the networks and to evaluate the networks using three key criteria: service to the patron, time taken to provide the service, and cost of that service.

Swank, Raynard C. *"Interlibrary Cooperation, Interlibrary Communications, and Information Networks—Explanation and Definition."* In Proceedings of the Conference on Interlibrary Communications and Information Networks. Edited by Joseph Becker. Chicago: American Library Association, 1971. Available from American Library Association, 50 E. Huron St., Chicago, Ill. 60611 ($15). 30 pp. ED 057 847.

Information networks are defined as having information resources, readers or users, schemes for the intellectual organization of documents and data, methods for the delivery of resources to users, formal organizations of cooperating or contracting information agencies, and bidirectional communications facilities. The major concerns of the conference in each of these broad areas are explained.

Weber, David C., and Frederick C. Lynden. *"Survey of Interlibrary Cooperation."* In *Proceedings of the Conference on Interlibrary Communications and Information Networks.* Edited by Joseph Becker. Chicago: American Library Association, 1971. Available from American Library Association, 50 E. Huron St., Chicago, Ill. 60611 ($15). 57 pp. ED 057 852.

The most significant trends in interlibrary cooperation are summarized and some early examples and developments to the present day are selectively reviewed. Except for a small section on international library cooperation, the concentration is on cooperation among public, state, special, academic, and federal libraries of the United States. The paper is divided into two parts: cooperation by type of library organization and cooperation by function, and in each part the major problems are briefly identified.

APPENDIX 2
LIBRARY SERVICES AND CONSTRUCTION ACT

(United States Code Annotated, 1974 Suppl., Title 20,
S. 351a-351e, 361-364.)

§ 351a. Definitions

The following definitions shall apply to this chapter:

(1) "Commissioner" means the Commissioner of Education.

(2) "Construction" includes construction of new buildings and acquisition, expansion, remodeling, and alteration of existing buildings, and initial equipment of any such buildings, or any combination of such activities (including architects' fees and the cost of acquisition of land). For the purposes of this paragraph, the term "equipment" includes machinery, utilities, and built-in equipment and any necessary enclosures or structures to house them; and such term includes all other items necessary for the functioning of a particular facility as a facility for the provision of library services.

(3) "Library service" means the performance of all activities of a library relating to the collection and organization of library materials and to making the materials and information of a library available to a clientele.

(4) "Library services for the physically handicapped" means the providing of library services, through public or other nonprofit libraries, agencies, or organizations, to physically handicapped persons (including the blind and other visually handicapped) certified by competent authority as unable to read or to use conventional printed materials as a result of physical limitations.

(5) "Public library" means a library that serves free of charge all residents of a community, district, or region, and receives its financial support in whole or in part from public funds. Such term also includes a research library, which, for the purposes of this sentence, means a library which—

  (A) makes its services available to the public free of charge;

  (B) has extensive collections of books, manuscripts, and other materials suitable for scholarly research which are not available to the public through public libraries;

  (C) engages in the dissemination of humanistic knowledge through services to readers, fellowships, educational and cultural programs, publication of significant research, and other activities; and

  (D) is not an integral part of an institution of higher education.

(6) "Public library services" means library services furnished by a public library free of charge.

(7) "State" means a State, the District of Columbia, the Commonwealth of Puerto Rico, Guam, American Samoa, the Virgin Islands, or the Trust Territory of the Pacific Islands.

(8) "State Advisory Council on Libraries" means an advisory council for the purposes of clause (3) of section 351d(a) of this title which shall—

(A) be broadly representative of the public, school, academic, special, and institutional libraries, and libraries serving the handicapped, in the State and of persons using such libraries, including disadvantaged persons within the State;

(B) advise the State library administrative agency on the development of, and policy matters arising in the administration of, the State plan; and

(C) assist the State library administrative agency in the evaluation of activities assisted under this chapter;

(9) "State institutional library services" means the providing of books and other library materials, and of library services, to (A) inmates, patients, or residents of penal institutions, reformatories, residential training schools, orphanages, or general or special institutions or hospitals operated or substantially supported by the State, or (B) students in residential schools for the physically handicapped (including mentally retarded, hard of hearing, deaf, speech impaired, visually handicapped, seriously emotionally disturbed, crippled, or other health impaired persons who by reason thereof require special education) operated or substantially supported by the State.

(10) "State Library administrative agency" means the official agency of a State charged by law of that State with the extension and development of public library services throughout the State, which has adequate authority under law of the State to administer State plans in accordance with the provisions of this chapter.

(11) "Basic State plan" means the document which gives assurances that the officially designated State library administrative agency has the fiscal and legal authority and capability to administer all aspects of this chapter; provides assurances for establishing the State's policies, priorities, criteria, and procedures necessary to the implementation of all programs under provisions of this chapter; and submits copies for approval as required by regulations promulgated by the Commissioner.

(12) "Long-range program" means the comprehensive five-year program which identifies a State's library needs and sets forth the activities to be taken toward meeting the identified needs supported with the assistance of Federal funds made available under this chapter. Such long-range programs shall be developed by the State library administrative agency and shall specify the State's policies, criteria, priorities, and procedures consistent with this chapter as required by the regulations promulgated by the Commissioner and shall be updated as library progress requires.

(13) "Annual program" means the projects which are developed and submitted to describe the specific activities to be carried out annually toward achieving fulfillment of the long-range program. These annual programs shall be submitted in such detail as required by regulations promulgated by the Commissioner.

June 19, 1956, c. 407, § 3, as added Dec. 30, 1970, Pub.L. 91-600, § 2(b), 84 Stat. 1660, and amended Oct. 19, 1973, Pub.L. 93-133, § 4(a), 87 Stat. 466.

§ 351b. Authorization of appropriations; availability of appropriations

(a) For the purpose of carrying out the provisions of this chapter the following sums are authorized to be appropriated:

(1) For the purpose of making grants to States for library services as provided in subchapter I of this chapter, there are authorized to be appropriated $112,000,000 for the fiscal year ending June 30, 1972, $117,600,000 for the fiscal year ending June 30, 1973, $123,500,000 for the fiscal year ending June

30, 1974, $129,675,000 for the fiscal year ending June 30, 1975, and $137,150,000 for the fiscal year ending June 30, 1976.

(2) For the purpose of making grants to States for public library construction, as provided in subchapter II of this chapter, there are authorized to be appropriated $80,000,000 for the fiscal year ending June 30, 1972, $84,000,000 for the fiscal year ending June 30, 1973, $88,000,000 for the fiscal year ending June 30, 1974, $92,500,000 for the fiscal year ending June 30, 1975, and $97,000,000 for the fiscal year ending June 30, 1976.

(3) For the purpose of making grants to States to enable them to carry out interlibrary cooperation programs authorized by subchapter III of this chapter, there are hereby authorized to be appropriated $15,000,000 for the fiscal year ending June 30, 1972, $15,750,000 for the fiscal year ending June 30, 1973, $16,500,000 for the fiscal year ending June 30, 1974, $17,300,000 for the fiscal year ending June 30, 1975, and $18,200,000 for the fiscal year ending June 30, 1976.

(4) For the purpose of making grants to States to enable them to carry out public library service programs for older persons authorized by subchapter IV of this chapter, there are authorized to be appropriated such sums as may be necessary for the fiscal year ending June 30, 1973, the fiscal year ending June 30, 1974, and fiscal year ending June 30, 1975, and the fiscal year ending June 30, 1976.

(b) Notwithstanding any other provision of law, unless enacted in express limitation of the provisions of this subsection, any sums appropriated pursuant to subsection (a) of this section shall (1), in the case of sums appropriated pursuant to paragraphs (1) and (3) thereof, be available for obligation and expenditure for the period of time specified in the Act making such appropriation, and (2), in the case of sums appropriated pursuant to paragraph (2) thereof, subject to regulations of the Commissioner promulgated in carrying out the provisions of section 351c(b) of this title, be available for obligation and expenditure for the year specified in the Appropriation Act and for the next succeeding year.

June 19, 1956, c. 407, § 4, as added Dec. 30, 1970, Pub.L. 91-600, § 2(b), 84 Stat. 1662, and amended May 3, 1973, Pub.L. 93-29, Title VIII, § 801(b), 87 Stat. 58.

§ 351c. Allotments to States; minimum allotment; population basis for distribution of remaining funds; reallotment

(a) (1) From the sums appropriated pursuant to paragraph (1), (2), (3), or (4) of section 351b(a) of this title for any fiscal year, the Commissioner shall allot the minimum allotment, as determined under paragraph (3) of this subsection, to each State. Any sums remaining after minimum allotments have been made shall be allotted in the manner set forth in paragraph (2) of this subsection.

(2) From the remainder of any sums, appropriated pursuant to paragraph (1), (2), (3), or (4) of section 351b(a) of this title for any fiscal year, the Commissioner shall allot to each State such part of such remainder as the population of the State bears to the population of all the States.

(3) For the purposes of this subsection, the "minimum allotment" shall be—

(A) with respect to appropriations for the purposes of subchapter I of this chapter, $200,000 for each State, except that it shall be $40,000 in the case of Guam, American Samoa, the Virgin Islands, and the Trust Territory of the Pacific Islands;

(B) with respect to appropriations for the purposes of subchapter II of this chapter, $100,000 for each State, except that it shall be $20,000 in the case of

Guam, American Samoa, the Virgin Islands, and the Trust Territory of the Pacific Islands;

(C) with respect to appropriations for the purposes of subchapter III of this chapter, $40,000 for each State, except that it shall be $10,000 in the case of Guam, American Samoa, the Virgin Islands, and the Trust Territory of the Pacific Islands; and

(D) with respect to appropriations for the purposes of subchapter IV of this chapter, $40,000 for each State, except that it shall be $10,000 in the case of Guam, American Samoa, the Virgin Islands, and the Trust Territory of the Pacific Islands.

If the sums appropriated pursuant to paragraph (1), (2), (3), or (4) of section 351b(a) of this title for any fiscal year are insufficient to fully satisfy the aggregate of the minimum allotments for that purpose, each of such minimum allotments shall be reduced ratably.

(4) The population of each State and of all the States shall be determined by the Commissioner on the basis of the most recent satisfactory data available to him.

(5) There is hereby authorized for the purpose of evaluation (directly or by grants or contracts) of programs authorized by this chapter, such sums as Congress may deem necessary for any fiscal year.

(b) The amount of any State's allotment under subsection (a) of this section for any fiscal year from any appropriation made pursuant to paragraph (1), (2), (3), or (4) of section 351b(a) of this title which the Commissioner deems will not be required for the period and the purpose for which such allotment is available for carrying out the State's annual program shall be available for reallotment from time to time on such dates during such year as the Commissioner shall fix. Such amount shall be available for reallotment to other States in proportion to the original allotments for such year to such States under subsection (a) of this section but with such proportionate amount for any of such other State being reduced to the extent that it exceeds the amount which the Commissioner estimates the State needs and will be able to use for such period of time for which the original allotments were made and the total of such reductions shall be similarly reallotted among the States not suffering such a reduction. Any amount reallotted to a State under this subsection for any fiscal year shall be deemed to be a part of its allotment for such year pursuant to subsection (a) of this section.

June 19, 1956, c. 407, § 5, as added Dec. 30, 1970, Pub.L. 91-600, § 2(b), 84 Stat. 1662, and amended May 3, 1973, Pub.L. 93-29, Title VIII, § 801(c), 87 Stat. 58.

§ 351d. State plans and programs—Prerequisites for allotment of basic State plan in effect, submission of annual program, and establishment of State Advisory Council on Libraries

(a) Any State desiring to receive its allotment for any purpose under this chapter for any fiscal year shall (1) have in effect for such fiscal year a basic State plan as defined in section 351a(11) of this title and meeting the requirements set forth in subsection (b) of this section, (2) submit an annual program as defined in section 351a(13) of this title for the purposes for which allotments are desired, meeting the appropriate requirements set forth in subchapters I, II, III, and IV of this chapter, and shall submit (no later than July 1, 1972) a long-range program as defined in section 351a(12) of this title for carrying out the purposes of this chapter as specified in subsection (d) of this section, and (3) establish a State Advisory Council on Libraries which meets the requirements of section 351a(8) of this title.

Provisions of plan

(b) A basic State plan under this chapter shall—

(1) provide for the administration, or supervision of the administration, of the programs authorized by this chapter by the State library administrative agency;

(2) provide that any funds paid to the State in accordance with a long-range program and an annual program shall be expended solely for the purposes for which funds have been authorized and appropriated and that such fiscal control and fund accounting procedures have been adopted as may be necessary to assure·proper disbursement of, and account for, Federal funds paid to the State (including any such funds paid by the State to any other agency) under this chapter;

(3) provide satisfactory assurance that the State agency administering the plan (A) will make such reports, in such form and containing such information, as the Commissioner may reasonably require to carry out his functions under this chapter and to determine the extent to which funds provided under this chapter have been effective in carrying out its purposes, including reports of evaluations made under the State plans, and (B) will keep such records and afford such access thereto as the Commissioner may find necessary to assure the correctness and verification of such reports; and

(4) set forth the criteria to be used in determining the adequacy of public library services in geographical areas and for groups of persons in the State, including criteria designed to assure that priority will be given to programs or projects which serve urban and rural areas with high concentrations of low-income families.

Approval of basic State plan by Commissioner

(c) (1) The Commissioner shall not approve any basic State plan pursuant to this chapter for any fiscal year unless—

(A) the plan fulfills the conditions specified in section 351a(11) of this title and subsection (b) of this section and the appropriate subchapters of this chapter;

(B) he has made specific findings as to the compliance of such plan with requirements of this chapter and he is satisfied that adequate procedures are subscribed to therein insure that any assurances and provisions of such plan will be carried out.

.(2) The State plan shall be made public as finally approved.

(3) The Commissioner shall not finally disapprove any basic State plan submitted pursuant to subsection (a) (1) of this section, or any modification thereof, without first affording the State reasonable notice and opportunity for hearing.

Long-range State programs; development; provisions

(d) The long-range program of any State for carrying out the purposes of this chapter shall be developed in consultation with the Commissioner and shall—

(1) set forth a program under which the funds received by the State under the programs authorized by this chapter will be used to carry out a long-range program of library services and construction covering a period of not less than three nor more than five years;

(2) be annually reviewed and revised in accordance with changing needs for assistance under this chapter and the results of the evaluation and surveys of the State library administrative agency;

(3) set forth policies and procedures (A) for the periodic evaluation of the effectiveness of programs and projects supported under this chapter, and (B) for appropriate dissemination of the results of such evaluations and other information pertaining to such programs or projects; and

(4) set forth effective policies and procedures for the coordination of programs and projects supported under this chapter with library programs and projects operated by institutions of higher education or local elementary or secondary schools and with other public or private library services programs.

Such program shall be developed with advice of the State advisory council and in consultation with the Commissioner and shall be made public as it is finally adopted.

Termination or limitation of payments to States by Commissioner; procedure; grounds

(e) Whenever the Commissioner, after reasonable notice and opportunity for hearing to the State agency administering a program submitted under this chapter, finds—

(1) that the program has been so changed that it no longer complies with the provisions of this chapter, or

(2) that in the administration of the program there is a failure to comply substantially with any such provisions or with any assurance or other provision contained in the basic State plan,

then, until he is satisfied that there is no longer any such failure to comply, after appropriate notice to such State agency, he shall make no further payments to the State under this chapter or shall limit payments to programs or projects under, or parts of, the programs not affected by the failure, or shall require that payments by such State agency under this chapter shall be limited to local or other public library agencies not affected by the failure.

Judicial review of Commissioner's final actions; procedure

(f) (1) If any State is dissatisfied with the Commissioner's final action with respect to the approval of a plan submitted under this chapter or with his final action under subsection (e) of this section such State may, within sixty days after notice of such action, file with the United States court of appeals for the circuit in which such State is located a petition for review of that action. A copy of the petition shall be forthwith transmitted by the clerk of the court to the Commissioner. The Commissioner thereupon shall file in the court the record of the proceedings on which he based his action as provided in section 2112 of Title 28.

(2) The findings of fact by the Commissioner, if supported by substantial evidence, shall be conclusive; but the court, for good cause shown, may remand the case to the Commissioner to take further evidence, and the Commissioner may thereupon take new or modified findings of fact and may modify his previous action, and shall certify to the court the record of further proceedings.

(3) The court shall have jurisdiction to affirm the action of the Commissioner or to set it aside, in whole or in part. The judgment of the court shall be subject to review by the Supreme Court of the United States upon certiorari or certification as provided in section 1254 of Title 28.

June 19, 1956, c. 407, § 6, as added Dec. 30, 1970, Pub.L. 91-600, § 2(b), 84 Stat. 1663, and amended May 3, 1973, Pub.L. 93-29, Title VIII, § 801(c), 87 Stat. 59.

§ 351e.   Payments to States; prerequisites; Federal share; promulgation by Commissioner of Federal share

(a) From the allotments available therefore under section 351c of this title from appropriations pursuant to paragraph (1), (2), (3), or (4) of section 351b(a) of this title, the Commissioner shall pay to each State which has a basic State plan approved under section 351d(a)(1) of this title, an annual program and a long-range program as defined in section 351a(12) and (13) of this title an amount equal to the Federal share of the total sums expended by the State and its political subdivisions in carrying out such plan, except that no payments shall be made from appropriations pursuant to such paragraph (1) for the purposes of subchapter I of this chapter to any State (other than the Trust Territory of the Pacific Islands) for any fiscal year unless the Commissioner determines that—

(1) there will be available for expenditure under the programs from State and local sources during the fiscal year for which the allotment is made—

(A) sums sufficient to enable the State to receive for the purpose of carrying out the programs payments in an amount not less than the minimum allotment for that State for the purpose, and

(B) not less than the total amount actually expended, in the areas covered by the programs for such year, for the purposes of such programs from such sources in the second preceding fiscal year; and

(2) there will be available for expenditure for the purposes of the programs from State sources during the fiscal year for which the allotment is made not less than the total amount actually expended for such purposes from such sources in the second preceding fiscal year.

(b) (1) For the purpose of this section, the "Federal share" for any State shall be, except as is provided otherwise in subchapter III and subchapter IV of this chapter, 100 per centum less the State percentage, and the State percentage shall be that percentage which bears the same ratio to 50 per centum as the per capita income of such State bears to the per capita income of all States (excluding Puerto Rico, Guam, American Samoa, the Virgin Islands, and the Trust Territory of the Pacific Islands), except that (A) the Federal share shall in no case be more than 66 per centum, or less than 33 per centum, and (B) the Federal share for Puerto Rico, Guam, American Samoa, and the Virgin Islands shall be 66 per centum, and (C) the Federal share for the Trust Territory of the Pacific Islands shall be 100 per centum.

(2) The "Federal share" for each State shall be promulgated by the Commissioner within sixty days after the beginning of the fiscal year ending June 30, 1971, and of every second fiscal year thereafter, on the basis of the average per capita incomes of each of the States and of all the States (excluding Puerto Rico, Guam, American Samoa, the Virgin Islands, and the Trust Territory of the Pacific Islands), for the three most recent consecutive years for which satisfactory data are available to him from the Department of Commerce. Such promulgation shall be conclusive for each of the two fiscal years beginning after the promulgation.

June 19, 1956, c. 407, § 7, as added Dec. 30, 1970, Pub.L. 91-600, § 2(b), 84 Stat. 1665, and amended May 3, 1973, Pub.L. 93-29, Title VIII, § 801(d), 87 Stat. 59.

§361.   Grants to States for older readers services

The Commissioner shall carry out a program of making grants to States which have an approved basic State plan under section 351d of this title and have submitted a long-range program and an annual program under section 363 of this title for library services for older persons.

June 19, 1956, c. 407, Title IV, § 401, as added May 3, 1973, Pub.L. 93-29, Title VIII. § 801(a), 87 Stat. 57.

§ 362.   Uses of Federal funds; Federal share

(a) Funds appropriated pursuant to paragraph (4) of section 351b(a) of this title shall be available for grants to states from allotments under section 351c(a) of this title for the purpose of carrying out the Federal share of the cost of carrying out State plans submitted and approved under section 363 of this title. Such grants shall be used for (1) the training of librarians to work with the elderly; (2) the conduct of special library programs for the elderly; (3) the purchase of special library materials for use by the elderly; (4) the payment of salaries for elderly persons who wish to work in libraries as assistants on programs for the elderly; (5) the provision of in-home visits by librarians and other library personnel to the elderly; (6) the establishment of outreach programs to notify the elderly of library services available to them; and (7) the furnishing of transportation to enable the elderly to have access to library services.

(b) For the purposes of this subchapter, the Federal share shall be 100 per centum of the cost of carrying out the State plan.

June 19, 1956, c. 407, Title IV, § 402, as added May 3, 1973, Pub.L. 93-29, Title VIII, § 801(a), 87 Stat. 57.

§363.   State annual program for library services for the elderly

Any State desiring to receive a grant from its allotment for the purposes of this subchapter for any fiscal year shall, in addition to having submitted, and having had approved, a basic State plan under section 351d of this title, submit for that fiscal year an annual program for library services for older persons. Such program shall be submitted at such time, in such form, and contain such information as the Commissioner may require by regulation and shall—

(1) set forth a program for the year submitted under which funds paid to the State from appropriations pursuant to paragraph (4) of section 351b(a) of this title will be used, consistent with its long-range program for the purposes set forth in section 362 of this title, and

(2) include an extension of the long-range program taking into consideration the results of evaluations.

June 19, 1956, c. 407, Title IV, § 403, as added May 3, 1973, Pub.L. 93-29, Title VIII, § 801(a), 87 Stat. 58.

§ 364.   Administrative coordination with programs for older Americans

In carrying out the program authorized by this subchapter, the Commissioner shall consult with the Commissioner of the Administration on Aging and the Director of ACTION for the purpose of coordinating where practicable, the programs assisted under this subchapter with the programs assisted under the Older Americans Act of 1965.

June 19, 1956, c. 407, Title IV, § 404, as added May 3, 1973, Pub.L. 93-29, Title VIII, § 801(a), 87 Stat. 58.

INDEX

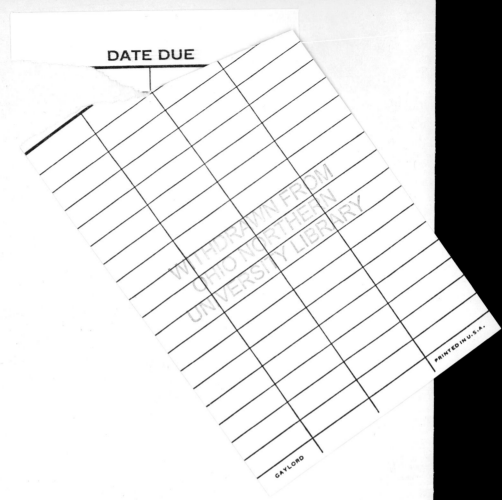